Rentschler .

I WOULD LIVE IT AGAIN

JULIA B. FORAKER
(1932) Eighty-four years old

I Would Live It Again

MEMORIES OF A VIVID LIFE

BY

JULIA B. FORAKER

(MRS. JOSEPH BENSON FORAKER)

ILLUSTRATED

HARPER & BROTHERS PUBLISHERS
NEW YORK AND LONDON
MCMXXXII

TO

MY HUSBAND

AND TO

MY CHILDREN

T A B L E   O F   C O N T E N T S

ILLUSTRATIONS

I WOULD LIVE IT AGAIN

"I know not how it is with you—
I love the first and last,
The whole field of the present view,
The whole flow of the past."

—R. L. STEVENSON

PRELUDE

ONE snowy January night, 1907, two or three hundred men sat down to dinner at a famous Washington club. The club was strictly a good-fellowship affair for chosen souls.

That dinner never got beyond the quail. When the waiters appeared with those trifles they were frantically waved away. Something was happening that had startled the guests out of all thoughts of birds, bottles, and brotherly love:

The President of the United States, reaching into the blue, had hurled a forensic bomb at the senior Senator from Ohio, and the Senator from Ohio was sending back at him from his own well-stocked arsenal, stinging shot for shot; and Heaven knew how the affair would end.

The affair never ended while the national life of Mr. Roosevelt and Foraker ran together. From that night at the "Gridiron," when the President challenged his least malleable henchman in the arena, a drama of temperament was played in American politics as uncompromising as anything since the days of Alexander Hamilton.

Chief of opposed issues between Roosevelt and Foraker, and brandished by Mr. Roosevelt on the occasion of which I speak, was the "Shooting up of Brownsville."

That Texas mystery, involving a negro Dreyfus, sprang out of the night, baffled the country for years and died unsolved. But its effect was sinister; it reached far ahead. For a long time afterwards men stumbled over the wreckage that "Brownsville" left on the shores of the Republican party.

Foraker came home at two o'clock in the morning from the "Gridiron duel," as Mr. Pierpont Morgan afterwards spoke of it (he was there with Mr. H. H. Rogers; the President shook his fist at them). My husband looked white and fagged, but not defeated—on the contrary! —and told us the whole story over the library fire. The fire had gone out; we put on fresh logs; it was oddly symbolic. Everything afterwards served to add to the flame of discord between the Gridiron duelists, once friends.

Memories of those days, other political memories, very far off, come back to me as I look down through the years. They crowd together; I hardly know which to greet first. They crowd together, phantom-like. All are gone who once brought vitality and desires and wealth and power to those scenes. The pageant over, now I may tell my impressions of it from an excellent vantage; recall the principal players and their infinite little ways. To none can it any longer matter.

Retrospect touches the first term of my husband's Ohio Governorship—when the salary was four thousand dollars and we paid our own house rent; it leaps to

Washington in the glittering 'nineties; wilfully then it turns back to youth when romance gave me its flower and tragedy was a dark thing that happened to other people. Tragedy was Lincoln dead, whom I saw.

I am tempted to linger over the earliest years, so stark, so cruelly shadowed yet beating excitingly with promise. Soon, none who went through the last half of the nineteenth century will be left to tell how it all was. But the political current rushes me on. Always it has rushed me on. From the 'fifties, when, a little girl in pinafores, I flew around the dinner table with the biscuits (every day men of affairs stopped at our farmhouse for the twelve-o'clock meal and to feed their horses)—from the time when I was there with the Whig biscuits and between relays an entranced listener of the new "Republican" talk, politics have set for me an absorbing pace.

Shrewd, slouchy "Buckeyes" made up that early political circle, descendants with many of the traits of speech and manners of the New England Ohioans, the Kentucky and Virginia Ohioans who settled in the rich valley upon the opening of the Northwest. Whigs all, I thought that first crowd; father was a Whig—what else could one be? But as "Free Soil" became more and more the battle cry I learned that one could be, mercy! all sorts of queer things, depending upon what part of the country you came from: "Know-Nothing," just a plain bigot, that one; "Barnburner," if you were of the New York Democrats that nominated Van Buren; "Scala-

wag," if you lived below "Mason n' Dixon"; "Come-
outer"——

"Come-outer," I wrote in my first diary, "a kross man
who will not vote."

Everybody then seemed to me a little cross with things
as they were. Ohio, "first free child of the Mother of
States," was solidly for the new party out to beat the
arrogant Democrats, and to end this evil of "men owning men."

Long, long after my political début I was given the
privilege of casting a vote. By that time, having taken
the Republican Party to my heart when I was ten, and
it not so old, having made my whole life in it and of it
and feeling just a little possessive, I confess to a rather
mixed emotion about the ballot. I am afraid that I had
never missed it. I was glad that the concession had been
won; but I remained uncontrollably calm. In seventy
years so much had happened, such acres of bright water
and dark had raced under the bridges.

Washington society in the 'nineties was as brilliant as
any that ever America has produced. The administrations had a certain ceremonious glory; there was an arresting group of men in the Senate, with a few remarkable leaders; the diplomatic set was distinguished and
delightful and romantically mysterious in the old-time,
Old World manner; the rich, spectacular New York-
crowd-with-the-names came over, took big houses, gave
extravagant parties and exotically quickened the pace.

Ambassador Bryce spoke of this period to me as the "shattering 'nineties." This was after they were over and one could tell.

In the 'nineties, too, our country's cornucopious bounty seemed to overflow. Never again shall any of us see such abundance and cheapness, such luxurious well-being as prosperous Americans then enjoyed. The Age of Plenty was rounding the peak.

Politically, the 'nineties were one long, fierce joust. One looks for conflict in politics, of course; it is another way of going into battle. But in this decade and on, around the bend into the new century, the privileges of combat were pressed to the uttermost. From the election of President McKinley to the election of President Taft it was war.

The period closed without olive branches. But as the years go by, these emblematic greens take hold, tempering at last with their shade the too-staring page of memory. I have much happiness to record in these chapters of my life. If I have something, too, to say of strife, it is only because —— But my husband used to tell a war story which expresses the point I have in mind here better than I am able to express it:

Foraker was with General Slocum on the march through the Carolinas in 1865. They were anxious to locate the boundary line between North and South Carolina and asked every native they met if they had crossed it. But weary mile on mile the line remained always far ahead. Finally they saw an old man standing in front of a log house set some distance back from the road, silently watching the marching column. General Slocum rode up to him. . . .

"I suppose you are a Union man?"

No, the man said, he wasn't a Union man.

"Then you are a Secessionist."

No, he wasn't a Secessionist, either.

"If you are neither a Union man nor a Secessionist, will you please tell me what you are?"

The old man looked at the general with faded blue eyes.

"I am a rebel."

General Slocum turned and rode back to his staff. . . .

"We have crossed the line," he said.

For me, it is a little like that. My political war is over; Time has signed the peace; yet poignant in my remembrance are certain things which I cannot but eternally protest . . .

I am a rebel—at eighty-four.

J. B. F.

Cincinnati
Autumn, 1931

THE 'SEVENTIES
AND BEFORE

CHAPTER I

MORNING YEARS

MY HUSBAND never forgave my father for tears in his eyes at our wedding. . . .

"Particularly," said Captain Foraker, "when you are doing so well."

I was all for this view myself. It was apple-blossom time in Ohio when the affair began; there was a new moon and I remember seeing it aslant, through birch branches, yet feeling happily defiant. How little I had to fear! With youth, love, and life ahead that moon could hold nothing for me but luck.

This was the great Grant year, 1868. The second Republican Party was fourteen years old; the political current was proving almost too strong for that troubled bark when the General sent it forward with his powerful arm. It was a time of many new stars in the state sky. Foraker, rounding out college years after the Civil War, was tempted to begin a little faint rising on his own.

I have reason to remember a certain speech leveled at Horatio Seymour, the Democrats' candidate against Grant. The speaker was young and needed a hair-cut, but he inspired me with a curiously heightened interest in the campaign. I thought I'd attend all the meetings.

"That there's a smart feller," said an old farmer, as we filed out. "He'll go fur."

There was no crystal ball on the crochet mat in the parlor of my girlhood. Had I ever looked into one, caught there a hint of my part in Foraker's progress, I should have been unimpressed. Boys had all the future then; girls were supposed to stay in the appropriate, sheltered niches in which it had pleased God to place them, and to thank Him.

Until I was sixteen I lived the isolated life that had engulfed my mother and her mother; it was unlikely that Destiny meant to look me up with an offer of anything more dashing. I was born in a log farmhouse at Wellston, Ohio, June 17, 1847. That country then was almost as lonely as when my mother's father, David Paine, built the house in 1808. The property was grant land secured from the government. I have the original parchment deed signed by President Madison and still own fifty acres around the original log-house site.

Grandfather Paine was a New Englander of lively Revolutionary ancestors and descended from Henry Adams, founder of the illustrious Adamses. He married one Abigail James. "Nabbie," as they called her, seems to have been a keen sort, alert as David to the call of the Northwest; the two made their wedding journey a start towards that promised land. The house they built, duly, was midway between, and the only one between two county seats—or so the surveyor's trace said—McArthur in Vinton and Jackson in Jackson. The site was chosen because of the presence of "salt works" or mines, essential for cattle. The house stood in magnificent beech woods once the great beauty of Ohio, and between it and civilization stretched miles and miles of wolf-haunted timber.

My mother was born, lived her life, and died there. The property was part of her dower; when I came along it was almost as lonely as Eden and stock-still primitive. Living conditions had changed little, what with the hills and the mud. I remember an incredibly old man—he wore a coonskin cap and had fought Indians under William Henry Harrison—who came to our house; a great story-teller. He used to speak of the "Braddock cussin'" to which good men were driven who tried to cross Ohio with a five-horse team. The oaths bequeathed by Braddock to a far-flung posterity may have relieved the pioneers, but they didn't improve the roads. That mud made Ohio history for fifty years.

Only, by my time the mythical county seats had come to life. My yesterdays really begin here, for to the trafficking come-and-go between Jackson and Vinton I owe my first political memories. In a wide stretch of country without a single tavern, and no other house, our farm became the meeting center, a sort of political exchange for travelers riding cross-counties. My father,

Hezekiah Sanford Bundy, was a Congressman from Whig days, and to stop at "Bundy's" was to get, besides a good dinner, the latest slant on the fierce issues of the day, perhaps meet a big man. I don't know what men would have done without such a forum. Things were happening then that just had to be talked over.

I remember Log House as clearly as though only yesterday I had walked out of it—out of the door and across the spring and through the orchard . . . the pippins falling *plump*! . . . the creak of a cider-mill somewhere . . . on to the big honey locust to wait for my father coming back from Hamden with the mail. He'll be over the hill in a minute, riding with a slack bridle . . . he is reading the *Cincinnati Weekly Gazette*.

The house was built of walnut logs, full tree size (walnut was cheap then; pine was dear); the logs were fitted and numbered; no metal was used; even the door hinges were of wood. It had the dignity of two stories, a real staircase, and numerous rooms that grew into wings as my father's means mounted and his hospitality ran further and further away with him. There was something of feudal charm about the thick walls, the clay fireplaces, an enormous one in the kitchen cluttered blackly with crane-hung kettles, spiders, and pothooks; something decidedly feudal about the spilt-Burgundy liberality that pervaded living. I have planned and lived in several delightful houses, I adore house planning, but my first

Mrs. Foraker's Early Home, Wellston, Ohio

A political center in the Civil War period

home had qualities of beauty like a palace: the mellow look of it; the candlelight-firelight flicker on the dark beams; the puncheon floor scrubbed to dazzling and checkered by the blues, greens, and rose of home-dyed-and-woven rugs into something Eastern and lovely. If the picture runs the danger of being brightened by time's flight, I must be given that handicap. Who can tell the Bible-truth about his youth?

We were always prepared for extra folks at Log House and every day they came. I remember the horses hitched all over the place, being fed, too. Every day (except Lord's Day, when the universe seemed to be struck dumb) the long table hummed with argument drawled and stressed in the burred accent of Southern Ohio, a speech oddly composite of all the dialects of backwoodsmen ancestors, and flecked with quaint turns.

The year that I appeared, California and New Mexico came along, too, and the winning of these rich new lands must have set everybody off on an eternal theme—the ban on slavery in new territories. We were too far off the track for me to have had, as a child, many visual impressions of the approach of Civil War. But the first talk I can remember, and this because my father fixed it by explaining it to me, was that Ohio meant to keep the Northwest free—"and don't you forget it." That was a little the tone. And unspeakable indeed were the Southerners who opposed certain new lands as territories be-

cause we weren't going to let them keep slaves there.
Yet they thought they had as much "say" about this as
we had, having fought as bravely to win the new country.

More arresting were the stories told by men who had
seen run-away slaves in the depot at Cincinnati, being
taken back in chains to their owners, the people crowding and pushing for a look. This didn't happen often
enough to lose excitement; the Fugitive Slave Law was
flouted in Ohio; most people tried to help the blacks
who managed to get across "Mason and Dixon" to reach
Canada or a free state, and rarely was anybody punished.

It took the most dramatic happening of that time to
pierce my childish unconsciousness of the volcano beneath our feet. I came riding home from school one
early December dusk. A sullen, red sky. Father was
standing there. He lifted me off my horse.

"They've hanged John Brown," he said.

I grew up in that moment. Here was a hero and a
martyr to touch the imagination, to make of "anti-
slavery" a passionate reality.

I was to see the earliest volunteers drilling on the com-
mons of our two country towns; and on one occasion in
the first year of the war get a glimpse of what an army
looked like. This was when three thousand troops marching down our road, broke ranks, and began foraging the
country for horses and food. Crowds of hungry soldiers
swarmed into our farm at four o'clock in the morning,

stood their rifles against the trees, and demanded breakfast. They got it. I was watching the soldiers ride off
when one of them, an officer of a Chillicothe division,
leaned over and handed me his gold "turnip" watch and
chain.

"Keep this for me till I come back, will you, sissy?"
he said.

He never came back.

Perhaps the most exciting events in my memory of the
Civil War was Morgan's raid. One mid-July day in 1863
a tall, ganglin' fellow, neighbor of ours, dashed up to our
farm. He was carrying his boots, one in each hand, and
he was breathless. Between gasps he told us that Morgan's men, "thousands of 'em," were on their way down
our road from Jackson! Then he was off again to warn
others. (He had taken off his boots so that he could run
faster, but they always told it on him that he was so
scared o' Morgan he ran clean out of his boots!)

Maybe we didn't fly around! Everything valuable was
stored out of sight. I remember them hastily piling silver
and other small treasures into a brass-studded leather
trunk and taking it down to hide in the willows. The
men rode off to the woods with every horse on the
place. . . .

At the cross-roads—it was so near to our farm that we
could hear the clatter of the cavalry—a scout met the

raiders and reported that Union troops were coming into Hamden, two miles south, by trainloads. At that Morgan and his riders wheeled around and went somewhere else to strike as unexpectedly as they had come upon us, and to get away scott free. But, oh dear! I'd like just to have *seen* those hotspurs!

Morgan on the loose was an object of terror to the countryside. We had heard of his plunderings in Kentucky and Indiana: ransacking country stores and farmhouses, taking anything he wanted . . . burning and destroying everything before him. He helped himself to horses whenever he could get them. The farmers were wild. The Confederate cavalrymen had left Kentucky mounted on the best blood of Blue Grass. But they rode so hard, they were so hotly pursued by our militia with every man who could ride and shoot joining the chase, that to escape capture fresh horses were a vital necessity.

The man who owned the finest horses in our county was a detested Copperhead. His sympathies did not prevent him, however, from hiding his entire stable deep in the woods. He was certain Morgan would not find them. But Morgan did find them, and took every horse, and left in place the exhausted steeds he and his staff had been riding. Of course all that those thoroughbreds needed to "come back" was rest. And to them the fine strain of Kentucky horses to be found through southern Ohio owed its start. I remember a horse racily mixed up with my early Cincinnati days, a beautiful sorrel with a blazed face, that was proudly distinguished as of "Morgan stock."

It was when I was thought old enough to "help wait" that I began to catch the drift of table talk and pick up convictions of my own. I learned what a "black Republican" was when I was spelling Republican with a k, and I heard the contemporaneous debate between "a Mr. Lincoln and the great Senator Douglas" so thoroughly gone into that I knew the house-divided-against-itself speech before I could decently write the maxim in my copy-book. I remember forgetting to refill the sugar-bowl for Judge Joshua Gidding's lettuce through listening entranced to an account of the Prince of Wales' visit to the President's house. The narrator, a Democratic sheep who had strayed into our fold, had just been on to Washington to see Mr. Buchanan himself.

"The President didn't have to dress up none for the Prince," he drawled, "'cuz he wears a white tie common."

Casually, too, as party crystallized, I got my first lesson in political diplomacy. Whisking around the table and keeping my eyes and ears open, I caught the difference between gimcrack politicians with bottomless appetites (symbol of that coming horror, the office-hound) and important men, to whom, as if by instinct, one "handed" pie first—and oftenest. ("Vinegar pie" was a delectable mystery of those days, made particularly for

deserving souls like William Dennison, Governor of
Ohio when Civil War was declared. There was a knack
about it.)

In 1860 the life of the open hand became too much
for Log House. Father started building a larger one on
the near-by foundations of a house built by my great-
grandfather Paine. It took a long time to finish the Fine
House. We fed and lodged this crowd; we were in for
that whenever we had extra work done. When they had
finally gone, a man came to paper and paint at three
dollars a day and board. He was so conscientious—or so
comfortable?—that he spent a year with us.

La, sir, what grand people we were in the Fine House!
Inside shutters were perhaps the most dashing of our
positive novelties, but a hot-water heater attached to a
stove next the kitchen fireplace, and the first sink the
countryside ever saw, made it for the year '60 a very modern house. The parlor was an immense and quite beautiful room; decorators, I see, are reproducing that room
today: wall-paper of oyster white with gold fleurs-de-lis;
haircloth-covered rosewood furniture of pleasant simple
design but set around the walls as though it were being
disciplined; a mossy-green Brussels carpet with medal-
lions all abloom with vast pink roses; heavy crystal can-
delabras—always candles in this room—and a mantle-
piece arrangement of a white marble clock (it remained
ever at twenty minutes past six), flanked by bouquets of
wax flowers under glass globes tied with green chenille.

When the fire was lit the room *was* lovely. Another thing about that house that gave it distinction were the huge lumps of coal blazing in every fireplace. There was a vein of marvelous coal on land about four miles from us; the men used to go there and dig it out in great chunks. We, living within that lucky area, burned coal before most of the people in that part of Ohio had ever seen it.

But with all our smart span-newness, life on the distaff side remained much as it had been: Early Colonial—the last phase. The transference of the production of domestic staples to factories, the magic erasure of distance which brought modern life in with a swing—there was none of that. We were to all practical purposes as isolated as when Daniel Boone complained that a thirty-five-mile farm hardly gave a man elbow room. To break one's last needle was a tragedy; to lack hooks and eyes for the placket of a new dress meant an embittering postponement of social triumph. Woman's serenity depended upon complete confidence in the placket.

Money was negligible then; man was the power. On occasions barrels of flour and sugar and "N'yorleans" molasses were rolled into the storeroom; sacks of green coffee beans appeared, and smaller amounts of gunpowder tea. Everything else that furnished our table we made ourselves. I heard a great deal about generals in those days; but for cool head, foresight, and efficiency I think that my mother and my father's mother who lived

with us outgeneraled all of them. There was nothing
these two women couldn't do—and they did everything.

Memories of harvest time carry the faint echo of a bell
followed by a ghostly *tramp-tramp*. The "hands" are
coming in to dinner. They must be fed on the stroke of
twelve; dinner couldn't be a second late for that crew of
fiercely hungry men working in the fields since five.
Then, hurried along, came our own dinner. We were always a large family, cousins, "in-laws," ancestors, and
aunts profiting by my father's generous paternalism. And
there were the usual "orphants" to be found in so many
prosperous country families of that time. These were
Tommy (lovable but what a fighter!) and Jennie, twelve
and fourteen, children whom mother had calmly brought
home with her one day in response to the beseeching look
in the eyes of a dying woman to whom my mother had
been good. No organized charity then; just this dis-
orderly humankindness.

Besides the regular rooftree crowd and the inevitable
extra brigade, that second dinner often ran into a third.
I remember one devastating day (the porch chairs were
already occupied by men, chewing the slippery elm of
appetite) when a wagon-load of dear friends arrived,
unheralded, from another county, hurraying and hungry. How different from today when hospitality works
on the principle of "Telephone first!" The chickens that
fell in those crises! . . . the tired wrists from beating
eggs! . . . the Mississippis of milk and buttermilk and

cider that flowed! . . . the biscuits, eternally, hotly the biscuits! The epoch takes on picturesqueness now, but women were ground up in it, in the ceaseless concern with food, raiment, and warmth. I am sure that the modern woman's bolt from the kitchen and the home, so solemnly deplored, has very deep roots in woman's drudgery past, in a life that men would have gone down under, would, rather than keep it up, gratefully have seen their sex die out.

Spring calling! A very cyclone of cleaning swept the land, taking slight account of the young man's untimely fancy or the magic of the wild-flower woods. Reluctant windows opened to the sweet air; brilliantly crazy quilts and "kivers" and the mad red family flannels rollicked on the line like banners. . . .

"She is not afraid of the snow for her household: for all her household are clothed with scarlet."

Even the spring-house stones were scrubbed whose lives had been so pure. There was mush for supper, sure sign of dead-beat fatigue. The moon came up divinely and everybody hurried to bed "so they could get up."

In this rhythm the dressmaker began her stay. Miss Abby and her patterns arrived from Fifteen Mile and settled down by the window in the little spare room for four months. The sewing-machine was already out, but it was very expensive and the time was not yet when farmers' wives fell upon it with that frenzy which gave them, besides a completely new set of diseases, the thrill of their lives. It took Miss Abby the whole of a perfect May afternoon to set a crinoline; the longest, loveliest day in June found us knee-deep in plush.

Through the smiting heat work pell-melled. Mercy! the katydids have begun a-hollerin'! . . . half summer's gone already! A rush now before fall, the real "busy time." Cheese-making: I can see the creamy stream running from an iron kettle into great wooden molds. In a vote for the most deliciously remembered morsel of childhood (everybody has one) I should be for a lump of that cheese fresh from the whey. The spring house belongs to this picture. An elaborate care, yet one would like to look upon such a place today—deep, dim, cool; the wide, flat, mossy stones; the circle of shallow crocks, their yellow, wrinkled faces telling of Jerseys worth their weight in butter; the perpetual *lap-lap* of water coming from far hills.

The whir of the loom sounded then, for the loom stood in a cold room and it was make hay while the sun shone, and the spinning-wheel sang to the hum of bees. On this film flashes suddenly the picture of my little Grandmother Bundy walking back and forth, back and forth, manipulating the thread. It is a hot day and her terribly old-lady's cap (she would be about forty-eight then) has got a little pushed back. I am startled to see how young she looks, her blue-black hair, without a gray thread, growing in a widow's peak over a very white brow. We had a fine sheep-hill and at one time all our woolens were carded, spun, and woven at home. I wore linsey-woolsey dresses; very gay patterns, some of them. I have the big wheel used by my Grandmother Bundy and my mother's smaller wheel. They will end in a museum, they that once sang to us and kept us warm.

Forward, in fruity chronology, went the "putting-up." I had spoken a piece at school:

> "What wondrous life is this I lead!
> Ripe apples drop about my head
> The luscious clusters of the vine
> Upon my mouth do crush their wine:
> The nectarine and curious peach
> Into my hands themselves to reach . . ."

Poet Marvell we now translated in terms of the measuring-cup. Vitamins were lying low; the natural use to make of fresh fruit was to narcotize it with sugar. The catacombed fruit-cellar gleamed glassily; a wine-colored glow pervaded the universe. I remember when any of my mother's friends called that at a given moment everyone rose and went down "to see your fruit." The visitors' lips moved silently as they swept the display with appraising eyes. They were counting. The cult called for two things: to put up more than one's neighbor and to put up at least five times as much as ever possibly would be eaten. The year inscribed on jelly labels often ran into history.

On the back porch with its curtain of blue morning glories, candle-dipping went on all through pleasant weather. "Company candles" were made in molds, twelve at a time, but weren't much fun, as you couldn't be praised as you were for getting your dipped ones smooth and symmetrical. On rainy days, if a let-up in men folks promised, we made soap, oceans of it. It is an irony that hurrying progress was to discount the dull, meticulous thrift that so long ate up women's leisure for things broadening and bright. With a mug of the unctuous liquid we put cleanliness as near to godliness as we could get it. It wasn't without a certain poetry, you know, that Ohio Saturday-night bath: heated rain water, soft as milk, the cool roughness of home-woven huckaback, the ceremony proceeding before that last wild thing, an open fire.

In the fall woman's work piled mountainously. I remember with special poignancy the apple-butter making. We made enough for eternity it seemed, yet never too much. Family, visitors, everybody took turns stirring the bubbling caldron that hung in the fireplace; there was a mediæval, long-handled spoon with a paddle on the tip of it that swished round and round the bottom of the kettle. Boiling hot the butter went into two- and four-gallon stone jars and was instantly sealed over with brown paper. Little Julia, six, leaned on one of these jars and went in. My hands and wrists were badly scalded. My father dressed the burns with sweet oil; it hurt terribly and always he looked as if he suffered more than I did, which helped very much.

Indian summer, when the Ohio Valley is of a winey loveliness and enticement, was before all else "hog-killin' time." These rites over, the smokehouse fairly sagged with tawny treasures—enough sausage for hundreds of icy-morning breakfasts. Nothing to do now but bury the vegetables deep in their pit below frost and call it a season. Covering that cache meant sealing up summer.

It was the moment to sit down for a spell. But as in the spring when the men were too busy to lay out a flower-bed (I remember my mother fluttering about wistfully with a design for a new one called the "Northern Star"— from *The Ladies Floral Cabinet*), so at winter's edge and on, Satan's interest in idle hands was sternly countered. Under the impression that we were on holiday we knitted and quilted between the everlasting baking and boiling. My Grandmother Abigail Paine could card, spin, and knit a pair of socks in one day; you couldn't see her take off her stitches; the affair was nothing but click and gleam. I wasn't such a wonder as all that, but I was pretty smart. Whatever child-education lacked in the last century, and I understand this was practically everything, certainly it didn't lack knitting-needles. The baby sacks and socks and "mitties" and "throws" I helped to pile up would have embarrassed an orphan-asylum. In the "tidy" lists, too, I left a record. There was nothing else to do. My little sister and I had no playmates but each other; mature interests were the only ones provided us. For dashing moments there were the fascinating flummeries of ladies' home work: making artificial flowers, most admired of all by country folk; making other dust-catchers in beads, shells, and what not. Or, oh, beautiful! interpreting "Peterson's styles." I made a "modesty frill" for my mother's Christmas. It was to go inside a V neck, concealing all immodest suggestion of a white throat. I made a "cloud," or "fascinator," for a spinster cousin—the color was a sensibly-provocative pink. In effect, I was "kept occupied." Anything rather than an idle child!

Few books. Religion, cookery, and diseases covered the range. Sometimes fiction fluttered in, but, mercy! what gaudy trash was fed to the imagination-starved men and women of the farms:

Through Fire and Water, by the Author of *The Heir Expectant,* or *Her Lord and Master,* by the Author of *From Dreams to Waking.* I don't remember in those dark ages of my girlhood ever hearing a writer mentioned by name; only as th' Author-of. Classics were being produced then, but no Aurora Leigh, no Clive Newcome, no Adam Bede nor Little Dorritt found their way into our Bœotia. We did read *Barchester Towers,* by a Mr.

Trollope. But only because the novelist's mother some years earlier had settled in Cincinnati and opened "Trollope's Bazaar of English Fancy Goods." People were cold to English fancy goods, and Mrs. Trollope left, saying very "mean" things about Ohioans; more, she printed 'em. Naturally, the Trollopes, having slandered us, interested us. I don't believe, though, that *Barchester Towers* was considered so good as the other book that circulated in the county that year. Could this have been *A Passion in Tatters* by the Author of *Wed in the Morning, Dead at Night*? A sentimental kinsman of ours had an unbridled taste for such books. He used to tell the plots. Once embarked on a plot, nothing on earth short of sudden death would have side-tracked him. He couldn't make his farm pay, but how he enriched his life with vicarious romance!

When I was eleven, and my sister eight, Art came to our house: my father bought a piano; a Bechstein "square"; the legs were a riot of leery cupids; it came all the way from Chillicothe. It was the first and for a long time the only piano in our part of Ohio. A music-teacher was then imported; she remained two years in our house. At the end of that time, since I could play "The Mountain Stream Waltz," and my sister "Convent Bells" (very tricky for the left hand), there really seemed no reason why teacher should linger. A small friend had spent the winter with us in order to take lessons. She lived only six miles away, but over quite impassable roads. The whole countryside heard of "the instrument at Bundy's." People came from everywhere to hear it, or, what must have been even more pleasurable, just to see it.

Mrs. Trollope said that Ohio women were "quiet but not gentle." My mother was both. It remained for my Grandmother Bundy to set the high pace at our house. She was the vividest person I ever knew, and left imprints on my character of such worldly and spiritual value that I owe her the most honorable mention.

A little woman, five feet, perhaps, yet always managing to look tall; shining blue-black hair wound in braids around her small head, the darkest eyes, the whitest skin, and teeth like a row of even young corn. She had a good deal of the aristocrat in her, great intelligence, hardly a trace of fear (during a thunderstorm she hid the scissors, but what was that), and the most primitive culture. She ran us all.

Born Adah Melinda Nicholson of Dutchess County, New York, grandmother had come through just a few things. When she was sixteen she eloped with Nathan Bundy, a man much older than herself. He had been dickering with her father about a sale of land; it ended by the alluring creature (he had silver buckles on his shoes and wore his hair in a queue) selling great-grandfather the Dutchess County farm for five thousand dollars. The next thing anybody knew he and Adah Melinda had raced off in a buggy.

They had not gone many miles, only just beyond the first parson's, when Adah Melinda's mother overtook them. She had the faster horse. But she was not in pursuit to fetch her erring daughter home. On the contrary. Good suitors were scarce in Dutchess, and I imagine she thought that a man smart enough to get five thousand dollars out of paw could be trusted with her daughter. She was merely taking her some silver spoons, a feather bed, some hand-woven linen sheets, and an "E Pluribus Unum" coverlet without which no girl at the beginning of eighteen hundred could be thought soundly wed. These and a God-bless-you together. There was a little kiss and the wedding journey was resumed. In a two-horse carriage now. The bridegroom had very alertly made this swop when he saw his bride's wedding presents piling up.

They were half a mile on their way once more when the clatter of hoofs and some one calling made them look back. Mother again! She had forgotten something she wanted to give to Adah Melinda; it was a little silver bird; you clamped it on a table and it held your work in its mouth while you sewed. At the sight of this dear trifle that she had always seen near her mother as she worked, tears came into the little bride's eyes and she would then have gone back. But her mother, with a queer brusqueness, drove off, and the man sitting beside her, with the silver buckles on his shoes and his stockings bulging with her father's money, whipped up the horses, and soon her mother's buggy, which she watched, disappeared in the dust.

Grandmother never saw her mother again, nor any of her people; nor heard, ever, but one word from them. This was when she learned that her brother, on his way to bring her her share, twelve thousand dollars, in her father's estate, had been murdered at Cleveland. Just laconically murdered. No details, no investigation, no news ever again. And no money.

Nathan and Adah Melinda ended up at Marietta, the first settlement in Ohio. Nathan had planned to take up a valuable grant land farther south in the state, but the so-called roads were so utterly horrible he could not reach it. My father was born at Marietta; when he was two years old they moved on—it was the fever of the times— to Athens. Thirty miles from Marietta to Athens by rail today; to my grandmother in 1819 it must have seemed thirty thousand. They traveled horseback. There was no wagon road; just a thread of a path between blazed trees. My grandmother rode with her feather bed, her dishes, and other household effects packed around her horse, and carried my father on her lap. The child got so restless that he was always standing up! Athens then had little to it but its fancy Greek name. The log house they built there was in a real wilderness. Panthers screamed around it at night; they burned sulphur to keep off the bears. But the pioneers were of tough, indomitable fiber and they prospered. The day that they cut down the big walnut in the lower pasture, things on the Athens farm looked pretty bright.

The tree fell badly and Nathan was killed.

Hard times now began in earnest for the mother and her little boy. Through a flaw in the title she found she could not hold on to the property. My father left school and went to work. Any work. There was the time he drove a flock of sheep to Marietta; he started back, breakfastless, at four o'clock in the morning, stopped about eleven at a farmhouse and asked for something to eat. The farmer allowed it wasn't meal-time at their house. Well, a little bread and milk then, please, said my father. They gave him a pint of milk. "It'll be nineteen cents," said the farmer. That was exactly a day's pay for the boy as sheep drover. The milk was sour. My father said that he watched that man's career afterwards; he felt that he was a twisty one. During the Civil War the man, true to form, made a fortune selling "shoddy" as woolen to shivering soldiers.

Another man, a rich farmer named Miller, paid the lad twelve and one-half cents a day and board for chopping cordwood. Father was always a little pernickety about food, but his mother was a tempting cook. Now, wood-chopping made him ravenous. The board the farmer's wife conceded was parsimonious and bad. Father stood it as long as he could; then, embarrassed by being constantly reproached for not "eating up his plate," and half starved, he cleared out. He didn't wait for a "Good-by, ma'am," nor to collect his week's pay—ninety-seven and one-half cents. And never thought to see the farmer again.

Years afterwards my father walked into a board meeting at the Athens hospital. There sat old Miller. He screwed up his eyes at the sight of him.

"Whadye go off like that fur?" he said, just as if the thing had happened yesterday.

Father told him. They parted cordially.

By the time father and I met, his hardships were over in the sense that we were living like lords at Log House. Father was Congressman from Whig days; reëlected as a Republican again and again; he was one of the Lincoln Electors in 1864. I heard so much about Washington as a little girl I came to confuse it with heaven; farther off for me, of course, but probably much the same sort of place. (I was somewhat mistaken about Washington. I wonder if I shall find that I've been misled about heaven, too?) My father campaigned six counties on horseback, spoke at cross-roads, county fairs, general stores, under sycamore trees, at every sort of meeting-place—except a barroom. He knew every farmer's family, had a great eye for crops and a memory for the babies' names. He was "Uncle Bundy" to everybody, witty, mercurial, gentle as a woman, generous, and wildly hospitable.

It was only when he worked to repeal the Ohio "Black

Laws" that his popularity went into complete if temporary eclipse.

I don't suppose many people remember today that for
forty-five years—from 1805 to 1850—we had on the stat-
ute-books of Ohio a blot and a disgrace known as the
"Black Laws of Ohio." The "Black Laws" were statutes
which, among other things, forbade any colored man to
testify in any case in court in which a white man was a
party. One day a white school-teacher came to our house
and told my father a curious story. She had occasion to
go to the house of a colored family living in Gallipolis,
father's district. As she came towards the house she saw
a white man whom she knew enter the barn and then
come out, leading a horse. The man, colored, who owned
the horse was not then at home. When he returned and
found his horse gone he was in a state of emotional excitement about the theft. But there was no redress—and
he knew it.

My father took up this man's case, gave himself to it,
worked to have the Black Laws repealed. And they were
repealed. And father got a sentence against the white
horsethief, and the colored man got back his horse. But
it cost father his return to the legislature the next term,
and it cost him for a while the friendship of that whole
countryside. Father weathered it. And when people came
again crowding to his table he greeted them as if no
bitter period had intervened.

My grandmother delighted in her son's seignioral

spirit bubbling up out of an arid youth. She played up to it extravagantly. She adored clothes; in her young days she wore her dresses "flossed" (embroidered) to the knees; she was as neat as a cinnamon pink. She kept a reverence for form that was remarkable, considering the bitter, homely grind she had come through. I remember her hurrying downstairs, dressed in her black silk and her brooch, to greet my father returned from one of his Washington sojourns.

"And how was our kinsman, Governor Sprague?" Her tone was that of a person who dines with royalty and thinks nothing of it.

"Drunk—all the time," said father.

It was this teasing love of taking the wind out of his mother's grand sails that, over her protest, made him send me to district school when I was seven. My first school was little and red, of course, and only a mile away; I tramped there one winter in boots, literally wading through the mud. Then came the Big School, three miles off. I rode there—the soft southern Ohio snow didn't help the roads—unsaddled my horse "Patience," found a branch low enough to tie her to. I ask nothing more exciting than those schools. The things that *happened* . . . !

There was the time a fiery little girl, Lizzie Jane, goaded by a boy who called her mother "nothin' but a shoutin' Methodist," picked up her sled by the rope, swung it a couple of times around her head and brought it down on the insulter. He recovered—but we gave religious differences a wide berth after that. And there were those tall, lanky, mischief-inventive boys who were always slouching over the little, low desks; they'd sullenly straighten under teacher's constant, exasperated command to "Sit up!" then instantly slouch again. Teacher sent one of these boys out one day to cut switches; as he went through the door he gave a marrow-freezing Indian scalp-cry (he knew he was going to "get it," anyway). The children were so startled they screamed and dropped their slates with a great clatter. Teacher got very white. then darted after the boy and gave him a beautiful licking then and there in the snow, with all of us, big and little, crowded at door and window to see.

And there was the fun of playing "Andy over" (ah, what a game if you could throw a ball!) with the boys during the long noon recess. And, spring come, swinging up and up into the gloom and tickling of the tall trees (Thank that school board for those splendid long ropes!) or playing "I Spy" in the dense brush. I feel sorry for my great-grandchildren; they've got no primitive advantages whatever in their so-perfect modern school.

District school was certainly a man's job, but a picture of that period flashes here that still charms me—and puzzles me. This is of a slim girl with soft eyes who rode into our farm one summer day on a big roan horse. Her skirt almost dragged on the ground, she wore a lit-

tle round green hat with a feather. She said she was out
"looking for a school." She was fifteen years old. I
handed her up a glass of milk, all she wanted, and she
rode off, her long skirt puffed out by the wind. At the
gate she looked back and waved. I wonder if she ever got
her school? and how she managed the big boys? and
where she is now?

But while school was giving me thrills grandmother
said I wasn't learning anything she could see; more important, I was in daily danger from playing with the
children of "shif'less" people. Shiftlessness: own cousin
to drink; in wickedness six to one, half a dozen to the
other.

You worked your farm smartly; kept up the imple-
ments and the barns; maintained a properly-stocked
larder; everybody on the place worked, worked with
that sense of unity, of family pride in "standing" without
which nobody could expect to hold up his head; and the
better blood you were and the more money you had
the more proudly this was true. Grandmother never
flinched from this code. She had the pioneer woman's
pathetic, defensive snobbishness. Wasn't she of eastern
Dutchess, a sprig of the same family tree as Peter Stuyvesant, an early Governor of New York? Were not the
Spragues of Rhode Island and the Sanfords of Connecticut her kin? Likely she'd see this nobility contaminated
in her grandchild by shiftless contact!

In the end, except for brief, glorious winter terms, all

that I learned until I went away to school I learned from my father's political friends and from my grandmother. Adah Melinda taught me "manners," clever dodges with my hands; made me observant, made me "write down things." We didn't use highfalutin words like "diary." Above all, she drilled into me that no matter how good you were or, secondarily, how "learn'd," you couldn't afford to slight certain worldlinesses. Lily-white hands were her fetich. Possibly they wouldn't make a lady of you if you weren't one; certainly you couldn't be a lady without them. She made very clever gloves out of white linen; never lifted a hand without putting a pair on, and saw to it sternly that I wore them when I helped. They were always drying ghostily outdoors; the syringa bushes burgeoned with them.

Crooning helped housework. Fragments of an old ballad ring in my ears yet to the rhythm of the churn:

> The sun had sunk behind the hill
> When across yon dreary moor,
> A weary lad,
> All tattered and sad,
> Came up to the farmer's door.
> "Can you tell me," said he,
> "If any there be
> Who would likely give employ?
> To reap or to sow,
> To plough or to mow,
> To me, a farmer's boy.

I don't remember what happened next; only that, happily,

> The lad he grew to be a man,
> The good old farmer died;
> He left the lad with all he had,
> And his daughter for his bride.

We liked dreary ballads, funerals, and things. Perhaps because our hearts were gay.

Speaking of gloves, women made everything that covered the human form divine; often they didn't know how to make it, but they made it. Their amateurishness gives the caricatural look to old daguerreotypes. Distant neighbors sought grandmother to show them the way about in the tortuously turkey-tracked patterns of the period. Church brought out the sartorial stars. I remember a tense-mouthed, tiny woman with six tall sons whom she drove into the meeting-house ahead of her, like a marshal. The stalwarts all wore gingham pants. Their mother made these interesting garments. When she got her brood into the pew she produced from her reticule six squares of unbleached muslin and gave one to each, with a warning look. This clan were always the last to arrive; the preacher waited for the handkerchief ceremony to be got through with, then rose briskly and lined the first hymn:

> "How tedious and tasteless the hours
> When Jesus no longer I see;

Sweets prospects, sweet birds, and sweet flowers
Have all lost their sweetness for me."

Usually the singing was tangled up by a set old man of ninety-four who *wouldn't* wear spectacles and who finished each verse half a line behind everybody else. As for the little mother of the gingham giants, she was a queer one in many ways. There was a dark rumor, never denied, that she kept her pies in the linen-closet.

The Sundays when the circuit-rider was due at our little red-brick chapel, three miles away, and the county funerals brought the community its only social life. To miss a good funeral for any reason was a tragedy second only to dying oneself. Sermons were sulphuric. I remember one preacher who worked himself into a magnificent "pulpit sweat" over something called the "continental Sunday." As we were cut off by distance and doctrine from everything resembling amusements, I hardly know why preacher thundered at us about the levity of "furriners" on the Lord's Day. But I am sure that no profane pleasure of the "continental Sunday" ever afforded the zest of our sacred and only one of church. It was more than a temple; it was bread and the circus.

Grandmother Bundy, burning up with ambition and a love of elegance, had fifty years of the drab routine of the farm. How did she stand them? But the only careers open to women then were the home and invalidism. Women were either draft horses of endurance or they gave in to life and "enjoyed poor health." You asked them how they were and they told you they were "right complaining." We all knew as many invalids half a century ago as today we know women who are happy and successful in highly competitive professions, either because they are toughly and beautifully fit or because the spirit of the age persuades them that they are. In 1841, when William Henry Harrison was inaugurated President, Mrs. Harrison did not go to Washington with him. She was an invalid. She remained at the Harrison homestead in North Bend, Ohio. President Harrison, you remember, died one month after his inauguration; his wife survived him twenty-five years. The announcement of her death surprised the public. It had thought her long gone.

"Old age" clapped its black Chantilly-lace cap on grandmother before she was forty. Besides the terribly-dating dress of the period and the experience, fatally-aging to any woman, of living with a married son (though the sweetest of men), Adah Melinda had sacrificed her beautiful teeth on the vague surmise of an itinerant dentist that they caused her "neuralgy." Dentists and "face painters" traveled by once a year and reaped a harvest. I always regretted that the artists in "oil-paint work" who portrayed certain members of my family did not, instead, make a portrait of my vital little grandmother and leave the dentist to do the others. But whatever else the old darling lost, she kept a tight grip on worldly convention. She was often tried by our green

HARRIET LANE, niece of President Buchanan and mistress of the White House during his administration, 1857

KATE CHASE, daughter of Chief Justice Salmon P. Chase, a celebrated beauty of the 'sixties and 'seventies

KATE CHASE
With General John J. Abercrombie and staff
Civil War days

Molly from County Mayo. My mother had found Molly, young, pretty, quite savage, somewhere in Vinton. I remember the implike way she slid down off a gray horse at our door the day she came—to stay for years. That Molly *would* bring the boiled potatoes to the table in her apron, squeezing them. We told her we didn't do that . . . she kept on squeezing the potatoes in her apron. Grandmother went perfectly wild.

"Suppose you came in squeezing the potatoes in your apron when Governor Dennison was here?" she blazed, "or Judge Benjamin Wade? . . . or Judge Giddings? . . . or General Butler? . . . or Judge Chase? . . . or . . ."

She managed to stop just short of mentioning the Almighty.

Most of the men whose names grandmother hurled I came to know as I grew up. Lincoln was my father's personal friend, though I never saw him until he lay dead in the rotunda of the capitol at Columbus, but Salmon P. Chase, ever with poaching eyes on the Presidency, and whose daughter Kate (she married Governor Sprague of Rhode Island) was the toast of the nation, was of that early circle; so were "Free Soil Giddings" and Ben Wade. I remember the rough-hewn challenging look of Wade, his ferocity in argument (also that he took sugar in his buttermilk), and Rutherford B. Hayes (he remained always a dull stranger to the livelier public, but he was the most courteous of men), and the two noble Shermans, and others whose names I have forgotten.

Judge Chase, Salmon P., was invariably brought into the talk. A great man, of course; one couldn't keep off the subject. I remember particularly a roar of laughter that greeted a new Chase story told at our farm round-table by the chief actor in it. This was a popular parson, the Reverend Granville Moody of Ripley, Ohio. He was chaplain of a regiment largely made up from that neighborhood. A few months before Lincoln was re-nominated for President, Moody was in Washington on leave. The Capital then was at its most disloyal; Mr. Chase, Secretary of the Treasury, was occupied as usual with his own boom as candidate for President. He asked Moody for breakfast; didn't say what hour. The chaplain, an early riser, turned up about seven-thirty. Why not? Mr. Chase was in his dressing room. When told of Moody's arrival, he sent for him, said how glad he was that he had come early; he'd wanted to have a confidential chat.

"You'll excuse me if I go on shaving," said the Secretary; "Well; a number of my friends are coming to breakfast. We want to fix on a plan for my candidacy. What I'd especially like you to do, Chaplain, is to tell these men exactly how the boys in blue feel about Mr. Lincoln. You've just come from the front. You tell them."

Moody said for once in his life he kept still and listened. Listened to the President's Cabinet officer com-

ment on the soldier's lack of confidence in Lincoln;
listened to his conclusion that it would be an admirable
thing if the men who wanted to see him, Chase, nominated, were told how completely without illusion about
Lincoln were the boys in blue. So on, thus. Moody just
listened.

Duly, a large party sat down to breakfast. Mr. Chase
called upon Dr. Moody to ask the blessing. The Chaplain was now pretty hungry. But he didn't slight that
grace. He made, on the contrary, quite a prayer of it in
which he took occasion to tell the Lord how completely
beloved and believed-in Abraham Lincoln was by the
boys in blue. There wasn't anything the boys in blue
wouldn't do for that man, Lord.

Moody never mentioned his host's nomination for the
Presidency. And it was a delicious breakfast, too. Trust
Kate Chase to see that her father's board glorified the
flesh-pots!

Moody was more than a chaplain. He could forget the
cloth if necessary, and with what evangelic tact! It was
at Lookout Mountain, I think, that the Colonel of
Moody's regiment went tearing up and down the lines
yelling to the troops—"Give 'em hell, boys." The chaplain was at his heels, yelling too, "Do as your Colonel
tells you boys. . . . Do as your Colonel tells you."

Of many meetings with Salmon P. Chase I remember
particularly one in the railway station at Columbus,
Ohio: a May night, 1868. I was with my father, on my

way home from school. That was the spring of Andrew
Johnson's impeachment trial. The two men talked and
talked. About the impeachment (it was sure to fail and
thus divide the Republican Party) but only briefly, and
as it related to the perennial subject: Mr. Chase's candidacy for the Presidency. Chase had sent for my father
a few days before to talk this over with him; they were
close personal friends. He was Chief Justice then. "But
also," he said, "I feel that I am the servant of the people
and should they call me to preside for four years over the
destiny of our country I doubtless would feel it my duty
to comply." How familiar I was to become with that diffident little protocol!

The Chief Justice's plan was to secure the Presidential
nomination on the Democratic ticket; failing this he
would "enter the arena" as an independent candidate
against Grant. "Of my success," he told father, "there
can be no doubt." He always appeared like a very great
man to whom nothing could be denied. Which is part
of being so.

Father was shocked, he told me, at what he felt was
the Chief Justice's treason to the Radicals. But I found
Mr. Chase charming. Why shouldn't he be President?
So polite, so flatteringly interested in unimportant me.
Did we girls read that amazing woman, Mrs. Browning,
at college? Ah, but we must! Read that one, anyway,
about "The swan's nest among the reeds," he said, with
an odd smile. Then he was off again on the subject of

Chase for President. The announcer began to roar my
train, but the Chief Justice, entranced by White House
dreams, held father like the Ancient Mariner.

Of Grant none of us had ever heard until the war. But
as his star arose he seemed to pulverize every other topic
save that of Grant, Grant, Grant. Where he was; what
he was doing. What he was likely to do, that was something else. Nobody could say. Mystery in a person, what
magic it has for us! I remember so clearly, it might have
been yesterday, Grant's appearance in Cincinnati after
his return from a trip around the world. There was an
avalanche of applause; the great crowd was blue with
Union veterans. He was quite unmoved by it all, as if he
cared not that people applauded him. He looked dead
tired. His eyes were like tapestry eyes. Yet in spite of his
listlessness one felt that stubborn, granite force, felt that
which made the man, as Henry Adams said, "the greatest
general since Napoleon."

Late in the summer of 1863 I took part in a remarkable demonstration that grew out of the war bitterness
which so deepened in intensity that year. Treason to the
government was everywhere; rage against the hated
"Copperheads" swept loyal districts like a storm. Over
at McArthur in Vinton there was to be "a big day" showing how we felt about the war. Our county, Jackson, hit
upon a spectacular expression:

Thirty-six girls, each girl dressed to represent one of

the thirty-six states—West Virginia had just come in—
rode the ten miles across country in an immense open
wagon drawn by sixty yoke of oxen. Through that roll-
ing country the whole drive was simply up one hill and
down another. When we were on the crest of one hill we
could see the long line of oxen rounding the distant bend
of the hill beyond.

We "states" stood all the way over and back—a long
day's journey. There must have been seats in the wagon,
but we stood and looked over the top of the high boards
that inclosed it and watched the people pouring out of
the farms.

Men dropped their pitchforks and came running
across fields; women hurried from farmhouses, wiping
their hands on their aprons, little children stumbling
after them, old people coming up breathless. It must have
been a great sight—that line of beasts (they said the
sound of their hoofs could be heard for miles)—that colorful blaze of youth, and all that it meant. And how
people clapped and waved and cheered!

It was the loveliest moment of summer, the land filled
with the sights and sounds and scents of harvest. To this
day, if I catch the faintest fragrance of new-mown hay,
it brings it all back to me. I feel again the thrill of that
ride and the terrifying, powerful pull of those sixty ox-
teams.

That was sixty-eight years ago, yet I feel again the
thrill.

CHAPTER II

KISMET

ONE late-December afternoon, 1868, my sister-in-law, Kate Bundy, and I were making Christmas presents before the sitting-room fire at the farm. Kate was the widow of my half-brother, dead but a few months. She was twenty-three, with lots of spirit and charm, if not actual beauty. She had a two-year-old baby; we had put a buffalo robe on the floor and he was playing on it, good as gold. Winter set in early that year; already there were drifts of snow against the windows.

When a present was finished we would take it into the parlor and put it on the organ—a little rosewood organ; it was to be a Christmas present to Kate from my father. It had a number of cubbyholes, and we put small presents in them; the top was heaped with things and there were some cedar branches about that Kate had brought from the woods. The piece that they gave with the organ was on the rack—it was "The Strawberry and Cream Waltz." The room was very cold.

Kate had finished all her presents. The last one was a lamp-mat in bright orange wool. It looked like a dahlia. Kate took it into the parlor. There was straw under the ingrain carpet in the sitting-room; it rustled when you walked. I heard Kate playing a bar or two of the "Waltz"; she came back, shivering.

"It's like the tomb in there," she said. "I'll tell you— let's go over to town. It's only three o'clock. The stores'll look pretty all lighted up and tinselly."

But I was knitting a muffler for Captain Foraker; it wasn't anything like finished.

"You go," I said.

She believed she would. The horse we girls rode was out in the fields. Instead of ploughing through the snow to catch him, Kate decided she would saddle "Mountain," who was in the barn near the house. Mountain was a young, mettlesome horse that had belonged to Kate's husband. He was hardly broken, not a safe horse for a woman to ride, and I said so. But you couldn't stop Kate doing a thing once she had made up her mind. Time he was made safe, she said.

I remember watching her cross the snow towards the barn. She wore a little black pork-pie turban, her bright hair bundled into a net; a short fur jacket and an immense crinoline of some mourning stuff. Her skirt tilted smartly as she walked against the wind. I admired Kate.

I forgot to look when she rode out. I was lost in my muffler. It was pepper-and-salt, with a scarlet border and deep fringe at the ends. It was almost a yard wide and three yards long. You see men in Far West films today wearing those berserker things. I forgot time until I found

I couldn't see to knit, and I got up to light the lamp. The boy who did the chores came in with coal.

Suddenly—I can't explain it—I was seized with a panic of fear. Kate! She ought to be home by now! I fairly pushed the boy out of the house. He must go down the road and call out. The hired man came in with the milk. I hurried him off.

Grandmother appeared from somewhere—like as not, she said, Kate was just dawdling over folderols. Kate was like a child about Christmas fixings. But I could see grandmother was worried, too. I piled on the coal; the fire blazed up and made the room bright as day. It shone clear across the road. Kate would see it. Grandmother took up the baby and sat down in a low rocker before the fire. The baby went to sleep.

I don't know how long we waited there in the fire-light, I peering out into the night, grandmother's rocker creaking. I know that it had seemed a long time when I heard the sitting-room door very carefully opened. It was Belle, our hired girl. She beckoned to me. Grandmother didn't see her. I went out to the kitchen. At the storm-door stood an old farmer we knew very well. No, he wouldn't come in. He didn't say anything for a moment, just stood there stamping the snow from his boots and looking down. Then ——

"Kate's dead," he said.

He had found her lying face down in the snow, one arm over her head, her skirt spread around her like a dark pool. At the foot of the hill three hundred feet back was her hat, her purse, one glove—little things. She must have been dragged some distance. There was a frozen pond just there; boys coming home from school threw lighted firecrackers on the ice. The noise frightened "Mountain" and he ran away.

I didn't get Captain Foraker's muffler finished for Christmas. There were other things to do . . . all the presents to be removed from the reed organ father was giving Kate . . . all the greens. You couldn't have things like that about. I slipped the "Strawberry and Cream Waltz" into the big family Bible. It seemed to be the only place to hide it. Nothing of Christmas was left in that cold room.

I think now that this was a mistake. I think Kate would have liked to have about her the little things she had so loved to make.

That year, streaked by tragedy for me, saw also the bright adventure well on its way. In June I had graduated from the Ohio Wesleyan Female College at Delaware. The year that I entered this remarkable institution Joseph Benson Foraker, back to books after the Civil War, appeared at the "university" in the same town. That class was full of captains, majors and colonels all under twenty.

Now the kaleidoscope of destiny began, in my opinion, to turn to some purpose.

JOSEPH BENSON AND JULIA BUNDY FORAKER
On their wedding journey, 1870

We met.

We had been heading towards an encounter for a long time, Foraker and I. He had only a year's start of me in life and we grew up on farms but a short motoring distance apart today, but separated then, as by a continent, by the worst roads in the world. While I was learning my politics in pinafores he was already starting things over the hills in Highland County. This was a time when the Ohio legislature was holding its most telling conference under sycamore trees. The Republicans had fixed on their first Presidential candidate. Foraker had run up a flag on his father's farm at Reece's Mill, bearing the name of Frémont and Dayton. He had cut down a sapling for a pole, made the pennant out of bits from his mother's home-dyed "pieces"—and let it wave! It was one of the first Republican banners in Ohio, and the first and the only one then in that part of the State.

This alert new-party man was ten years old. Frémont, explorer "from whose camp fires have sprung cities," had captured the lad's imagination along with his Oregon Trail guide, Kit Carson.

Ben Foraker cried when Frémont was defeated. And by that varmint, Buchanan, too! Foraker was to play an important rôle in the election of later Presidents, but never with the heart-break grip of first love. After the flag episode Ben was indulgently regarded by the local Black Republicans as one of them; the miller, the blacksmith, the storekeeper and the farmers called him "our man" with a grin.

He did show statesman traits. He adored fishing. His mother was a born angler; when the fishin' mood possessed her the house could keep itself. She and her favorite boy would trail the best places along the Rocky Fork of Paint Creek for hours; she took Ben with her whether paw needed him or not. Over their dinner pail, sitting under a big willow, they talked. Of religion: "Professed sanctity" was a meeting-house schism then; some folks claimed a place among the "completely sanctified"; others were modestly content to be known as "merely justified." Well, they had no call to fight about it, had they? Of low tariff: it was a sin and a shame what the Ohio sheep-growers had to put up with, English wool coming in like it did. Of the gold rush: Ben, who wanted to go west and pick up a lot of nuggets same as everybody, must promise cross-his-heart that he never would. Just thinking of him on those dangerous new rail trains, his mother wouldn't sleep a mite. Better stick to the canals. Of slavery, of course: Ben read *Uncle Tom's Cabin* aloud. His mother couldn't help him much over the hard words; moreover, Uncle Tom only mildly excited her. Temperance was her passion. Of slavery she saw nothing, but drink was a common-stalking evil; it devastated communities all around her. She, along with several million other women of that day, was for going after drink and wiping it out. And they did go after it—

with prayers. Not until twenty years later was Carrie Nation to come along with her hatchet. But the saloonkeepers were even more confused and terrified by the praying women than by the hatcheteers. The gentle crusaders broke up business as successfully as their athletic sisters, and their methods had a more lasting effect.

Between the boy and his mother, with her fierce principles and her gentle nature, there was a quaint, tender bond that kept the two very close to the end of life. And the contemplative idling with a line which she encouraged gave Foraker a rare escape from his tightly-screwed existence on a farm. Lots of men, he found out, had come upon ways to change everything.

Books: Napoleon, the Indian wars, the Roman emperors. Ben read down all the dip candles in the house. When his brothers complained of this, his father—a tall, lean farmer with an Andrew Jackson profile and a bone-dry wit—said, "By the Eternal, the boy should burn all the candles in Highland County if he wanted to!" This was high talk in a God-fearing family. That year Ben squared things by learning 1,396 verses of Scripture and winning a prize, a small red Testament. His first majority.

It was quite against the design of the founders of old Delaware that "the sexes," students-under-the-elms, should meet. Boys and girls did not come there to meet each other. (Ah, but didn't they . . . !) A rule existed that forbade "females" to look at, speak to, write to, even dream of the university "men"—except on Saturday night from eight to nine sharp. That was reception night. Gentlemen might call. One hour! Girls who had no beaux to receive hung over the bannister—"reception door must always be left open"—and jeered with mischievous eyes. Mrs. Donelson, governess of the college, received with us during the whole of those racing sixty minutes. When nine o'clock struck her hand was already on a bell—irreverently, the "cow bell"; she rang it sharply. This meant, and we knew it, "All ashore that's going ashore"; in other words, the gentlemen were to leave. But it was much harder to get them to go than it was to get them to come. It ended by dismissing the girls to their rooms first, then dowsing the gas. There was nothing else left for our beaux to do but to go home.

And yet, how romance thrived in that old town! I think it was the famous sulphur spring on the campus that betrayed the authorities. It is uphill work trying to keep down romance when there is a spring to furnish an excuse for a short walk at any time. The waters, so pure, so healthful—and so dangerous! In spite of the Puritan fiat, President Rutherford B. Hayes managed to meet and become engaged to Lucy Webb at Delaware; Vice-President Charles Warren Fairbanks met his wife, Cornelia Cole, there; many other names which the public came to know figured in those Delaware matches.

As I look back upon it I think that life in that fresh-water college of the 'sixties was as quaint and wonderful as anything that ever was. To me, at sixteen, it brought my first contact with the world, with young friends, even my first railroad journey. No, not my first. That came off some years earlier. My father was going to Athens to hear McKee of Kentucky speak at a barbecue. What about my going with him as far as Zaleski, spending the night there with my friend, Mary Wills, and coming back with him the next day? A ride on a train! Well, I couldn't resist that. I had a wonderful time. Mary gave me a long green *barége* veil. She wore a veil, so I was crazy for one. I was at the station at four o'clock the following afternoon, as agreed, but father's train wasn't. It was waiting for McKee of Kentucky to finish. I didn't know what to do. Mother would expect me; worry if I didn't come. A freight train came along just then. "Take that," somebody said, and helped me into an empty car.

After a long, lonely time a man with a lantern came back, climbing like a cat from one car into another.

"Hello!" he said.

He hadn't expected to find a little girl all tangled up in green veiling. He said I must come forward to the engine and ride with him. He helped me over and over and over. Did I say it was a *long* train? When at last we got to the engine I found out something. My friend wasn't the engineer; he was the fireman. The engineer was drunk; very. The fireman pushed him aside and he

drove the train. My, but we went fast! The wind! My
veil stood straight out! At last it was my station. I still
had several miles in an ox-cart, the stars had come out
then, before I was home. Mother was standing in the
doorway, watching for me. She had a lamp in her hand.

When I first went to Delaware father put me in the
middle of the coach, saying in a sort of good-by-forever
voice that in case of an accident I had a better chance
there. They seemed to lack something, those much-
talked-about railroad journeys. Indeed, I took a number
before I was convinced that the engineer was not necessarily drunk, and that I *might*, in a pinch, sit at the end
of the car without feeling that I was flirting with the
grim reaper.

To resume with college (Horace Greeley said that the
way to resume was to resume): Social occasions at Delaware were so jealously conceded that each one had a thrill
beyond anything thereafter. Taboos were on all worldly
amusements. There was to be no dancing; above all,
there was to be no *waltzing*. "Huggin' up," our preacher
called it, "two strangers huggin' up." There were no
cards, no play-goings, no rope at all as we understand it
for our boys and girls today. I remember that one of the
divinity students was expelled in his senior year for attending a performance of "The Merchant of Venice."
The adventure took him to Columbus and made him
miss chapel the next morning. One of the old presidents,
Doctor McCabe, held that a student must be in chapel

unless dead. Foraker told me later that a roommate of his, troubled by the severe sentence on the man who saw Shylock, disposed of at a great sacrifice a ticket he had secretly purchased for Charlotte Cushman as Lady Macbeth. Another classmate was pitched out of the Methodist Church for attending a small town dance—he was eighteen at the time; the worst of it was that the boy never again entered a church. The next thing we heard of him was terrible—he was reading Tom Paine's *Age of Reason.*

Far more dramatic, more emotional than the theater of that day were the midwinter revivals. Church-college towns were swayed by them, and some of the great revivalists whom I remember had certainly, though their sincerity could not be questioned, the gifts of very moving actors. Always they drew crowds.

But do not imagine that fun with a rare edge did not flourish then quite "as if life held no tomb"—after Lord Byron's hint. Roastin'-ear parties when the woods were like flame and the air was like ice-cold new cider. Unearthly sleigh rides. Snow was snow then; often the driver had to set up a stake to see where in the drifts he was going. Not that we sleigh-riders cared! And lectures—we went not to be improved, but to see each other, of course! The shallow, sensational "lyceum lectures" were the rage immediately after the Civil War. Anybody who for any reason had become notorious through the newspapers was hired to lecture; a man who had been in state's prison for felony, and was now in the legislature, lectured. A woman who had been captured and outraged by the Ute Indians *lectured*.

Of the great speakers, I heard Dickens at Delaware during his second and last visit to America in 1868. I cannot think that anyone ever heard a person read with such inimitable realism and charm as this "foreigner" (they called him that) in a black velveteen jacket. I remember the jacket and the charm, but of what the author read only the unforgetable death of Little Nell, which provoked sobs. Anna Dickinson, who had written a shocking, immensely-read book with a black-and-white theme, appeared in ashes-of-roses cashmere with a long train, lectured on Joan of Arc, and created a havoc in hearts. What was a *pretty* woman like that doing in politics? And Bret Harte, the literary idol of muslin maidens, enchanted us. I think we went expecting to see a handsome "Jack Folinsbee" or a "Jack Hamlin" type, coolly insolent and fascinating. But Bret Harte had a scholar's quiet voice, poet's hair, a little long and parted in the middle, and wasn't it very gray? and young, dark eyes, brilliant almost as if with fever. He talked about the "Argonauts of '49"—and you could have heard a pin drop.

Everything was done—same old care—to make forbidden fruit tempting. We had no sports except croquet. There was, probably still is, a millpond where a fallen tree had created a dangerous current. It was put out-of-

bounds. Worse than dangerous, swimming was unlady-
like. After that the millpond became secretly and immensely the rage. The brightest girl in school (she had
promised, after repeated offenses, that she would never
go to the pond again) was drowned there; a girl with
her was miraculously brought back. The two had
clutched at each other's long hair, were wound and
bound in it. I find in my journal of '66 reference to a
rumor that "the room above the Olentangy engine-house
was to be turned into a gymnasium for the men." I don't
remember any talk of athletics for us girls. What would
we have done with sports in our tight stays, our crino-
lines, our preoccupation with "the crimp"—our
"switches"?

The college tried to ban switches. They might as well
have tried to ban the leaves from coming out on the trees.
It was the height of the woman's-crowning-glory-her-
hair ideal, hers or someone else's, it didn't matter. I did
not wear a switch, but it was only because I had more
hair than I knew what to do with, anyway. No woman
under ninety-five was free from hair vanity. One day my
history teacher, Miss Brown, thin, prim, and forty, sent
word that she wished to see me in her classroom at a certain hour. Very ominous. Now what had I done? Miss
Brown looked forbidding as I entered the room; she
asked me to close the door, then, guardedly—would I
lend her my switch for next reception night? I was so
relieved, I could have given her my hair! The switch

craze must have reached its height about 1873, when one phase of the panic of that year was expressed in advertisements of a "Crisis in Human Hair." Shop windows dangled with bargains.

Our graduation exercises were Spartan endurance tests for the audience. I have before me the "Order of Exercises" of that hot June 24, 1868. The program began at half-past eight in the morning and went on all day long. Every girl in the class of twenty-one read an essay. Interspersed were prayers and musical numbers, mostly polkas for four hands. The subject of the last essay on that day was "Who Are Waiting for Us?" The question fell on ears jaded by the reflections of sweet girl graduates for eight solid hours. And it was supper-time. I'm afraid that the number of those waiting for us was a little thin.

Apprehensively in 1877 the female college and the university were united. More rules: "Young ladies will not be allowed to walk more than one block with a gentleman going to and from recitations." The local paper followed this with a reminder that "the longest block is from the Court House to Lincoln Avenue." Delaware is today one of the greatest of co-ed universities. I believe there are few rules. The sulphur spring is said to retain all its old magic.

One event of Delaware days I shall remember forever. It was the night of an entertainment given by our dramatic club. The program depicted our country during the Civil War. A girl who represented the South was dressed in black and had chains hanging from her wrists. I was the North. I wore white and on my head a crown in red, white, and blue paper after the shield of the United States. I should not have remembered the occasion and the parts we played but for the fact that the next day the news came that President Lincoln had been assassinated. Our chapel was a small frame building with a bell in the tower. The bell was rung by hand. That day, April 15, 1865, the bell tolled all day long. We girls took turns at the rope. I remember pulling it until my hands were blistered.

Later, when Lincoln's funeral train went through the country on the way to Illinois, it stopped at all the places at which the President's train had stopped when he was on his way to his first inauguration. One of these towns was Columbus, twenty-five miles from Delaware. I went there, irresistibly moved, like thousands of others, to pay a last respect. The coffin was placed on a catafalque under the great dome of the State House, which at that time had entrances from the north, south, east, and west. The procession was formed four abreast and came from High Street, which is south of the Capitol. The lines passed through the door and divided at the bier, two going out of the eastern and two out of the western door. I do not recall that anyone I knew was with me. I only remember passing through and looking down at Lincoln's white face.

Washington always had a curious fascination for me. My father's years in Congress made him a fund of enthralling gossip about the capital and the shining lights there. Would I ever see that city beautiful, I wondered. I almost got there the winter after my graduation. Father had planned that I was to spend some weeks with him. Long and frenzied shopping at the great "Shillito's" in Cincinnati. Father liked pretty clothes and had a man's respect for quality above trimmings. He insisted upon paying so much for the black Lyons velvet for my long coat that there was nothing left for lace to trim it with. It should have had lace, of course. Other splendors: a black corded silk of the fashionable "Metternich green"; a fifteen-yard dress pattern was not too much—dresses were voluminous dreams—and a "plaid costume," a loud, pleasant fashion sent us by Queen Victoria from Balmoral.

After all, I didn't go. At the last minute I had to stay at home and take care of Kate's baby. Kate's mother was ill, my own mother had gone then, grandmother was too old; it was I who must look after Willy. No trained nurses to take family responsibility then.

But perhaps I enjoyed Washington all the more when I first visited it with my husband in 1878. And my Metternich green and my black mantle became merged with

my trousseau. Styles didn't change in the volatile manner
of today. As I was my father's housekeeper, he was pretty
tragic at the prospect of my leaving him to marry a pen-
niless young lawyer. The law was overcrowded in the
cities, he said. Foraker himself was a bit staggered to learn
that there were three hundred lawyers practicing in 1869
in Cincinnati. Three hundred lawyers! He made this
formidable number the subject of his graduation thesis;
he had gone to Cornell from Delaware, graduating in
the first class (eight in number) from that university.
Moreover, my father mistrusted a city with its devious
pitfalls for the feet of young men. If we stuck safely to
the farm, he argued, my husband might, with luck, some
day become judge of Jackson County. And look here!
stay at home and he would give me half of the farm,
lock, stock, and barrel, then and there. Coal cropped up
on our land a little later; one thousand acres sold for one
hundred thousand dollars. But Foraker and I thought
we'd risk anything that fortune had in store for us. Neither of us believed that this could be other than pure rose.

Father was a good sport. He gave me the grandest
wedding the county ever saw. Two enormous cakes
were sent from Portsmouth, fifty miles away; they were
a riot of angels, arches, real orange blossoms, tight sugar
roses, and little bride-and-groom figures, made in Ger-
many; very Bavarian indeed. The wedding was at nine
o'clock in the morning; not *Harper's Bazaar*, sacred authority on social usage, but the solitary Cincinnati train,

determined this October-frosty hour. My trousseau was
perhaps inappropriate for a girl marrying a young man
with his way to make. But then, as now, a trousseau was
a trousseau and it was nothing else. I was far from shops,
had no one to advise me; but with the color plates in
Godey's Lady's Book and "Danarian's" general store over
in Portsmouth ready to order anything under the sun
that one fancied, I imagine I missed nothing. Father,
though he assured me that I was breaking his heart, gave
me plenty of rope, and, I think, had as good a time as I
had.

Real lace was the lady's own hall mark then. I had a
shawl of white "llama"; I thought it was lovely draped
over my carriage dress of "dregs-of-wine" surah or my
apple-green "calling costume"; it added possibly twenty-
five years to my appearance, but that didn't worry us
then. And a Chantilly lace sacque, with angel sleeves
that caught on my heavy bracelets and tore every time I
wore it, gave me a sense of elegance as sustaining as spiritual faith. "Real Val" was, of course, the lace of laces. My
wedding collar was of "real Val"; when life sternly set
in, how gallantly that collar traveled from one black silk
to another! At a Grant reception I remember that nine-
tenths of the women wore black silk, sometimes with a
white satin bonnet; very elegant.

Some years later, when my husband and I were visit-
ing the Hannas at Cleveland, I was to get a thrill from
seeing "real Val" used as casually as rick-rack. Mr.

Hanna and Foraker had gone off to a banquet at which my husband was to speak. Mrs. Hanna and I didn't go; we waited up for our husbands in the library so that we could hear all about it. Mrs. Hanna sat there sewing *wide* "real Val" on a pair of pantalettes. On *pantalettes*! And I was proud to have enough to go around the neck of my best dress!

A great many wardrobes of that period owed their treasures in real lace to the tragedy of the Franco-Prussian war. I find in one of my early journals a yellowed clipping from *Harper's Bazaar*, January 7, 1871, containing the following announcement:

Laces and French Embroideries at Panic Prices:—Arnold, Constable & Co. are offering a large and valuable stock of these goods at *About One Half the Cost of Production*, having been purchased of the manufacturers at *Ruinous Sacrifice in Consequence of the Prussian Advance.*

It was not until I became engaged that I took an interest in the still new fad—the sewing-machine. My father opposed it (men did) as long as he could, then surprised me by a gift of the "Florence." It was complicated, awkward (the sewing-plate was raised very high) and costly, but I spent entranced hours at it. I had a romantic feeling just then about neatly-hemmed sheets, towels and tea-cloths. Otherwise I doubt if I should ever have had the patience to struggle with "Florence's" cranky temperament.

For the first period of our married life my father's

bounty took the form of many and frequent contributions to our household needs and to my personal ones. I never knew how rasped Foraker was by this until he began earning enough to provide things himself. If Foraker gave me a bit of jewelry or a new dress or something in china or linen, and, on its first appearance, it was commented on, perhaps, he would say, carelessly: "Yes, that's rather nice. Did your father give it to you?" He hated to receive things. He was a giver.

In Foraker's first year at the bar he earned six hundred dollars. We were engaged then and we wanted to get married. All Foraker's friends said, "Oh, you'll be sure to make twice that next year." We thought so, too. So we got married. And Foraker's income that first year of married life was exactly four hundred dollars. The following year it rose to eleven hundred, and the next to twenty-seven hundred. After that it was easy.

"My encounters with the wolf at the door those first four years," said Foraker, "are painful to recall. Let's talk of something else."

CHAPTER III

THE HAYES HYMNAL AND THE TECUMSEH KISS

THE 'seventies were not decorative years, but Opportunity strode through them. While Foraker competed with the three hundred lawyers, I rocked cradles, copied legal documents for my husband in an earnest, ladylike hand, struggled with the *Buckeye Cook Book* and other facers, yet in all was buoyed by the pleasantest of convictions, that of getting ahead. The period brought Foraker his first elective office, judge of the Cincinnati Superior Court, and me my first visit to Washington.

President Hayes was in the "Executive Mansion" then. It was President Roosevelt who restored the charming old name, the "White House." Through my father, who spent much of his life in Congress, I seemed to have known the Hayeses always. The striking thing about the domestic atmosphere they created was their temperance hospitality (ah, but didn't that take courage then!) and their Sunday-night hymn-singing.

Those Sunday nights were so often described to me that I knew every detail of the scene before I ever saw it: the heavy ebony furniture; the crimson satin curtains, fearfully and wonderfully draped; the potted plants scattered all about the room; the dripping candles; the hot

fire, one huge lump of anthracite! and Lucy Webb
Hayes, in hoop-skirted black velvet, illusion, and seed
pearls, at a gloomy Chickering square piano playing
hymns while the guests, a crowd of people, sang with
heart and soul . . .

>"A few more years shall roll"

or

>"There *is* a land of *pure* delight
>*Where* saints immortal stand"

or, even the grovelling "worm hymns" which preceded
Moody and Sankey.

My own Sunday night début at the Hayeses' was on
an occasion that was almost worldly. General Sherman
was there. He was a great star, very human, very lovable,
and wildly idolized. Whenever he appeared there was a
sort of riot to do him honor. And riot there was this
night. No one had need of hymns with "Tecumseh" to
worship; the Hayeses wisely didn't bring out the books.

I remember an afternoon reception, at Colonel Dayton's house in Cincinnati, at which there was an imposing
half-circle of women receiving. General Sherman appeared in all the Assyrian magnificence of military full
dress. He took in the long line with his keen, penetrating
eyes—kind eyes, but with grains of gunpowder lurking
in them—then advanced. The courage and strength of
will which led him to the assault of Kenesaw, to show
that he was not afraid to fight, stood him once more.

Grandly he swept around that ring—and kissed every woman in it! A young lieutenant who witnessed this feat wondered how long he would have to wait before he would be great enough to do that. Social life hasn't the same luster since those gorgeous old heroes went.

I treasure an early picture of General Sherman which he gave my husband at the close of the Civil War; a cruel, war-is-hell photograph—it might have been taken just after Vicksburg. Sherman saw the picture at our house when he was nearing seventy. "Great Scott!" he exclaimed. "I don't look as old as that now, do I? I don't look as old as that *now*?" His distressed vanity was sweet.

At the time of the Grand Army Encampment in Columbus in September, 1888 (ah, what an immense and stirring thing the "G. A. R." was then!), General Sherman's mail came to him in the care of my husband, then Governor of Ohio. In May following, my husband put his hand into the pocket of a suit not worn since the previous fall and touched two thick letters addressed to General Sherman. The forwarding of these letters, with an explanation, brought me a most touching note from the General. The letters were from his wife; he had greatly loved her and she had died in the interval. It was, he wrote me, like having long, lovely details of news from the dear dead, with little tender cautions about his health and reassurances of the affection that had sustained him for so long. The old soldier had the fire of romance.

Sherman night at the Hayeses' remains green in memory because of another incident connected with it, one of those domestic trifles that women never forget. We were stopping at the old Ebbitt House in Washington; my six-year-old son, Benson, was with us. We couldn't take him to the President's house, could we? So we put him to bed, my husband gave him his watch and chain for company, and we went off after locking the door. But a gold watch and chain suggested to Benson an opportunity to astonish the world which he decided should not be wasted. He got up, dressed, started to go out, most splendid!—found the door locked. It must have been immediately after this that an army officer and his wife heard loud demands to be let out—like the starling—coming from the next room. They had the door opened, and saw only a very little boy who said that he wanted to go "downstairs" . . . and did they know that it was thirty-five minutes to ten?

This question of what to do with the children had a great way, in the old days, of puzzling Northern parents when the engraved invitation came in, if not actually holding them up when the carriage was at the door. There were no trained nurses for children then; none but crude, kind-hearted, irresponsible "girls." A woman couldn't leave her children in such hands without wondering all the time if Delia or Sally were now dropping the baby (the Delias and Sallys never mentioned it if they did) or now forgetting to keep the guard before the nursery fire—or what *were* they doing? For myself, I can say that there were times when this anxiety was capable of spoiling the party. The Southerners had their slaves—their devoted mammies—always a mother for a child. The rich New Yorkers had servants of an imported class who were thought to be more trustworthy. Outside of these people the social complication of children was a real problem. Means had less to do with it than the nature of the nurse-supply.

Even a President's wife felt this. In September, 1879, the President and Mrs. Hayes honored Cincinnati by a visit. The chief event of their entertainment was an evening reception given by the William S. Groesbecks at their handsome country house whose view took in the Kentucky hills, the "moccasin bend" of the chocolate-colored Ohio River and was of a beauty quite matchless when the moon came up. The affair was formal and splendid, the hour fashionably late—as late as eight o'clock. Little Fannie Hayes, the President's twelve-year-old daughter, came along with her parents. "I had to bring her," said Mrs. Hayes, simply. "I couldn't leave her alone at the hotel." I can see the child now, rubbing her sleepy eyes.

Perhaps the "plain people," that carefully-respected political ogre of the last century, admired this democratic one-of-us-ness. Thanks to our seeing things more largely, and to other causes, the President's wife today may travel with one maid, or four maids, even on an official tour, and by doing so not, necessarily, imperil one bit her husband's chances for a second term. There have come to be other ways for her to do that.

There was something very fine about Mr. and Mrs. Hayes. They did unpopular things, as their wineless dinner-giving, but it was with such thoroughbred courtesy that no one could resent it. They stood quite simply by the principle which they had brought with them to the White House. The Presidency could not swerve them from what they believed to be right. I think, however, that total abstinence was more her creed than his; but he yielded to her on this issue as on others. It has been pointed out sufficiently that Rutherford B. Hayes was utterly lacking in the politician's sense of politics. Just did what his standards obliged him to do. Did that—and served three terms as Governor of Ohio! His disinterestedness disarmed the most ax-grinding ward heeler.

And Lucy Webb Hayes went along, pleading gently, courteously, and wisely for temperance whenever and wherever she could, keeping the White House filled with flowers and welcoming there the sheep and the goats, the worldly and the unworldly, with all the grace of some smiling, tolerant, beloved queen. It does not exactly glow in remembrance, the Hayes régime, nor will it in history. Yet the Cave Dwellers, those old Washington-Georgetown families whose verdicts on an Administration have fearful and lasting weight—the old Cave

Lucy Webb Hayes
Wife of President Rutherford B. Hayes, 1877

Dwellers to this day say that we never had a First Lady like "Lucy Webb." She is one of their legends.

The President's dependence upon her was infinitely touching. When she died he wandered, dazed, through the lovely gardens she had made at their Ohio home. The sight of an empty bird fountain distressed him. "Oh, Lucy wouldn't like that," he was heard to say, half to himself, and hurried to fill it. He was like a man in a dream.

There are comparatively few women who have been in public life who have had justice done them, apart from the men with whom their lives were associated. The nineteenth century imposed upon them the same "true female delicacy" about calling attention to themselves as women, individual personalities, as, in letters, it imposed upon the George Sands, the George Eliots, the Daniel Sterns.

A study of Lucy Webb Hayes, with insight, would reveal more about the real force, "the best" in American life of her epoch, than would all the biographies of her husband that have been or will be written. With all her pliancy and sweetness, her air of "just coming from vespers," she stiffened like a Roman woman before any taking of liberties with what was known to be right. I had occasion to learn this on one occasion when I was a young Governor's wife. The daughter of a distinguished American jurist was coming to Columbus for elaborate memorial services to be held in honor of her father.

"Jeptha's daughter," Henry Adams called her. She was a woman of extraordinary fascination, beauty, and distinction. She was cultivated to her finger tips, had the manners that come from exquisite breeding and a charming heart, and had been, all through her father's public career, a daughter of whom any man would have been extravagantly proud. She had married brilliantly but unhappily, and after a separation (or divorce; I am not sure) her interest rested, lightly or otherwise, upon another statesman, a rather hyacinthine person. Now, I, as the Governor's wife, was thought to be the one who should entertain this lady. The whole state was doing its best to honor the memory of her illustrious father. There was a flutter of excited anticipation over the visit of so celebrated and lovely a woman; nor was the flutter wholly restricted to her own sex.

Mrs. Hayes was in Columbus. We met at a friend's house. She drew me aside.

"My dear," she said, gently, "I have just heard that *you* are to entertain Mrs. X. Why should it be *you*? We must not judge her . . . let the Lord do that. But I think . . . in your position . . . to countenance even the appearance of evil is a mistake."

She spaced her words a little. That was all. She drifted away with a faint rustle of black silk, a faint fragrance of tea-rose. We did not speak of it again.

THE 'EIGHTIES

CHAPTER IV

"PRESSED BRICK"

IN 1883 Foraker was defeated on his first nomination for Governor of Ohio by Judge George Hoadley. Hoadley was a wet Democrat (the prohibition issue has been ever our hardiest perennial) and a sledge-hammer fighter, but a square one. He and Foraker put on the gloves and went for each other in the campaign, yet neither of them did anything or said anything that interfered with their remaining always most perfect friends. Oddly, Foraker seemed to gain rather than lose popularity by his defeat. The following year he was made delegate-at-large to the National Republican Convention to be held in Chicago. It was my first taste of the excitement that ferments in those great political gatherings. As my husband was chosen delegate-at-large six times in succession, I had ample opportunity to become a convention "fan."

A tragi-comicality of the 1884 convention occurred the night my husband made his speech nominating John Sherman for the Presidency. Going along at top speed, Foraker just happened to mention the name of Blaine. He had hardly got the word out of his mouth when the whole vast crowd went perfectly wild. They yelled

"Blaine!" for fifteen minutes. On the speaker's table was a cap with a white plume, placed there to call attention to the "plumed knight." During the pandemonium, the crowd, a mob now, got completely out of hand. Foraker stood, hardly knowing what to do; finally he picked up the Blaine cap, turning it around in his hands. Goodness! I thought, he isn't going to put it *on*? If he did that he would certainly, and disastrously, change the current of everything, including that of his own future. I began saying to myself with great intensity, "Don't do it! Don't do it!! DON'T DO IT!!!" After a moment or two Foraker put the plumed cap down. "Why didn't you put on the Blaine cap?" I asked him later. "You looked as if you were going to." "I was," he said, "but something, don't know what, warned me not to." I knew.

It always takes two or three days to prepare resolutions, make the platform, etc. In this interval there are speeches! speeches! speeches! Frequently there are many ballots, as at the Democratic Convention in 1924. The 1884 convention nominated James G. Blaine for President and John A. Logan for Vice-President. My husband was one of the committee sent to notify Mr. Blaine at Augusta, Maine, of his nomination. He took with him our twelve-year-old son, Benson. Benson said that Mr. Blaine didn't look a bit surprised.

Foraker campaigned Ohio with Blaine that year. A great reception was planned at Cincinnati for the presidential nominee. Who that heard him can ever forget

the speech Blaine made from the balcony of the Burnet
House that September night in 1884. Moonlight, and
Blaine's silvery voice. People were bewitched by Blaine;
it was almost uncanny. The man's curious hypnotic
power never lessened. It was just as "spellbinding" in his
last public speech, this was at "Ophir Hall," the Whitelaw Reids' country place, in the Harrison-Reid campaign
against Cleveland and Stevenson, in 1892, as in 1876,
when Robert Ingersoll likened "Blaine of Maine" to a
plumed knight with shining lance, smiting traitors in
the face.

In the 1884 campaign the Blaine Club, for some reason, failed to include the Vice-President in their plans for
receiving the presidential candidate. They were going
to give Logan a send-off all by himself, and later. But
Mr. Logan heard of the Blaine reception and came uninvited, unannounced, unmet. He made his way to a hotel
as best as he could. We heard that he was there—and
very mad. Immediately I called upon Mrs. Logan. She
was a beautiful woman with great poise, and fond of
dress. I remember how striking she looked in a tight-
fitting blue princess robe with a gray set-in, and a little
bonnet with a bird on it perched on her white hair. Snow
white. She was young then, and by rights a raven's-wing
brunette. She went through some sudden, severe shock
connected with the death of her father. When she returned home her husband met her at the train. "My God,
Mary!" he gasped. "What has happened?" She didn't

know what he meant and he was too petrified to explain. Arrived home, the door was opened by an old servant. At the sight of Mrs. Logan she threw up her hands, gave an Irish shriek, and fled. Beginning now to be a little irritated, Mrs. Logan sought a mirror. There it was, her hair had turned white in a single mysterious moment— just the way the thing happened in novels. "Like it, John?" she said, carelessly, to Logan, who had followed to catch her when she fainted. Yet indeed she must have been startled when she saw herself in the glass.

Logan's skyrockety temperament required exactly her management. When he raged in flashes at the treatment he was getting from the Ohio barbarians, she would pat his hand with a soothing there-there, dear old John, till John would simmer down and smile. In a political family somebody has got to keep calm.

.   .   .   .

I had a good deal of experience in state politics before I was to go to my next national convention. I drove for Foraker during the two campaigns against Governor Hoadley. We had a carriage called a "Rockaway." Governor Hoadley used a Rockaway and had been elected, so we thought a Rockaway was the thing. But it was our Rockaway that defeated Hoadley's when he ran against my husband in 1885. I had to go to the station, quite a drive from our home on Walnut Hills, at all hours of the night to meet my husband. That was the time of great corruption in Ohio elections: false registrations, negroes locked up in the calaboose on election day, ballot-stuffing, forged tally-sheets, hoodlum rule. It wasn't thought safe for me to drive alone at night; but I whipped up the horse on dark stretches. Mrs. Elkins had a similar experience in New York City during the Blaine and Logan campaign in 1884. Senator Elkins was on the Republican Committee and during the last few weeks and just before election there was so much rowdy wickedness staged by the roughs and toughs that Mrs. Elkins was warned that she must not be surprised any morning to learn that his body was suspended from a lamp-post. They were bad years, 1884 and 1885. I don't recall that since then the rough element has ever got the upper hand in elections.

Foraker's mother, a very old lady, attended his first inaugural as Governor; made the long, hard trip through the blizzard. Governor Hoadley, the retiring Governor, complimented her on the great honor conferred upon her son. "If he only comes out with as much honor as he goes in I shall be satisfied," she said, primly. One could hardly put it better than that.

Since politics and home-making are the things that have most interested and most occupied me in life, domestic incidents get intricately mixed with my political remembrance. During the four years Foraker was Governor of Ohio, 1886-1890, we lived in three different houses. The first one we took over from the Hoadleys; paid twelve hundred a year for it—out of a four-thousand-dollar salary. It was elaborate, expensive, considered handsome, and was the most inconvenient abode that a large family of small means ever struggled with. It was the first house in Columbus built of the then elegant "pressed brick"; each brick, brought from Philadelphia, came wrapped in tissue paper. The vast kitchen and the dining-room were separated by a meandering jungle of pretentious pantries; there was only a mere letter-box slide to pass the dishes through; stone-cold they were by that time. The chief ornament of the kitchen was a mammoth coal-range that looked like a mausoleum and would have taken the remainder of the Governor's salary to feed with coal. We never had a hot meal until I sent to Cincinnati for my own range. Good old "Miller." That range wandered around with us as we went from house to house; picture of the Governor of Ohio trying to keep a roof over his head!

We had a great visit that term with the Algers; he was Governor of Michigan. Their house party included a crowd of Senators—John A. Logan, Manderson, Palmer, also Michigan's two Senators, Horr and Conger. We talked politics from morning until night. There were dinners, banquets, and an afternoon reception of two thousand guests, all of us standing in line to receive. These affairs were punctuated by the usual fiery, intensely partisan speeches of the 'eighties. The trend of all of them was that the country would go to the dogs if the Republican Party did not get back into power. Grover Cleveland was our President then. One of the

terrible charges brought against him was that he went
fishing on Decoration Day! What a small thing that
now seems to us to have created such a tempest!

The Algers came to visit us a little later. The Governor
wanted to study Ohio state institutions. With the remembrance of all the elegance and luxury at the Alger house,
I was concerned about my meager collection of cut glass;
Mrs. Alger had masses of it. So I slipped out secretly and
bought four impressive and glittering bowls out of the
house money! Mrs. Alger warmly admired them. Ah,
tact! I loved that woman.

One of the things we did in those days was to take our
visitors to the weekly dance at the Hospital for the Insane. The Ohio capital has many state institutions.
Governor Alger danced with the patients. "I know now
how to distinguish between the sane and the insane," he
said to me, between waltzes; "the insane do not wear
corsets." The distinction has vanished.

Foraker was greatly interested in the reforms which
clamored for attention in the various state institutions;
particularly improvements in the prisons. His efforts in
that direction were responsible for placing him once in
an imperiling position at an important moment. And
"thereby hangs a tale." But before I go into that I must
recall a friendship whose story intervenes logically just
here, a friendship between my husband and an amazing
man who was to dominate the political scene from
now on.

CHAPTER V

MR. HANNA GOES SHOPPING

FORAKER and Mark Hanna first met at the National Republican Convention of 1884. Many men who were to shape American politics for the next quarter of a century met for the first time at Chicago that stormy, defeated year—and sized each other up. A friendship between my husband and the "Cleveland boss" began then that was to survive a twenty-years war. The warmth of their relation glows yet in many old letters from Hanna to Foraker; they are before me as I write. Portraits look out from them that have a place, perhaps, in the gallery growing around this Byzantine of the 'nineties.

Hanna often veiled a dislike, for strategic reasons; but if he "cottoned to a man" he had a childlike directness about letting him know it. Immediately the convention closed, and he had "got some sleep," he wrote my husband, "Will hope to be considered your sincere friend." And two days later, "I assure you, my dear fellow, that it will not be my fault if our acquaintance does not ripen, for I shall certainly *go for you* whenever you are within reach." He wrote these early letters himself; had a quaint habit of underscoring.

Of course he saw political promise in Foraker, too. Men he could start things with were his magnet. When, and if, his man arrived, he had an all-rewarding glow: he had beaten the other fellow. I heard Thomas B. Reed tell my husband that this fascination of "beating the other feller" was what lured him away from a golden law practice and into Congress. Hanna was a born beater. He used men, when expedient, without squeamishness about who a man was or what he did or what kind of a necktie he wore. But when with his political interest went his admiration, a simple gorgeousness shone in him that was unique. It was this quality, raised to an infinite power, that gave romance to McKinley's Presidency. Probably no other man, looking towards the White House, ever had such a friend. However, Hanna, whether he regarded men as tools or personally liked them, couldn't stage the simplest plan without doing it like a human being.

There were his famous Washington breakfasts; nothing like them before or since. Whenever he wanted to "gain the tender creature," he asked him to breakfast. (Purely business functions; no women were ever involved in Hanna's political spreads.) He asked all sorts of men to these breakfasts, sometimes very odd ones. In that haze of hospitality it was very natural, very agreeable, to fall in with what the man from Cleveland wanted. Perfect food and *mein host* whose straight-offness in getting to the point, interest in the commonplaces of the other man's life and knowingness about the other man's job, and who, moreover, put on no "airs"—all this made the rawest ward heeler feel at ease. The ward heeler went back home and told his wife about the corned-beef hash that was so remarkable and the lemon verbena in the finger-bowls and everything; and after that he wore a sort of nimbus when he went out—he had breakfasted with Mark Hanna. The corned-beef hash that "Maggie" made (Maggie, Hanna's marvelous cook, a great "man's woman") became an asset of the Republican Party.

All through these early letters there crops out his Oriental hospitality, his hatred of humdrum methods, his belief in cakes-and-ale for helping things along. He wants Foraker to join him and Charles Foster at Middle-bass Island to talk over the Blaine campaign: "The Toledo Club have a nice place . . . we could have a good time." He takes hold of Foraker's second campaign for Governor like a brother; there comes a string of pleasant suggestions: "I have a snug little place on the Lake Shore, five miles out of town, where I can keep you quiet between 'heats.' " "Your room in the Hanna house will be ready." "Let me know what time you will come and how many brass bands you want" (oh, the dear brass-banded 'eighties!). . . . "My carriage could meet you at the Viaduct depot and bring you to my house in neat time. . . . Claim you for dinner at six o'clock and will invite Amos [Townsend, later Congressman from Ohio] and a few fellows to meet you—'stag party,' see?"

"Whenever you feel like running away, telegraph me and I will be ready for you."

Not a fisherman himself, he plays on Foraker's fishing weakness by constantly proposing political conferences disguised to attract the compleat angler. There is Mr. Chisholm's invitation to the Chicago Club at Point Pelee: "This is the finest club on the Lakes, composed of some of the best men in Chicago. If the weather is fine we can have a jolly time, whether we catch any fish or not." (If Foraker hesitated, he was a hard-struggling young lawyer then, Hanna would write and telegraph and telegraph and write; he never yielded a point, or won it, without a steady bombardment of letters and wires; this whether it was a question of going fishing or appointing a man to office; he set his heart on things—and nothing was a trifle.) "You will find General Sheridan, Robert Lincoln, and a host of other good fellows. Don't let *imaginary* duties keep you at home."

In his own house he was a true manor lord to his friends: "Well, as the fishing is over and we can't have that excuse for a spree, I think you and Old Bushey had better come up and make me a visit as soon as we get into the country." ("Bushey," Asa Bushnell, who, as Governor of Ohio, took so maddeningly long to appoint Hanna successor to John Sherman in the Senate. Whirligig of friendship!) After an election: "You must be a used-up community. . . . When you want to get away from things, bring your wife and come up and spend a few days with us." And repeatedly, such beckonings as, "Whenever you are troubled about sleeping, telegraph me, take the first train, and come up. We are fortunate to get our share of the rain . . . our garden is smiling all over." And "I see you are snowed under with taffy. . . . When you get tired out and want a good, quiet rest (with good company) come up to my box on the Lake Shore and you shall have it." Or impromptus like, "Your visits do not come too often to please us. . . . Wish you could come for longer and bring the family." (Poor Mrs. Hanna! There were only six of us!) And then a glimpse of Hanna's sympathetic feeling for stage people: "Lawrence Barrett will be here Thanksgiving week and stay at my house. . . . Delighted to have you and your wife come up for a day or two that week and for Thanksgiving dinner."

It was kind of him to include me almost from the first. December 8, '84: "My wife says that it is her turn now to reap some of the benefits of my political tramps and show the pleasure of my dear friends. So we await your coming." Everything seemed to block that first visit, including scarlet fever. That came at a battling moment in Ohio politics and Hanna was greatly beset and bothered; yet instantly he writes:

"I regret to hear of the sickness of your little one and hope the others may be spared. It is a dreadful disease for children, for you never know when you are through with it. The great danger being what may follow. Careful nursing *long* after the fever is past is the only safeguard. We have been through it."

My Cleveland visit, when it came, was made unforgetable for me by the charm, grace, and elegance of Mrs. Hanna. She was a sister of James Rhodes, the historian, herself a woman of great cultivation who could have taken her position in any society in the world and appeared distinguished in it. And her devotion to her husband, her pride in him who could be so very much the rough diamond if he wished (I think there was a touch of the defensive in this; he hated fuss, so many people had it, he wanted to put them off), made their union take on a quality of pure romance. The luxury of life at the Hanna house was, I think, my first glimpse of things as they could be done. I have told about Mrs. Hanna sewing "real Val" on pantalettes; everything else was on a "real Val" scale, though no one could have been simpler about her money and position than my hostess. They talked a good deal of something called "Standard Oil" in Cleveland on that visit. I'd never heard of it before. We in southern Ohio knew nothing of this Golconda.

I don't know how much he minded his crucifixion by the caricaturists. I remember once (this was in the later Washington days, of course) when we were all together, his opening a newspaper at a particularly cruel cartoon of himself, one of Opper's or Davenport's—a swollen, evil-eyed monster with a dollar sign in the lobe of each enormous ear. He glanced at it . . . a queer shadow passed over his face for a thousandth of a second. That was all. I think he suffered only as the attacks on him hurt his wife; at least he suffered so much for her that for himself no response was left.

My happiest memory of Hanna—I cannot think of it now without a strange tenderness—springs from his charming, indulgent friendship for my son Benson. Benson was twelve, perhaps, when he went to Cleveland for a visit at the Hannas'. When the time came that had been agreed upon for his return, my husband received the following letter:

CLEVELAND, O., May 27, 1886

MY DEAR GOV.—Benson is having such a good time that I have not the heart to send him home. He said his wardrobe was a little scant for a long visit, so he and I went shopping this morning for collars and stockings and my wife says she can keep the shirts going, as our laundry runs all the week. So you see we can keep up his personal appearance. We are growing so fond of him that we will not want to lose him (he takes after his mother). Therefore, if you are willing, let him stay as long as he is contented. The weather is moderating and will soon be pleasant. Ruth* has commenced flirting with him and wants most of his attention. So there may be a chance of a family alliance. Tell his mother not to worry about any trouble to us, as certainly he will make his own welcome. I asked him this morning if he was contented to stay. Oh yes, he replied, but he didn't know but that his papa might be wanting him for something. His appetite continues good. The new steamer the *City of Clev.* gave an excursion today to invited guests.

---

* Now Mrs. Ruth Hanna McCormick, former member of the U. S. Congress.

I could not go, but sent Benson with Mr. Robbins (from our office) and some of my family. I think Benson will not lack for amusement. Guess we will hold him as hostage until his mother comes after him.

Sincerely yours,
M. A. HANNA.

Benson's own account of the shopping foray we heard more than once—in a child's dramatic monotone: "They bought lots of things, (it ran), and had lots of fun. . . . Mr. Hanna bought a bag of candy and they ate it and walked around . . . and there was a grind organ man and a monkey and Mr. Hanna took a lot of nickels and dimes out of his pocket and gave Benson a lot and they gave it to the monkey and the monkey took the money to the man and came right back for more and Mr. Hanna said the monkey could keep that up longer than he could . . . and a man with his collar turned up came along and Mr. Hanna said how is the baby and the man said the baby isn't any better and Mr. Hanna gave him a funny yellow-back dollar and said he'd seen some pretty sick kids pull through and the man just looked at the dollar and looked at it and didn't say anything . . . and Mr. Hanna said well, we'd better go home now if Bensy is going to make a dude of himself . . . he was always saying things to make a fellow laugh . . ."

And so on and on.

Benson was a hopeless Hanna man after that and Hanna played up like a schoolboy to the understanding that they were pals. He proposed a trip "up the Lakes" on one of his schooners for Benson—and "take another boy with you." References to this adventure constantly crept into letters otherwise foaming with political complexities: Are the German Republicans being difficult? . . . There is a rumor that Blaine's sympathy with prohibition has done it; Hanna breaks off to beg the Governor to "ask Bensy when he is coming up to see his new steel ship. She is nearly ready to launch and he should inspect her before she goes into the water." Do all the wrong men think they should be appointed? He writes his trenchant gauge of their merits and digresses to add: "Tell Captain Benson that the Steamer *Cambia* is in commission and that I have kept a place for him. She is running to Escanabe. He can come up any time and stay with me until he can catch her at Ashtabula." Hurrying back from Canton, where McKinley and John Sherman and he have talked all night, he postscripts his letter to inform "Skipper Benson that I will keep his boat running until he comes up. He will be very proud of her. She is . . . the fastest screw on the Lakes."

Skipper Benson had a marvelous time on that voyage. "The boss's pet," he was treated like a young prince. He came back with his pockets bulging with bits of iron ore —also a bunch of wilted wintergreen for his mother— and much talk of assays and ports and "our lines." Apparently they owned all the ships on the Lakes, "they" being Hanna and Benson. "All right, pard," chuckled Hanna.

Late winter of 1888 finds him in great distress over the illness of "my little girl" (Ruth Hanna). He writes absently; his grip is off things; he is distracted by anxiety. But instantly, at the happy turn, he picks up the old glove: "I'm not pleased with the conditions of the party in this state," he writes Foraker from New York. "If you get any overtures from Tom Platt and his gang, *set down on them*."

Hanna's liberality was tempered by a shrewd concern that "virtue, not cheek, should be rewarded." The epigram is his own (October 23, 1885). After a generous gesture on his part at a tight moment in Foraker's second-term campaign for Governor, my husband wrote him:

"If the victory was a splendid one, you greatly helped me to achieve it. You will remember the old preacher who always borrowed five dollars from a neighbor on Saturday night, to be repaid on Monday? When finally his neighbor asked him why he always made such a loan, he said that he found he could preach with much more power when he had money in his pocket than when he was strapped."

Hanna came back with: "Don't feel the obligation only to the extent of the friendship . . . I feel for you *personally*. . . . I fully appreciate your situation and know how much of a drain it is on your *fat salary*. . . . After hearing your story I am glad that the spirit furnished produced such glorious results. . . ." Then the old, kind refrain: "I'll bet you are tired out. . . . Wish you might come and spend a few days with me."

Hanna emphasized again and again in these letters that he doesn't want any office. Undoubtedly he meant this every time he said it—all but the last time.

"As I do not want any political favors, I want you to have all the glory." "While I lie down and let them walk over me (!) . . . I have no claims for myself." "I don't like public office. . . . I told McKinley that I only cared for you in this matter . . . not for myself." "I feel that you will mount the ladder rapidly and I will always be willing to stand at the *bottom* to keep it from *slipping*." The M in his name might have stood for Mæcenas, instead of Marcus; he got so much pleasure out of the thought of himself in that rôle.

When his favorite failed to win, however, he could switch to the man who *did* get in, with a rapidity that made whole wards blink. I recall the local excitement about the proposed appointment of a certain southern Ohioan to the wrangled-over position of state oil inspector. Hanna scorned the man as a common saloon-keeper. Well, the man's headquarters certainly were a famous Cincinnati over-the-Rhine beer-garden and a saloon, on the site of the present Hotel Gibson, appropriately called *The Mecca*. Quite aside from that, he had built up a powerful political organization, and further than that and immensely important, a reputation for

never forgetting an obligation and for always keeping his
word. But Hanna would have none of him. If that man
was appointed that day, he, Hanna, would quit town for
good and all.

The man was appointed. And when in '96 McKinley
was nominated for the Presidency at St. Louis, Hanna
and he (this man) walked into the convention hall arm
in arm. And always after that when the man was in
Washington Hanna invited him to breakfast. This con-
descending acceptance by royalty turned the man's head.
He began to look in an upward direction. And why not?
And in 1906 he and his wife sent a decorous silver ice
pitcher to Miss Alice Roosevelt on the occasion of her
marriage. There is nothing wrong with this story; it
only shows that Hanna had a very astute politician's
sensitiveness to the way the wind blew. Also, that a ward
boss who keeps his word gathers no moss.

There's a something ominous, minor, running
through these old letters. Hanna never could have been
a man of that iron health demanded by the dynamics and
drive that he put into affairs. Again and again he speaks
of being "completely worn out" . . . "dead beat" . . .
"half sick" . . . "quite sick." Yet he rarely slacked his
high-handed, ambitious, hard dictator pace: campaigning, raising money, pulling unsuspected wires, sounding
communities, launching booms. He must have over-
worked always. I recall Mrs. Hanna's constant solicitude
about him on this score. Of course the same sort of strain

breaks down practically every man who goes into public
life and attempts to meet its impossible demands. Yet
men like that have a come-back like cork. June 11, 1884,
he wrote Foraker about having to leave the convention
before the end and go to bed. Yet he showed a morning
keenness for herculean labors ahead. Nineteen years
later, in his last letter to Foraker, October 9, 1903, he is
still pressing:

"I have been doing very hard work in the campaign—
but hope to be able to go through with it."

Did he think then that all campaigns were so soon
to be over for him?

Somebody said—Senator Lodge, I think—that the only
stupid thing Hanna ever did was not to indorse Foraker's
nomination of Roosevelt for the Presidency at the Ohio
State Convention, Columbus, May 1903. For one stupid
thing in judgment there were a thousand clever kind-
nesses that sprang from the heart. Most of the letters from
which I have quoted were written in the years immediately following 1884 and before the two men went to the
Senate. Any rifts in their relations after those close, early
years, I think I have forgotten. Hanna's closeness to
President McKinley, his peculiar relation to that administration, gave him an excessive advantage in state matters that was historically unique. But in spite of any and
all official differences, Hanna and Foraker never ceased
to be friends. And when Foraker faced the dark skies of

1908 he said that there was one faithful hand-clasp that
he missed—Hanna's.

A man with a good deal of the boy in him, who would
take endless pains to please a child, was sorry when other
people were in trouble, liked dispensing happiness under
his own roof—and widely elsewhere with his left hand—
and who wore his love for his family most humanly on
his sleeve.

That Mark Hanna was not remotely related to a man
of the same name who was so pilloried in caricature that
he became a legend of corruption in his lifetime. In the
old Foraker-Governor period with which I am immediately concerned the Hanna that I knew was still just the
Happy Boss whose favorites had a way of winning.

CHAPTER VI

TWO O'CLOCK IN THE MORNING

WHEN Foraker was inaugurated Governor in 1886 Ohio taxpayers were under a great burden in the maintenance of the state penitentiary at Columbus. Moreover, the prisons were in a shocking condition, inside and out, and mediæval methods of punishment still prevailed. There was an average of eighty-eight punishments daily—punishments such as stringing up prisoners by their thumbs, putting them into bathtubs and shooting electricity into their bodies, other methods of incredible brutality. There were three hundred men in the idle-house. Labor unions made prison goods difficult to market. The people of Ohio were paying two hundred and fifty thousand dollars a year to run their penitentiary.

A Governor's record in the matter of the prisons is extremely important. Foraker worked hard for prison reform. He succeeded in appointing splendid boards. The whole condition of things was changed. Punishments decreased from an average of eighty-eight a day to four or five a day and on some days none. At the end of Foraker's two terms the prison was not only paying its own way, but ten thousand dollars from prison labor stood to the state credit.

In subsequent years, I may recall here, some of the old, abolished mediævalisms were revived at the prison. One very vicious prisoner was, I know, kept in a barbaric steel cage like a wild animal. There was serving a term in the penitentiary at that time a man of a highly superior type. They gave him clerical work. He interested himself in the unmanageable savage in the cage, and by intelligence and some strange human understanding succeeded in making him amenable to reasonable methods. The man's name was O. Henry.

There were a number of pardons during Governor Foraker's four years. One of them had a fantastic and momentarily annoying reaction on my husband. Three well-dressed women called to see Foraker one morning. They had come about their brother, twenty-eight years old, who was in prison. The boy ran away from home when he was twelve, and ever since then his sisters had been searching for him. The old father was still living; they did not want him to know that his son was a convict. The brother had told his sisters that he was not guilty of the crime for which he was in prison, although he had been in prison before. Governor Foraker advised them to get a lawyer, suggesting Judge Nash, who afterwards became Governor of Ohio. The result of the investigation proved the boy's innocence and he was pardoned. The sisters, whom Foraker never saw but once, were emotionally grateful, always sending the Governor fruit and flowers; their brother's pardoner became a sort of

god. At the National Convention in 1888 in Chicago
their gratitude took an embarrassing turn.

In June, 1887, President Cleveland, taking counsel
with his Secretary of War, Mr. Endicott, had ordered the
return to the Confederate states of a number of captured
rebel flags which were accumulating dust in the lumber-
room of the Department of War. As Congress had not
authorized this action and as President Cleveland had
not been, himself, a soldier, the announcement aroused
intense feeling, especially among ex-Union soldiers. From
one of these, an old army officer obviously excited by the
impression that the President's order included captured
flags in the State House at Columbus, Foraker received
a vigorous protest. In reply my husband sent the following telegram:

"No rebel flags will be surrendered while I am
Governor."

This message, broadcast, offended the Clevelands. It
was shortly afterwards, at the Philadelphia Centennial
Celebration, that Mrs. Cleveland, then a bride, administered her famous snub to the Governor of Ohio and his
wife. Doubtless a loyal bit of rudeness, but unwise. The
gesture antagonized a great many people who voted. At
the Toledo Convention, immediately following the
Democratic State Convention in Cleveland, July, 1887,
the battle flag incident seemed to be the main issue.
Everyone, delegates, alternates, and onlookers, an im-

mense crowd, wore badges with Foraker's picture, and printed beneath it the celebrated dispatch.

Foraker had had quite enough of this, I think, by the time he was to go to Chicago for the National Convention, July, 1888. Imagine his bored annoyance when just as he reached the platform to speak there was brought on an easel bearing an immense floral piece which spelled in red, white, and blue flowers the words, "No rebel flags will be returned while I am Governor." Gift of the three sisters, it was afterwards learned, whose brother Foraker had pardoned. The appearance of the floral slogan produced an uproar. The evil effect of the well-meant compliment was instantly sensed by my husband. He motioned to the ushers to take the flowers away. He knew what his enemies would say, and did say—that it was a cleverly devised scheme of the Governor's friends to call the delegates' attention to him as a presidential candidate. The worst of it was that Foraker could not explain the innocent source of that "tribute." To tell from whom and why the flowers came would be to put the story of the boy's prison conviction in every newspaper in the country. There was a great to-do about the affair. Foraker never volunteered one word of explanation.

Whatever his enemies said, or his friends wanted, Foraker had no thought of being a candidate for President. He was a Sherman candidate; Ohio was pledged to Sherman. Blaine was the other candidate in men's minds. His candidacy was potential, not official, it is true, but it was recognized as highly dangerous. As early as January of that year Blaine had written from Italy declining to have his name presented to the convention. Under the surface, however, people went on thinking a great deal about Blaine of Maine as our next President. Again and again delegates told me that they were voting for Sherman only because of their loyalty to Foraker.

I remember being greatly upset one day by an odd rumor. I was told by Mahlon Chance, who had been traveling through the states in the interests of candidates and getting the concensus of opinion as to the man the people wanted for President, that it would never do to nominate John Sherman; that the Democrats were already primed to fight him with a story connecting him with heavy investments in whisky before and after it was bonded, through which investments he had made a fortune. Whisky! All that was necessary to injure a candidate in those days was to connect his name in some way, any way, with that word. He may have been a teetotaler of the bluest, down, even, on barley water; but just let some fat boss instruct his creatures to spread the report that all the time he was a secret drinker, or a dark backer of a brewery or two, and people began to fall away from him. The whisky roorback was infallible. How well I remember my father coming to me one day, anguished. He had just read an account of a reception at the Governor's house at which there had been "punch." "Julia!" he cried, "surely you are not serving *rum*?" His tone implied that if I were, politically no less than morally my position was one of danger. Calm yourself, father; only lemon juice and pineapple with something else equally innocent to make it pink. "Rum" was the popular generic term for everything inebriative.

But to get back to Chance's story: I was so excited I could hardly wait to tell it to my husband. He smiled. "Don't you know," he said, "that Chance has been all over the United States in the interest of William McKinley? Hanna is wild to get McKinley in this year. The plan is, when the convention is deadlocked over candidates, to rush telegrams from all parts of the country requesting McKinley's nomination on his tariff record."

It was suddenly clarified for me then that Hanna in his heart of hearts was, and had been since first he and the Major met, for McKinley and only McKinley. I know that this opposes the view of many that Hanna was sincerely committed to Sherman's candidacy . . . that it was only when he saw that Sherman could not win that he threw his support to McKinley, whose loyalty to Sherman had so evoked his admiration. I know of all this. But remembering Hanna's transparent happiness in McKinley's personality, remembering Hanna, temperamentally a hero-worshiper, heart-set on his gods no matter how he might jib in political gales, it is my personal opinion that a very rare moment of Hanna's life flashed when, as Sherman dropped out, he could play openly his secret cards.

One day at luncheon, in the midst of the convention excitement, Senator Thurston of Nebraska said to me that we had reached a point where only a man with a soldier's record could save the day. "Why don't you take R. A. Alger?" I said. "He has a splendid war record." Thurston dismissed the suggestion. "Alger would be immediately charged with having sent money to buy seven delegates." I said that wasn't true, that all Alger had done was to pay the traveling expenses of men working for him. There was a lively buying-and-selling business at that convention. Foraker went into Hanna's room at the Grand Pacific one day. He found there a crowd of colored delegates, and Hanna buying their tickets and paying spot cash for them in the most open, business-like way. A regular trading-post in delegate tickets! It was so raw Foraker couldn't stand it; he expressed his contempt and disapproval to Hanna. Hanna resented this. His policy was to get what you wanted and get it quickly in any way you could.

A large number of men were on hand at the convention to entertain delegates and the crowd with speeches. Most of them had come prepared to speak; when called upon, the thing to do seemed to be to rise, all confused, thank the audience for the unexpected honor, blush, falter—and then produce their carefully-written speech from an inside pocket. It is a time-honored tradition that in speeches made at such a time in a convention the name of a candidate must not be mentioned. It must never be mentioned until the candidate is duly nominated. Robert Ingersoll, famous orator, was one of the speakers. It was such an opportunity and he was so enthusiastically received, that he was led into the unpardonable error of mentioning the name of his candidate, Gresham. An extraordinary scene followed. The vast crowd in the convention hall began hissing; they hissed for several minutes. When quiet was at last restored, Ingersoll commenced again, and again, unconscious of his enormous crime, he mentioned Gresham's name. Instantly the hissing broke out with renewed vigor, kept up until it drove Mr. Ingersoll from the stage. One could hardly believe eyes and ears. An ignoble and childishly insulting attack upon a distinguished man, unmatched, happily, by any incident of any convention since.

Convention week ended without having produced a candidate. On Sunday Mr. Blaine sent a cable withdrawing his name for President. At 2 A.M. on Monday Foraker and I, very sound asleep, were awakened by a knock on the door. It was Kurtz, my husband's secretary. He had a message from the Blaine men. They were outside waiting in the hall. They wanted to hold an immediate conference with my husband. Well, the only place to receive them was in that bedroom, the only thing for me to do was to leave, and the only place for me to go was the bathroom. So there I hid. The Blaine men crowded into the bedroom, led, I was to learn, by Senator Stephen B.

Elkins of West Virginia and the Honorable Samuel Fessenden of Connecticut.

The murmur of voices went on for some time. The bathroom was cold and I was very sleepy. At last I heard the meeting break up; I could go back to my room.

"What do you suppose they wanted?" said Foraker. "They've just come from a meeting of Blaine leaders where it was decided to throw the entire Blaine strength to me on Monday morning if I would accept the nomination for President."

"Oh!"

"I told them," he continued, "that I appreciated the honor and would have been glad to accept their support, but that I was completely committed to Mr. Sherman and couldn't and wouldn't accept the nomination unless Sherman asked me to accept it." There was more to his account of things than that, perhaps, but such was the gist.

"Well, it's almost three o'clock," I said, and turned out the gas.

Foraker's loyalty to Sherman threw the Blaine strength over to General Benjamin Harrison, whose vote had been so largely increased on the last ballot. So in the next President the country got its "man with a soldier's record." In a non-Gilbertian sense everything was lovely; the Republican goose hung high.

Husbands know best, that is understood; at the same time even had we been sure of nomination and election I

tremble to think of the unfolded future had Foraker been
in a position to say "yes" to that two-in-the-morning offer
of the presidential candidacy. We were a poor but popu-
lous family; what we needed most were some good legal
fees, not a conspicuous and costly eminence like the
White House. And yet, with the obvious wisdom of a
poor man with a growing family putting aside the presidential crown, the proffered honor remains the tempta-
tion of all temptations, saving your pardon, St. Anthony.
I remember talking with some Washington friends about
the Dewey presidential boom. Dewey was the shyest of
men. Had he not lingered in Manila for many months
after the Spanish-American war, dreading the American
ovation? A lady asked Francis B. Loomis, John Hay's
very able First Assistant Secretary, if he thought Dewey
would accept.

"Well, if he declines," said Loomis, dryly, "he'll be the
first man who ever did."

Whatever the four years do to the man, posterity's
guaranty to the President is full of glamour. He is securely lodged with fame. He's in the books! Forever he
is in the books! This dazzling perpetuity must balance
everything, even that dire drop with which the adventure ends. Something should be done to surround the
position of our ex-Presidents with appropriate dignity
and elevation and the grace of a fitting remuneration.
Their experience and matured judgment, it is thought,

might be very wisely applied in the Senate, though there the financial grace is something lacking.

The instance of an ex-President deliberately accepting, in the interest of pure service, an office that was felt to be beneath him, was given by John Quincy Adams. Ex-President Adam's eighteen years as a simple Congressman represents a selfless loyalty, a high-minded statesmanship, that is sublime.

CHAPTER VII

IT NEVER WILL HAPPEN AGAIN

I HAVE always had a good time at my own parties. But I never had a better time than in 1888 when the Grand Army of the Republic spent a week with us. Not quite the whole army. There were seventy thousands of them in Columbus that throbbing hot September. Not since the Second Review at Washington in 1865 had there been such a demonstration. Twenty-three years after Appomattox; the veterans might still be called young; there were still such immense numbers of them as to make their national encampment an event electrical, emotional, beyond anything in our national life.

It was a big thing for a governor to have the encampment at the capital. As I look back upon it I think I had good reason to feel that each one of those soldiers was our guest. All that summer, when my husband came home for luncheon or for the evening he brought news of the way the thing was growing. Requests for reservations were pouring in by thousands from every state in the Union. How were we to feed and lodge all those hordes of heroes? Columbus would have to be turned into a tent city. But would the private houses hold out in providing entertainment for the officers and other distinguished visitors and their wives? Besides the G. A. R. I may add that the encampment of the National Guard was to be held the first week in September and the Columbus Centennial, celebrating the Northwest settlement, was to be opened at almost the same time. Our house was to be filled with visitors for both of these events.

Well, we settled down to some serious planning. By August, as things seemed to be going forward, I decided to run up to Middlebass Island with my three little girls for a few days' breathing-spell. The Benjamin Harrisons were at the island that summer; many of our friends had cottages. I had just fairly settled down there when suddenly I was overcome by a panicky unrest (one of those middle-of-the-night panics). I thought of things left undone that ought to have been done . . . of all those dozens and dozens of people who were preparing to descend upon our household.

I packed up and started home. How hot it was! And Middlebass—how cool and blue! We went back, not delightfully by private car as we had come, but by a train which made us change cars at Newark at three o'clock in the morning and landed us at Columbus at four. My husband was there to meet us at that wicked hour. His greeting was quite, quite glowery:

"What in the world is the matter? Are you out of money that you could not stay in Sandusky overnight?"

No, it was simply that I couldn't be away another

minute . . . I had so much to do. But you can never
make a man understand those things.

After all, it went like a blaze. Every cranny and corner
of our house and grounds was turned into military quarters, and our hospitality drive had been so thoroughly
pushed that practically every other house in town was
prepared to receive guests. The adventure for me was not
without a touch of strategy. We were living in the
T. Ewing Miller house at the head of State Street. It was
a rambling, personal old house, ell-shaped, with a wide
hall in the center and immense porches on all sides. It
stood in three acres of pleasantly-laid-out grounds. We
had the house for one year only while the Millers were
traveling. They came home in April. Naturally they
looked to getting back their house. This would be in
September. I was dismayed. What! With the G. A. R.
coming! With all that entertaining planned for!

I couldn't give up that house, that was all there was to
it; there wasn't another suitable one to be had; those
were the days when the governors of Ohio faced a pillar-
to-post existence when they took office. I thought deeply,
then I invited the Millers to luncheon.

They came, charming with tales of their travels, and
yet, how nice it would be to be back in their own home
again! "East, west, home's best," Mrs. Foraker. Yes, of
course, I said, adding that she, Mrs. Miller, would be very
busy at first entertaining distinguished strangers who
were coming for the Grand Army review.

Mrs. Miller (instantly, coolly): "Oh, but, my dear, I haven't the slightest intention of opening my house to anyone . . . not to *anyone*."

At this I felt quite a glow stealing over me. As carelessly as I could I said that the plans for the entertainment of the encampment were all made; all made and officially indorsed. Every person who had a house was expected to take guests to the limit of capacity. Not only every house and every room would be in demand, but there would be tents on lawns, the occupants of the tents to be fed by the owners of the lawns: committees would inform householders of their obligations on this score.

Mrs. Miller looked at me a little oddly—then changed the subject to French oysters or something. We parted warmly. The next day I received a note from her saying that we could keep the house until late fall—and welcome!

There wasn't an inch of space unutilized in that old mansion by the time the soldiers came. We turned public rooms into bedrooms, added extra cots to bedrooms, canvassed all the porches and filled them with cots. The library, very small, and the dining-room were the only rooms that did not have beds in them. A closet with a window in the hall back of the back parlor was fitted up with washstands for the use of the two governors, Governor Hovey of Indiana and Governor Rusk of Wisconsin, who occupied this room. It was the first time

Governor Rusk had ever seen a folding-bed. He was fascinated by it—and a little suspicious:

> "Help me to live that I may dread
> My grave as little as my bed."

We spent some time opening and shutting the thing before the Governor concluded that it was not more dangerous than the shelling he had been through in the Civil War, and decided to chance it. (The following year Governor Rusk entered President Harrison's Cabinet as Secretary of Agriculture, a new portfolio.)

When all our guests had arrived the place was so full of generals, major-generals, brigadier-generals and colonels you couldn't have crammed in a corporal. Whatever a man's public position may have been at the moment, during that reunion his military rank became the only thing that counted. There was a great glint of silver stars.

In the upstairs bedrooms we added ever so many double beds. The Governor from Colorado, Thayer (Major-General; commanded a division in the Army of the Tennessee), was quartered up there; governors from two other states, too; can't remember them. Governor and Mrs. Alger from Michigan had a front bedroom; Colonel Fred Grant and Mrs. Grant another. Mrs. John A. Logan and her handsome son, Jack, also were our guests. By the window in the upstairs front hall I improvised a bivouac for an eleventh-hour arrival from Washington; he had come tearing back from somewhere in

Europe for the encampment and had no reservation. He might have come from Ephesus, the way he slept through the morning stir. I had fixed up the third-story rooms for my family—my father and my three daughters and their maid. Tents were erected all over the grounds, and my son Benson must sleep in a tent, of course. The boy was wild about being a real soldier.

Monday noon our first guest appeared—the Governor of Colorado. That night a large reception was held at the home of Mrs. Ewing for our idolized "Tecumseh." It was one of those joyously riotous Sherman first-nights; the soldiers acted like excited children about their old general—and how the ladies loved him! We didn't get home until one o'clock in the morning—shocking in the 'eighties. A telegram had come from the Algers saying that they would arrive about two o'clock. Benson went with the committee (by this time he was exactly the same age as the next Grand Army man) to meet the Governor and party. They learned that the train was in—but no Algers. At three o'clock the door bell rang. I went. There they were. Something about a later section.

"There's only one room left and it's yours," I said.

I was up at six that morning. About eight I happened to be passing the Algers' door; the Governor stuck his head out. "We have no water," he said. Of course the stationary stands would take just that moment to "act up." It meant going downstairs to find a servant, so—the wife of the Governor of Ohio fetched a jug of water for the Governor of Michigan. It was no time to be frilly.

Breakfast was laid for nineteen, and always there were two tables. Breakfast ran on all through the morning; guests sauntered in when they liked. Tuesday everybody was early; that was the day of the parade. Seventy thousand soldiers marched. There was a thrill about it unlike all thrills since. Between nine and ten o'clock the battle flags from the State House were carried past our house. Led by Mrs. John A. Logan, all the ladies went to the front gate to see them. All of us had keen memories of the battles that those banners had come through. Then we hurried off to the reviewing-stand erected in front of the State House. Eight hundred people, everyone of them somebody in public life, were on that stand.

The parade was one of those things one never forgets: brilliant sunshine: the trees that lined both sides of the street formed a green arch, a victory arch, indeed, through which came swinging to the sound of drum and fife and bursts of band music that endless line of men in blue. Just east of the reviewing-stand were five hundred children from the Soldiers and Sailors Orphans Home at Xenia; they were singing "Marching Through Georgia," the great song in Ohio on account of General Sherman, as the first column reached them.

The parade went on all day. We had brought our luncheons with us and just stayed where we were till after five o'clock. Ex-President Hayes was of our party. It was like a glorified picnic.

General Sherman was in wonderful form. Nobody could tell a better story than he, nor had so many good ones.

Only one thing happened that was in contrast with the General's high spirits and the good humor of everybody else: It was a very warm day and a presidential campaign was in progress. Some alert tradesman on the line of march had laid in a supply of palm-leaf fans with, on one side, his business address and on the other a picture of General Harrison, the Republican candidate. As a column passed his place he gave each man a fan. There were Democrats among the marchers, of course, but as column after column marched past the reviewing-stand the effect was of just one fluttering picture of Benjamin Harrison after another. This had gone on for two or three hours when Senator Allen G. Thurman, at that time Democratic candidate for Vice-President on the Cleveland ticket, rose blackly.

"I supposed that I was asked here to review a nonpolitical gathering," he said, stiffly, "but I find it's nothing but a damned Republican mass meeting."

He stalked off.

Everybody was distressed. We all liked Senator Thurman. Besides, it shouldn't have happened. That night at the principal "camp fire" General William H. Gibson, a most gallant soldier and a born orator, made a speech. He knew how to talk to soldiers, and when he reminded the G. A. R. that theirs was not a political army, but an army devoted to brotherhood, charity, and loyalty, and that, as they all knew, when they came to an encampment they left their politics at home—when he had rather sentimentally embellished this thought the men looked properly solemn and impressed. In conclusion the General referred to the fan episode, regretted it, said the thing was purely accidental, and handsomely apologized to all whom it may have offended. Then some perverse imp of humor possessed him:

"But, my comrades," he said, "if on such an occasion as this you *should* happen so far to forget yourselves as to 'holler' for anybody, be sure that you 'holler' for Harrison."

How they roared!

Among the number of handsome women at that review, quite the star of them all was Mrs. Fred Grant. Really, Mrs. Grant was most beautiful. I can still see her warm, lovely face, her delicate brilliance, her grace. She wore a Paris "calling costume," a pink-and-green-striped silk overdress over green cloth, and a mysterious little pitched-up bonnet of shirred rose. This finery was a gift from her sister, Mrs. Potter Palmer, she told me. Mrs. Grant always carried a small black leather bag on her arm; never stirred without it. In it was her very valuable collection of jewels.

Mrs. Alger had an expression of such serenity and

loveliness, one thought of her always as a beauty. She and Governor Alger had had a great romance; she was Annette Henry and had given up the luxurious life of a rich man's daughter to go with her husband to a Northern lumber-camp and share his hardships. They lived in a cabin; she cooked his five-o'clock breakfast. Alger made a fortune, but his wife "held the rope."

Colonel and Mrs. Grant arrived during the day from the East and were met and escorted to the reviewing-stand by Foraker's secretary, C. L. Kurtz. The Grants excited immense interest. Whenever we tried to drive in the town (in a hack, top down), such crowds surrounded the carriage that it was impossible to move. When we tried to walk I had to carry Colonel Grant's hat, hold him by the left arm and fairly push him forward. His right hand was very much swollen by hand-shaking. This excitement was not only because he was his father's son; the old soldiers had a tremendous feeling about him personally.

Colonel Grant talked interestingly about his life in the White House while his father was President. When Grant first took office the salary was only twenty-five thousand dollars a year. Before the General's second term the salary was raised to fifty thousand. (It remained at fifty during the Roosevelt administration.) Colonel Grant told me that when his father left the White House, after eight years, he had managed to save so little that he could do but few of the things he would like to do for the old soldiers. Many of them were very needy. The President estimated that it would take one hundred thousand dollars to meet the demands made upon him yearly. I could understand this; we ourselves were learning about the levies made on public men.

In this connection I may recall that it was not until Mr. Roosevelt's Presidency that Congress granted an addition of twenty-five thousand dollars for traveling expenses. After Mr. Taft was elected, before his inauguration, at his request this twenty-five thousand traveling fund was added to the fifty thousand, making the salary seventy-five thousand dollars. Very soon after Mr. Taft became President he received an invitation to visit some place; he casually remarked that he couldn't afford to pay his expenses. So Congress again came to his rescue and added an additional twenty-five thousand for traveling expenses. As it now stands, the President has one hundred thousand dollars yearly at his disposal. At the same time, if not all of the twenty-five-thousand traveling fund is used during the year, the balance returns to the government. Next to President Roosevelt, President Taft was our great traveling President, and he probably excelled the former President by many thousands of miles.

During that week of the reunion, each morning at eight o'clock different Grand Army posts marched up the walk of our house to call upon the ladies. They came with drums and fifes and colors flying, marched through the wide hall from the front door to the back door, then back to the front door where we all stood in line to receive them—Mrs. Grant, Mrs. Alger, Mrs. Logan, and myself. As the old warriors came to Mrs. Logan and took her hand, tears came to their eyes. She had nursed many of them on battlefield and in hospital. She had a marvelous memory; never forgot a man's name nor the circumstances in which she last saw him. It was: "Well, well! if it isn't Bill Gates! I haven't seen you, Bill, since that night after Shiloh. You had a close call then, Bill." Lightning recollections like this followed one after another. She talked with every man, cried with him, recalled old scenes and times and brave men they had both known and loved and who were gone. It was very touching.

What reunions within reunions there were that wonderful week! When those old boys who had faced battle and death together met around this peace-time camp fire it was almost impossible for them to bring their reminiscences to an end. I've mentioned that small library. The men would crowd into that room and would have stayed there till morning, "swapping" stories, the air thick-blue with pipe smoke—if I had let 'em. But I felt that it was my duty to order "lights out" at some sort of reasonable, no unreasonable, hour. There was another day coming.

With that enormous crowd on hand, about two hundred thousand extra visitors all told, some things had to go wrong. Many people did not get their baggage at all.

The railroad station was hopelessly swamped with trunks and suitcases; trying to find anything in that mountain was a needle-in-a-haystack affair. People gave it up. Governor Hovey of Indiana was with us. Even though I had crowds of social affairs to attend, I could not forget my duties as hostess, and I tried, personally, to look after the comfort of each guest. This brought to my knowledge the fact that the Governor of Indiana traveled extremely light. Owing to the jam at the station, all that he seemed to have with him was a small paper bag of collars.

On the day of Governor Hovey's arrival I had a harder time than usual to get the boys to call it a day. They were on a rampage. I took the paper bag of collars to the library door and held it up.

"Do you know what this is?" I asked. "It's poor Governor Hovey's baggage."

There was a sympathetic laugh—most of the men were in the same boat—and the men scattered, some of them going off arm-in-arm, singing "We're tenting tonight" in a cheerful 1-A.M. voice.

There was one day so hectic that I did not have a chance to see my cook in the kitchen (basement) until after three o'clock in the afternoon. The weather was scorching; cook weighed about two hundred pounds. I felt a little anxious about her—now what if this mainstay were to be "overcome"? As I went down the stairs I called out:

"Lizzie, are you all right?"

Her answer came back like a peel of bells, "I never was better in my life, ma'am." I turned and flew back upstairs. "Good-by, Lizzie," I cried. "That will do! . . . I'll see you later."

If things hadn't been all right in the kitchen, that party would have collapsed.

The only extra servant we had in those days was a colored man to look after the stable. My husband and I both liked good horses, but with bands on every corner we decided not to take our horses out that week, but to depend upon the hired hacks which were always lined up at the gate. We brought the coachman into the house to run errands. And didn't he run them! Patriotism is a great appetizer.

I had made all plans beforehand, arranged with the servant staff to carry on the housekeeping during the week; I did not give it many thoughts, myself—just entered into all the daily, and hourly, festivities, knowing that things would go like clockwork. And they did. At least no criticism or complaint came to my ears.

Late Thursday afternoon a committee arrived from Cincinnati, bringing an invitation to my husband and his house party to attend the Cincinnati Centennial Exposition (also a Northwest celebration) the next day. I must digress a moment to recall a quaint circumstance of the opening of that Centennial, which had taken place on July 4th. It was a great century-of-industrial-progress display. Mrs. Polk, widow of President Polk, at her home in Nashville, Tennessee, touched the button that started the machinery. She was a very old lady then, eighty-five, still with traces of the Andalusianesque beauty for which she was remembered when she came to the White House in 1845 and routed drink, dancing, and gallivanting with her stern Moravian principles. Now, almost a half-century later, she sat at a marble-topped table in her shadowy, stiffly-elegant Southern parlor, and with trembling old fingers pressed the modern disk of magic. The table was inlaid with an American eagle and many-colored stars; gift to President Polk from the Consul of Tunis.

Back to my Grand Army guests. Very early on the morning of September 14th we were off to Cincinnati in Governor Alger's private car. I found myself dead for sleep—there had been a good deal of that cannon's-red-glare-and-bombs-bursting-in-air sort of atmosphere around me during the last few days. The ladies insisted that I snatch this chance to "catch up," and what a siesta I made of that ride to Cincinnati! I was as fresh as new when we got there, and a good thing, too. There were more reception committees, carriages, ceremonies, bands, flowers, general houp-la.

We were escorted to the Burnet House, then *the* fashionable hotel. Afterwards to the Exposition and to seats of honor on the platform. The Mayor of the city gave us an address of welcome. The president of the Exposition welcomed us again. Then Governor Foraker was made master of ceremonies.

The Governor of Colorado was the fourth man called upon to speak. As I remember him he was a very solemn man; no one would ever accuse him of having laughs up his sleeve. He began by saying that something most outrageous had happened at the Governor's house in Columbus. He, the Governor of Colorado, knowing that he would be called upon to speak, had carefully prepared a speech, written it out, and then, while he went in to breakfast, left it upon the library table. When he came back, what was his surprise and indignation to find his speech gone! He had not known what had become of it until he heard the three preceding gentlemen speak: They had divided his speech among them! The Governor sat down. Polite applause.

Colonel Grant was next. He put his hand in his pocket and produced a scrap of paper.

"Ladies and gentlemen," he said, "I can testify to everything the Governor of Colorado has said. The three gentlemen referred to not only stole his speech, but, worse, all that they left me was this bit—'I thank you for your kind attention.'" Now the audience was on and there was a roar of laughter.

People called out, "We want to see Mrs. John A. Logan." Mrs. Logan was introduced and made a tiny, sparkling little speech.

"Wait," said Governor Foraker. "We have more ladies

in our troupe," and he presented, one by one, our whole
string of beauties. As the audience now seemed to be having a lot of fun, Foraker kept it up.

"There is one more lady here," he said, "and I won't
go back on her even if she is my wife." So I made
my bow.

Then the grand tour of the Exposition, and a most
elaborate banquet. Governor Alger sat on my right. He
spoke of the past few days in Columbus, said that he and
Mrs. Alger had talked over everything, what a picturesque time it had been. She and he had traveled all over
the world, but they never had enjoyed anything so much
as the G. A. R. week as our guests. Well, that was very
nice. I had enjoyed it, too, I said.

"I know you did," said the Governor, "and that's what
I admire—the management that doesn't seem to
manage."

The Encampment rather overshadowed other events
of that tumultuous September. But several diverting incidents of the Centennial hold their own with me. Among
our guests was General Dalton, one of the Massachusetts party. There were forty-eight in it; same number
that had settled at Marietta in 1788. The General was an
old-time stickler for precedence. Every day when we left
our house for the Centennial, General Dalton held up
the procession until he had seen to it that each carriage
was in line strictly according to rank. Not then having
had my Washington revelation of the sacredness of prece-

dence, I was inclined to be amused by all this punctilio. The Massachusetts men wore quite gorgeous gold badges, larger than a silver dollar. When they were all lined up to say good-by, General Dalton presented me with one of their badges in a very pretty speech, in which he said, "I am presenting this to the real Governor of Ohio." It is treasured among my collections of badges, some two hundred and fifty, from state and national conventions which I have attended. When the McKinley Memorial Building was dedicated at Niles, Ohio, I sent forty McKinley badges, no two alike. They were in bronze, tin, silk, satin, cotton, celluloid, and of every color imaginable. The collection includes badges from every state in the Union and represents all the presidential candidates as well as governors since 1884.

Why does one always forget the instructive side of those old centennials and remember only the laughs? There comes back to me an "Art Exhibit" in which was a large photograph of myself ardently tinted by a local artist. I happened to overhear two women commenting on this masterpiece:

"*Mmm!* the Governor's wife. . . . Ain't she innocent-lookin'?" said one. "Not so innocent," said her friend. "Too flushed."

Another feature was a bust of Governor Foraker done in butter. Every time I went to the Centennial I had to see my husband in butter. He never melted during the entire five weeks.

It amuses me to recall those quaint days lost in a past when a Governor and his lady could, on so little, give such perfectly gorgeous parties and have so much fun. To misquote Riley,

> Let's go back to Griggsby's Station
> Where we were so happy and so poor ——

We did go back. But in Foraker's second term as Governor of Ohio the salary leaped from four to eight thousand dollars. What we did with all that money becomes less of a mystery as you read on.

CHAPTER VIII

BABY McKEE AND HARRISON TOO!

THE Harrison administration, beginning in 1889, was marked by one of the strangest personalities that ever found a place in the sun. Benjamin Harrison was a Presbyterian with a firm, doctrinal belief, which he was heard to express, that he had been predestined to occupy the presidential chair. Unfortunately, predestination failed to provide for a second term; indeed, it hardly insured the predestinee temperament enough to get him through the first. If "anything in the shape of a human being" interested Abraham Lincoln, nothing much in the shape of one brought a gleam to the eye of our aristocratic twenty-third President.

This lack of human sympathy, personal magnetism, what you will, was emphasized by the excessive magnetic charm of the Secretary of State. Blaine was idolized as no other political leader ever was, within my knowledge. Rather an over-rival for any man—the "plumed knight." But the difference between the Secretary and his chief was of the heart, which made it quite hopeless.

I remember once during the governorship when we were on a flying visit to Washington, my husband came back to the hotel looking as if he had had a chill. It was thus: business matters that day had taken Foraker to the State Department to see Mr. Blaine. He found the Secretary obviously overwhelmed with affairs; crowds of men were waiting to see him. Foraker at that time was concerned about the grave condition of his father's health. The newspapers were reporting this anxiety. Blaine saw my husband at once; came out to greet him; instantly detached himself from the scene, from everybody.

"Tell me about your father," he said, drawing Foraker into a private room: "Do you know that I've always thought of him as a tall, spare man? I never thought of him as a man who would have a stroke."

Foraker was so touched that he could hardly speak. Blaine had never even seen his father, but he knew how Foraker loved him and he kept him a long time to hear about their life together.

Then the Secretary plunged into politics, discussing, with complete knowledge and understanding, the condition and the needs in all their variations of the eighty-eight counties of Ohio. Blaine, Secretary of State—his hands full of our virgin-new foreign relations—had the facts about each one of those eighty-eight Ohio counties at his finger ends; knew all about them, couldn't have known more if that state had been his chief, his only interest. The President, like his Secretary, was a demon of energy, and doubtless his intelligence was as fine as Blaine's; but it was Blaine who radiated glamour and warmth when he did things. Had he been a woman, people would have rushed off to send expensive flowers.

When the Secretary and the Governor's talk ended, Blaine insisted that Foraker must have his, Blaine's, carriage to take him wherever business called him further, waved aside protests, ordered it immediately. And then it was a warm good-by with a "Do you know I have a feeling, a very strong feeling, that your father is going to pull through," and a handclasp that showed that he meant what he said. I think the secret of Blaine's extraordinary charm was that he really did care.

Glowing and happy from his visit with the Secretary, Foraker went directly from the State Department to the White House to pay his respects to the President. Mr. Harrison was very much himself.

"I've got all these papers to look after," he said, glancing at his desk, "and I'm going fishing at two o'clock." He snapped his watch.

It was not that the President was unfriendly to Foraker—far from it. It was just his way of being nice to the Governor of Ohio. Decidedly I thought my husband had had a chill when I saw him shortly afterward. I wondered what I ought to do for him. This benumbing frigidity in Harrison was what made him so good a friend to Cleveland in 1892. I don't think there was a single Republican who had the slightest idea that Harrison would be re-elected. How could he be? He had a

CAROLINE SCOTT HARRISON
Wife of President Benjamin Harrison and first President-General
of the Daughters of the American Revolution

trick of turning a Republican into a Democrat that was almost sleight-of-hand.

Harrison spoke extraordinarily well; probably no presidential candidate ever spoke better. He was always clear, forceful, vigorous, and always fresh. My father, who was in the thick of the campaign and heard hundreds of the speeches, said that Harrison *never once* repeated himself. This was a remarkable record, perhaps an unequaled one. Harrison was the first to make popular the front-porch campaign which later McKinley carried on at Canton. Each delegation was received with a speech that directly appealed to the district it represented and which captivated by its sympathetic, intimate understanding of individual conditions and its mastery of facts. The fine Harrison homestead in Indianapolis was devastated by the crowds which flocked to hear the candidate speak; Republican fans even carried off the fence. Harrison in 1888 did as much by his front-porch eloquence to help his cause as McKinley did to help his in 1896. If people could have just heard those splendid speeches, just heard Harrison, and then gone straight home and remembered how fine it was and never, never tried to shake the speaker's hand that was so like a wilted petunia—well, history might have been different.

In my collection of political souvenirs is a rough piece of hickory bearing a painted-on-satin portrait of Benjamin Harrison, "A Chip Off the Old Block," with Morton and the American eagle, all three looking

equally confident and florid. This was a replica of the
"Tippecanoe and Tyler too" badge of 1840.

When President-elect and Mrs. Harrison went from
Indianapolis to Washington for the inauguration the
Governor and I met them at Piqua, Ohio, traveling back
as far as Columbus in their private car. There was a
great presidential crowd on this special train; the Harrison party was mostly family, as I remember: their daughter, Mrs. Mary Harrison McKee, with her two children,
one being the famous "Baby McKee"; Mrs. Lord, Mrs.
Harrison's sister, and her daughter, Mrs. Dimmock,
whom Benjamin Harrison married after he left the
Presidency. The Harrisons were finishing dinner when
we boarded the train and we were invited to join them
for ice-cream and coffee. Afterwards Mrs. Harrison relieved the nurse of "Baby" McKee and we all went into
the other car. The President and Foraker went straight
to the far end of the car, obviously to discuss political
affairs undisturbed. Mrs. Harrison followed them down
the aisle and deposited the baby in her husband's lap.

"You hold him, Ben," she said, sweetly.

For the rest of the trip Mr. Harrison, looking like a
very black but entirely submissive thundercloud, dis-
coursed upon the newly-admitted Western states and the
Indian troubles with Our Baby clawing at his hair, unty-
ing his cravat, and using him as a toboggan slide. When
we said good-by Mrs. Harrison charmingly filled my
arms with flowers from the heaped-up bouquets on a

table. The President-elect regarded this incident thoughtfully, then added a posy of pansies on his own. "Must always have pansies," he said. He had small, very bright eyes; in that little moment with the flowers they suddenly flashed warm and kind. What a strange man!

We went on duly to the inauguration with a large party of Ohio officials, and stopped at the Ebbitt House. That famous hotel was thronged by an illustrious inaugural crowd, apparently everybody one ever heard of. The registers of the old Ebbitt must read like party roll-calls. McKinley lived there, I may recall here, all the years that he was in Congress; lived in two rooms, with the door between his workroom and his wife's room always open.

Harrison's March 4th was the wettest within my memory. It poured slanting cats and dogs all day. Mrs. Harrison told me afterwards that her husband wore a complete armor of chamois leather under his suit that day. "No inauguration pneumonia for him!" Governor Foraker rode in the parade with his staff, Benson one of them, carrying the Ohio marker—blue and gold. The saddle and bridle Foraker used were a gift from his staff officers. His horse was a beautiful coal black, but a craven creature. After he had mounted he found she couldn't lead. So the Governor changed horses with one of his officers; the officer's saddle was an army saddle with Mexican stirrups (which the Governor's were not); luckily, for at the close of the day Foraker's feet were dry, anyway. To me, sitting on the presidential platform, the men saluting the President, hat in hand, looked crow-like, plastered by the drenching rain. But who minds in-auguration weather?

The inaugural ball that night opened with a bit of comedy that still brings to my remembrance a smile. We were in a private room with the President's party, wait-ing for the grand march. Mrs. Harrison was seated, wearing a regal, stand-alone brocade—and a look of misery. On the floor beside her lay a pair of glittering satin slippers, very tiny satin slippers. "They're too small," she whispered to me, faintly, "and I didn't bring any old ones. How *ever* am I going to walk around that room?" But she did; and none in all those thousands of people guessed her torture.

The procession to the ballroom had already started, all of us in proper precedence, when something very funny happened. Lackeys came on the run, shouting: "Make way! Make way for the Vice-President of the United States!" The Mortons had been forgotten! They had been waiting in another room, a mile or so away—this was in the vast Pension Building—and hadn't heard the band. Wildly we all backed to the wall: Cabinet officers, Supreme Court Justices, Diplomats, Senators and ladies.

Mr. and Mrs. Morton came very quickly indeed. She was a large woman, but she ran down the long stairway like lightning and on the very tips of her toes, her long dress gathered up into billowy satin wings. We watched

. . . and held our breath . . . it seemed as though she must fall. But in another minute they were both in their places behind the Harrisons. The music crashed and we were off again. But, oh, that scramble to make a gangway for Their Excellencies! I was wearing a black velvet dress (my "best black" for years) of flowing yards and yards, the basque so boned and wasped-in and heavily weighted with gold passementerie and jet that to move in it pell-melly was to say good-by to grace. All the ladies had exciting struggles with their trains. Carnival! A very pompous justice made the tour of the ballroom, blandly unaware of a torn length of white lace wound 'round his leg.

> ". . . the female Ivy so
>   Enrings the barky fingers of the Elm,"

quoted young Mr. Lodge of this gleeful incident.

Mrs. Harrison held a unique place in the hearts of patriotic American women. She was the first President-General of the Daughters of the American Revolution. The prestige gained by this association gave the new society a start which brought in members by the thousands.

CHAPTER IX

THE NIGHT THE ELECTORS CAME

I HAVE a woman's reason for remembering in particular the Harrison nomination. It's backing a little to tell it here, but I must be forgiven.

We were at luncheon—this was Saturday, January 12, 1889—when my husband mentioned the fact that the twenty-three Ohio Republican presidential electors had arrived. "I'd like to ask them to dinner tonight, if you can manage it," he added, casually.

It was pretty quick work getting ready for that dinner party. It never occurred to us that we might more easily entertain the electors the next day. Ah no! that was the Sabbath. It would be a dull day, too, for the electors were in Columbus over Sunday simply to be on hand to cast their votes before noon on Monday. But we didn't give Sunday dinner parties in the 'eighties.

"There will be twenty-seven men," said Mr. Kurtz, the Governor's secretary. T-shaped tables were my scheme, with special provision at the ends for the fat men. One of these inevitables, a huge person, came uninvited; liked the idea of dining at the Governor's house with the electors. He was state auditor so I put him on my right.

"That your cook?" he asked, pointing with his knife to one of the maids, serving.

"No," I said. "I have five servants."

He put down his knife and gave a long, low whistle. Something very dramatic happened at that dinner: two men unexpectedly came face to face who had not met since they were in Libby Prison together, twenty-five years before. One was George B. Fox, elector from Hamilton County. Don't remember the other. Neither of the men could have known whether the other was alive or dead, for when they met they stood transfixed for a moment, just staring into each other's faces, like ghosts. Then a flood of emotion swept over them that almost broke up the party. They put their arms around one another; they cried; they laughed, and cried again; they forgot where they were, forgot everybody else who was there, forgot to eat; they talked excitedly and both at once. I cannot recall what they said, but with the help of Lieutenant-Colonel Cavados' *Libby Life*—I read it in 1865, I have just read it again—it must have run something like this:

"R'member Christmas dinner at 'the Libby'? . . . the smell of rancid bacon soup 'n' ——"

"Flavored with tar smoke! Lord! Everything tasted o' tar. R'member ——"

"R'member that queer fellow below us? . . . slipped us up a bottle through a rat-hole?"

"*Mmm!* That 'u'd have been 'Drake's Plantation Bit-ters,' wouldn't it? Yes, I r'member. Skinny hands that fellow had ——"

"Terrible hands! I can see 'em now, coming up through the floor. R'member the 'Fresh Fish' fighting for places at the window when they thought 'the Libby' was on fire?"

" 'N' we were only trying to look at a woman going by in the street below. I r'member that. R'member ——"

"R'member the rain? . . . the doggone, everlasting sound of rain on the tin roof? My, but it was mournful! . . ."

Thus it went brokenly on and on, a torrent of passionately-recalled misery that ended by drawing in everybody. The presidential electors dropped politics for a past that flamed with Chickamauga, Chickahominy, Shiloh, Gettysburg. Almost every man at the table had been a soldier.

It was no new thing to have Civil War veterans run off with the honors at a Republican gathering. The Republican Party had saved the Union. It was the Union.

Something great, simple, fiercely solidifying has gone from politics with the passing of the Grand Army man.

CHAPTER X

THE MUGWUMP AND THE CARPENTER

IN EFFECT, variety, shaken from the political sleeve, did what it could for us in the 'eighties. Foraker, four times nominated for Governor of Ohio; a defeat to start off with, a defeat to end, and two lively terms for the sandwich filling. The order left me uninstructed in few of the defenses of political life.

The first defeat never touched my buoyant husband. The fourth nomination distressed me; I felt, in the way that a woman flairs disaster, that it was a mistake; felt this from the moment at the Ohio State Convention, June, 1889, when after eight ballots Major McKinley climbed up on a press table, only place for him, so great was the crowd, and seconded somebody's motion to make Governor Foraker's nomination unanimous. Foraker's name had not been presented until then, and was not then presented in the usual way necessary for nomination. *He was not a candidate.* He was "voted in" on McKinley's seconding. A nice distinction.

The table went down with the Major. Didn't hurt him. The cheering for Foraker kept up for twenty minutes. Yet he lost at the polls. The paradox proves nothing but that immense personal popularity may be used as an excellent smoke screen for the maneuvers of a man's enemies. That convention was enormously attended; it was more like a national gathering than a state; crowds of candidates. A month earlier was the Johnstown flood, May 30-31. In this appalling disaster Governor Foraker had acted with great energy and dispatch. Governor Beaver of Pennsylvania, unluckily, happened to be absent from his state at the time and could not give official relief until after Ohio trains, loaded with workers and supplies, had poured into the stricken valley and hundreds of tents marked "Ohio" had been set up. Ohio was proud of her Governor, proud of the other states' praise of him.

Very pleasant, all this enthusiasm. Yet that 1889 nomination made me perfectly sick. We had had four delightful but devastating years at Columbus. Now I knew that it was time to go home. My husband knew it, too. He had no thought of running for a third term, and but for the counties' landslide that voted him in never would have run. A dark horse against his will. He had got through his first term on a salary of four thousand dollars, paying out of that sum twelve hundred dollars for house rent. Even the increase to eight thousand the second term hardly amounted to dizzy affluence with a family of growing children. Now Foraker felt that he ought to get back to his neglected law practice and make some money. Once, around 1883, my husband had received a ten-thousand-dollar fee, his first. Upon my soul it was a lovely sight! One that I could wish to see again. This was the thought that raced through my mind while the crowd cheered. Cheers are not so good taken on an empty pocketbook.

Foraker's first impulse was to refuse the nomination. But what a hue and cry went up at that! "He owed it to the state, etc., etc.," to take a third term. Dear old plea! Today I believe they call it "hokum" or something. Whenever a group of men are heard solemnly assuring a public official that he "owes" something or other to his country, you may be sure that the solemn ones have some extremely personal axes to grind.

And was I not right? Late in the summer a prominent banker named Sessions called on me. He came with a telling-it-to-you-for-your-own-good look in his eye. He began by saying that, while he had no reason to like my husband (they differed about taxes), he hated to see him double-crossed by his "Republican friends." A plot was brewing to banish Foraker once and for all. Foraker seems to have been the Alcibiades of the Republican Party! The plotters called themselves the "Touch Elbows." Hanna, McKinley and the Sherman crowd were in it. Also our warm personal friend, T. Ewing Miller. What happy times our families had had together under the stars at Middlebass Island! Well, in politics it is a mistake to depend too much upon friends—or stars.

Personally, I regard that defeat as the best thing that could have happened to Foraker. For some time Mark

Hanna had been moving heaven and earth to push William McKinley towards the Presidency. Had Governor Foraker been reëlected in 1889, he would have been undeniably in McKinley's way, whether he wanted to be or not, and for the second time brushed by the wings of a presidential nomination. This was just twice too often for my own wishes and ambitions for my husband or my children. McKinley and Foraker were about the same age; both had fine Civil War records. But McKinley, although not rich, had many rich friends who would devotedly have put their resources at his disposal; and he was childless. Foraker, oppositely, had a single-handed way to make and was rich only in children. For these and other excellent reasons I never completely yearned to live in the White House. And was I not happy to quit the Ohio Capitol that good-bye-to-the-'eighties winter and get back to Cincinnati and stop being the Governor's wife and become just a woman bossing the architect of a new house which, after having lived in five different houses in five years (the Governor paid his rent, but he moved around just as if he didn't!) was to be at last our own?

And yet, who would not have been glad to have been alive and in it during the event-strewn 'eighties! Old heroes still on hand to see young Modern Life showing the top of its head over the horizon: The Panama Canal, the Koch germ, the Brooklyn Bridge, the harbor goddess that the French gave us, the first electric railway running before open-mouthed crowds at Baltimore. And for horrors and sinister things, to make us uneasy in spite of our gay spirits, fire, earthquake, battle, and sudden death: The Opéra Comique fire; the Exeter, England, theater fire; and Kingston, Jamaica, wiped out; the Haymarket riots; the New York panic (1884); Java quaking, Charleston, S. C., quaking; the great Chinese flood taking almost a million lives; and the mad Eastern blizzard of 1888; Roscoe Conkling dying of it, but seeing, happily, before he went, Blaine, whom he so poisonously hated, defeated for the Presidency; and Garfield elevated, elected, villified, assassinated; Grant failing to make the third term; the Mugwumps rising and padding heavily out of the Republican Party; at the National Republican Convention, 1888, Robert G. Ingersoll being hissed, as I have told, not for atheism as many have thought, but for mentioning irregularly his candidate's name (Gresham). And, at Johnstown, Pennsylvania, a dam bursting.

Nobody alive then has forgotten the grisly horror of the Johnstown flood. The rivers carried a realistic pageant of that disaster past hundreds of miles of banks lined with spectators. For days the Ohio raced with the wreckage of the two thousand drowned, their houses, their farms. Entire populations camped on the shores to watch the Johnstown flood.Governor Foraker, taking charge in the absence of Governor Beaver, had, among other

things, to cope with the morbid sightseers who thronged
the desolate valley. He made General Axline military
commander. The problem of getting supplies to the sufferers, complicated by that mob of the curious, became
acute. General Axline placed men at the bridge with
orders to let no one cross unless he carried a load. Coffins
were terribly in demand. At one time any person who
tried to cross the bridge could do so only if he carried a
coffin. One burly holiday-maker got very mad. "Who
tells me I've got to carry a damn coffin across this
bridge?" he said. "The Governor of Ohio," said the
guard. Benson, an aide, brought back with him a book
that had been found clutched in the hands of one of the
victims. It was a little old photograph album.

A woman's remembrance of political contests must include many incidents, homely and humorous, that the
man, center of the battle, has missed. Children give the
saving turn. Usually, in those governor campaigns, just
as I had got the baby to sleep and the other children
quieted down, a band of serenaders would appear under
our windows. And the temperamental baby would wake
up and add her voice to the general *allegro*, and it was
farewell to rest. Political talk was mother's milk to my
children. They very early conceived the idea that "being
good" and being wide-awake scouts for their father and
his supporters were one and the same thing. There was
Florence, an adventurous infant, who strayed into a po-

litical gathering once on her way home from primary school, felt the anti-Republican tone of it, and decided to remain and pick up what points she could. It was a Democratic campaign meeting for Allen G. Thurman for Vice-President.

"They think Thurman is stronger than Harrison," she brought back. "They spit tobacco, and they have never washed their hands." Hogarthian picture of a Democratic gathering! One night during a local campaign drive—Benjamin Butterworth for Congress, I think was the cause of it—my eight-year-old son Benson stayed out so late that I got very anxious. Foraker didn't seem to worry. At eleven o'clock Benson came in, grimy and sleepy and smelling horribly of kerosene. He had been in a torchlight procession, trudging all over town, and then they had assigned him the care of Butterworth's suitcase. And, Casabianca, he stuck by the suitcase until Butterworth was ready to go to bed, when he found Benson sitting on it, blinking but true. And so perverse is memory that when I try to recall the historic trimmings of Governor Foraker's first inaugural what I see clearest of all is Julia, youngest Foraker, sound asleep during the whole of her father's inaugural address. The day was that of the great blizzard, 1886, eleven below, and the snow so deep that our train did not reach Columbus until after two o'clock. Ever so often they had to stop and clear the drifts from the tracks. Myself, I remember as the noblest words of that occasion those spoken by Mrs. Hoadley, wife of the retiring Governor, who murmured something about "hot coffee" when we arrived tired, hungry, and half frozen. I think it was after that first nomination that Benson said to his father, eying him severely from the dining-room rug, "Do you realize the responsibility of this great office?" Foraker, a little dashed, said meekly that he hoped he did. Oh, one has to keep up to the mark with children!

Louise was another of our precocious, politically-minded jewels. Asked by her teacher to write something from James Russell Lowell on the blackboard, she stood there, chalk in hand, and wrote nothing. The teacher waited, then commanded again.

Louise (politely): "Do you think anyone really cares what that old mugwump said?"

Foraker got a "note" about his insubordinate daughter. In reply he wrote, "Just wait till you get Julia." Excuse for these mosses from an old nursery is in Lincoln's reply to the lady who complained of the old-fashioned woman who *would* talk about the bright sayings of little Mary and little Johnny. Lincoln admitted that she was pretty bad, that there was only one type worse; that was the woman who *wouldn't* talk about little Johnny and little Mary.

One of the most amusing women of those days was Lida Powell, daughter of Bishop Thompson, president of Ohio Wesleyan University for many years, and wife of Thomas E. Powell, opposing Democratic candidate for Governor against Foraker in the campaign of 1887. She was an old school friend of mine, like myself of staunch Republican stock, and, husband or not, Lida stuck to the party. Before a certain important election she and Powell agreed upon a method of celebrating the outcome. They divided their house. If the Democrats won, her husband was to light up his half; if the Republicans won, his wife was to light up her half. The Republicans won. When Mr. Powell returned home, rather depressed, he saw the entire front of his house ablaze with light, gas burning from one end to the other.

"What does this mean?" he demanded. "I thought it was to be only one half?"

"Yes, of course," said his wife, brightly, "but my half is the front of the house."

We politically-partnered women, if we didn't have the vote then, had plenty of homage; some of it of the sort that went out with the horse and buggy. One day an old soldier was ushered into my husband's office. He was carrying a large wooden panel; this he stood against the wall, raised the shade for better light, and looked, all triumph and expectancy, at Governor Foraker. On the panel was painted in bright house paint a portrait of a lady, larger than life and wildly unnatural.

"Y'r wife," said the old man. "Ought to be good. . . . Painted from a cut in the *Gazette*. . . . Present from the boys in blue."

The soldier—he had lost an eye at Bull Run—had

done the creature on the panel himself. "Me and the carpenter at the 'Home,' " he explained. "Hoped the Governor 'u'd like it and hang it in his parlor."

Under the anxious eye of that dear, shabby old comrade, Foraker looked at the staring, rubicund female with flat eyes the same size and the same piercing blueness as the flat buttons that, in a stiff serpentine meander, nailed down the flat bodice. Looked at it—and spoke a few throatily choked words of thanks. And the old soldier went away and left his painting (and the carpenter's) leaning against the law books. Thence it was removed, being too violent a challenge to the self-control of all who saw it. For long afterwards the portrait of the "Gov's wife" was, when things threatened to become a little slow, mischievously brought out by one or another of my children. It never failed to produce unbridled and unmitigable hilarity.

Very useful for a public man's family to have such private reserves of fun.

CHAPTER XI

PARADE

POLITICALLY, 1889 might be called the end of the houp-la. The partisan clamor of the years following the Civil War was to be subdued by the new problems of the 'nineties. We lost zest after that for expressing and explaining everything with silver-tongued oratory and brass bands. Torchlights went out.

Perhaps because it marked the eclipse of an epoch, the memory of the New York celebration of the first inaugural of George Washington still dazzles. New York said it knew how to do it—and it did. Solemnly the governor of each state issued a proclamation that let the children off from school April 30, 1889. Gayly then the governor himself set forth. He went escorted by crack state troops, and the flower of his state's most beautiful women and bravest men picked up and went after him. If you couldn't go to New York that spring you consoled yourself as best you could. It was a cold spring, anyway, and they did say that New York's tall buildings, ten to fifteen stories high, some of them, shut out the sun.

We Forakers left Columbus brilliantly, but there was a canker in the rose. Foraker, guest of honor on the special train of the Cleveland Greys (their thoroughbred horses were on that train, too), was suffering from a painfully injured foot. He could hardly move now. What about after he got there? Louise, my second daughter, had sprained her ankle. But Foraker carried her off willy-nilly; decidedly Louise could go if he could. I joined another special party: the Governor's staff officers, their wives—other Ohio bigwigs. I had Florence, my eldest girl, and Julia, the baby, with me. "Thith Wathington Thentennial," said Julia, "ith an education in itsthelf." Nobody else took it so gravely. We were on holiday, one after our own hearts.

At Baltimore our train ran into the one from Washington carrying Vice-President Morton and party in his private car. Everybody was shocked, but only the baggage-car really hurt. Out of that wreck our Adjutant-General and aides pried our trunks and flung them on to our relief train just as it pulled out. Ohio had its clothes. Why I remember the red straw bonnet and the long bewilderingly-braided coat in which I entered New York I don't know. But Ohio must have looked all right.

We found the Governor and Louise already limping about in front rooms at the Fifth Avenue Hotel. Thanks to a surgeon on their train, and Fannie Hayes, daughter of the ex-President who made the tenderest of nurses, and Benson—and "science"?—the sufferers now scorned solicitude. People were pouring into the hotel: sombreroed Western governors with huge parties, and Southern governors and planters in soft hats with frou-frouing, creamy-voiced ladies. Everybody had written you-all for "rooms on the Avenue" and there was a great to-do when the clerk could not make them go but just so far. The parade was to pass that hotel; the President's reviewing-stand, shaded by the chestnut trees of Madison Square, was just opposite, and all around that quarter the great people of the land were entertaining other great people. Above the entrance to Vice-President Morton's lavishly-decorated house at Fifth Avenue and Sixteenth Street fluttered a small blue flag with the coat-of-arms of the United States in white. It told the world that the Commander-in-chief of the Army and Navy of the United States was there. The "President's flag." Whenever people appeared on the balcony of the Morton house hundreds of spy-glasses were leveled upon them from surrounding balconies. The balconies of the Victoria Hotel, Fifth Avenue and Twenty-seventh Street, where the Grover Clevelands lived since they left the White House a few weeks ago, blossomed with provocative groups. The town was triumphant with arches; the particularly beautiful one by Stanford White gleamed against the green of Washington Square.

Festivities opened April 29th with a naval pageant, Admiral Porter, grand marshal, over the same route that Washington, one hundred years before, had traveled "in a magnificent barge escorted by thirteen masters of vessels." This was from Trenton to "Elizabeth Point." By mid-morning on that century-later April day, fully a thousand boats of every sort lay in the "Kill" off Bergen Point. They waited there for the President of the United States, who was coming on the *Dispatch* to lead the five-mile parade up the bay. Every boat was packed; then only about half could go who expected to. We steamed off on the *Erastus Wiman*, leaving at the pier about two thousand people looking ruefully at their too-tardy tickets. Luckily, we found places on the hurricane-deck and had a faultless outlook. The sight presented by New York Harbor was just one of those things that one remembers and talks about for the rest of his life:

A white, green, and black picture. An April sky, now sun, now cloud; the shores delicately plumy and for miles swarming with people who had come with bands, without bands, in carriages, wagons, on foot, hundreds of thousands of Uncle Sam's people; and that most beautiful sheet of water covered, gleaming, with a myriad of boats. There seemed not room to dip an oar between them. There was a little breeze that didn't know its own mind; one minute it whipped up white caps, the next it sighed languorously, then rioted again. We put on furs. Too warm. We took them off, and shivered. April!

Near the Statue of Liberty (a novelty then) lay a long line of warships. Between them and the goddess the *Dispatch* was to pass. When she was sighted, brilliant as an Eastern barge, a tremor seemed to run through the fleet. And now the real pageant began: steamers; all sorts of sailing-craft from majestic four-masters to snowy little cats that with other small fry swooped after the big boats like gulls; Crœsus yachts; democratic ferry-boats; tooting tugs—everything under the sun made to float all maneuvered into the President's wake. It was as pretty a game of follow-the-leader as ever was.

As the President and his fleet passed the men-of-war— color from deck to main truck—something very thrilling and beautiful took place. The bluejackets swarmed up the ratlines to the yards and stood there, hand in hand, outlined, up and up infinitely against the blue sky. People went crazy over this sight, but cheers were drowned by the roar of the great guns which now began to break loose. The salute of the guns was in more than one sense a moving thing; people reeled—but they loved it. A cannonade from the huge *Chicago* was like nothing that ever had happened since Genesis. All America was in it.

With us on the *Wiman* was "Gordon of Georgia." This battle-scarred old ex-Confederate thunderbolt (who was thought to have been one of the original "Cyclops" of the Georgia Klan and whose weakness for Jeff Davis long interfered, and publicly, with his homage to Abraham Lincoln), had now mellowed into a Union man without losing any of his Southern charm. He became extremely emotional as the patriotic panorama unfolded. He stood with uncovered head murmuring ecstatically to himself while the guns boomed, the bands banged, and the crowds yelled. Suddenly he wheeled around and addressing the whole group on the deck, as one renewing a confession of faith, exclaimed, "I thank God I am an American citizen."

Another person with us was as much affected by the scene as General Gordon, and as adequately expressive. This was a little old, lace-and-lavender mother of some tall colonel. She looked from the surpassing spectacle of the bay to the young sailors poised against the sky, from the glittering craft that bore her President to the far-flung peopled shores, from the benign goddess, holding aloft her torch for all, back again to the lads in the air. It was too much. "Oh, la!" she cried. She ducked her head against her colonel's shoulder. He put his arm around her.

Washington landed on a mud bank, at the foot of Wall Street, East River, New York. His barge was rowed all the way from New Jersey. President Harrison made his landing from a barge and on the same spot. The barge was manned by a crew of shipmasters from the Society of the Port of New York; Washington's crew in 1789 were members of the same society.

Far to the south one saw two dark, delicate spans flung spider-webwise from shore to shore. It was the Brooklyn Bridge, black with people.

That night was the ball. There have been great balls; there will be great balls. They perfume history. But there hardly can be another one graced by the presence of so

many women bearing distinguished Colonial names and
so amazingly "heirloomed" as that April ball in our
first President's honor.

The Inaugural Ball in 1789 took place in a plain
wooden structure, the "City Assembly Rooms." There
were three hundred guests. For the Centennial Ball (and
banquet the next night) a huge wing had been added to
the Metropolitan Opera House. Mr. Ward McAllister
managed it. He had just said something about there
being but four hundred people in New York society.
Some eight thousand crowded to the Centennial func-
tion. All around the wall were boxes for the especially
invited: military and naval heads, governors of all the
different states. Everybody came. When the ball reached
its height there wasn't room for an official Cinderella.

The ball's great feature was the quadrille. Old, historic
families were drawn upon. Mrs. William Astor hurried
back from Paris to take her place, landing the day the
Centennial opened, and bringing with her a ballgown
that expressed what M. Worth, in that year of grace,
could do for an Astor with white satin, black lace, and
silver-embroidered *point d'esprit*. (It seems to me there
were cascades of roses, too: old-pink, winy-red and yellow damask roses—"very French.") Withal, one detail
of the costume gave me rather a shock. *Mrs. Astor wore
a sham!* A sham, you know, was a part of the skirt made
of cheaper material because concealed by drapery or
flounces. When Mrs. Astor danced the sham showed.

"Would you have believed it?" Reminiscing ladies gasped for a long time at that touch of thrift.

It may be interesting, even to this year's débutantes, who will be dowagers, alas! at some future Centennial, to know who danced in that quadrille forty-two years ago. Here they are, penciled on the back of my program of square and round dances, still dangling its pink pencil: Mesdames William Astor, Alexander S. Webb, A. Gracie King, Frederick J. de Peyster, Bayard Cutting, Levi P. Morton, S. Van Rensselaer Cruger, Elbridge T. Gerry, A. Newbold Morris, Alexander Van Rensselaer, Robert F. Weir, Edward Cooper, Mrs. Herbert of Washington, Mrs. Edward F. Jones, wife of the Lieutenant-Governor of New York, Miss Louise Lee Schuyler and Miss Carola Livingston.

Beauty and birth further shone, of course, in that brave assemblage. It was useful to have Colonial aristocracy identified for me by New York friends who came to our box; but truly the dresses worn that night were even more distracting than Norman blood. Clothes were really clothes then, remember; ballgowns were our poetry— and Paris was their prophet. In my rather scrambled journal of that metropolitan adventure I find dress notes cropping out irrelevantly among references to the Centennial's more serious ceremonies. As this, in my midnight-jottings down after the banquet (following night): "Prayer of grace by Bishop Potter; very impressive, all standing, heads bowed. Ball: water-green *moiré* with

embroidered *mousseline de soie*, same shade; white lilacs
and green grasses left shoulder and skirt. Lovely! Who?"

I never learned the name of that siren "Who" in
green *moiré* and grasses; but with the help of yellow clip-
pings which fall out of my 1889 diary as I open it, I am
able to link certain other remembered gowns and garni-
tures (loved old-timey word) with their wearers. Except
by the dancers in the quadrille, short dresses (to the floor)
were generally worn, and on Empire, Louise Quinze,
or Marie Antoinette lines after the exotic craze of those
years. A great ribbon-time. I never saw so many runaway
sashes and coy shoulder-knots, such babblings of "baby
ribbon." And "ladder bows"—who remembers them? A
far western Senator's wife, stout, languid lady, wore a
"ladder" of perhaps twenty-five pink-satin love-knots,
rich-man-poor-man, down the front of her dress. Young
girls in white tulle dancing-frocks cascaded with pink
roses, a garland of rosebuds in their hair, *à la Taglione,*
lent a mid-Victorian touch, prim and charming, to a
scene that gave us something to talk about after we got
home (and the children were out of the room) in "these
new terribly low necks." Posies dangled from fans; in
silver posy holders when the dancers had inherited or
borrowed them. Waists, by the way, were still waspy.
There still burned in New York society the fashionable
ambition to have a waist "smaller than Mrs. Ogden
Mills'." Over-zealous ladies fainted now and then. Not
that it mattered. It was smart to swoon. The mission of

the bustle (elegantly, the "improver") was, of course, to make the waist look even smaller.

While many brocades were copies of eighteenth century designs made in France especially for this ball, the most arresting costumes were those made wholly or in part from genuine old brocades worn during the Washington administrations, worn, some of them, at the First Inaugural Ball. Often priceless heirlooms adorned them. The earliest brocade was that worn by Miss Louise Lee Schuyler. The dress was made in 1782 for General Phillip Schuyler's daughter, she who married Stephen Van Rensselaer, "last of the Patroons." With it the 1889 Miss Schuyler wore a diamond brooch containing a mortuary design wrought from a lock of Alexander Hamilton's hair. As if this were not enough to make any coming-on D. A. R. turn perfectly green, Miss Schuyler wore, also, a pearl locket containing a lock of Washington's hair.

The train of Miss Carola Livingston's quadrille costume was of century-old pink brocade thickly embroidered with silver thistles. Mrs. Carlton H. Way, of New York, wore a Spanish tortoise-shell comb that an ancestress, Mrs. Ezekiel Park, was said to have worn at the 1789 ball, at which she danced the minuet with Washington. (Incidentally, the beautiful Mrs. Maxwell is also credited with the honor of being the President's partner in that dance.) A story went with the comb; it was that Washington begged Mrs. Park to remove the comb for

fear it might be broken. Whether she took his prudent
advice I do not know. My own opinion is that she did
not. Mrs. Robert Weir (a descendant of Washington's
brother) wore diamond clasps that once Washington
had worn; she wore also miniatures, surrounded by diamonds, of President Madison and the vivacious "Dolly."
Beautiful old stuffs were in the gowns worn by many
other ladies whose names themselves were richly embroidered with historical association: Mrs. Newbold Morris
I remember, and Mrs. Van Buren and Mrs. Alexander
Webb. How many others there must have been!

Of that scene two figures remain brightest in my memory. One was Mrs. Levi P. Morton. In the *quadrille*
d'honneur Mrs. Morton's train was of old brocade so
lovely it was not to be believed: clusters of rosy-red wild
strawberries caught with bows and ends of faintly-violet
ribbon were carried over a darker violet ground shot
through with silver. The wife of the Vice-President had
a great air; in pearls, a marabout aigrette in her beautiful
gray hair (though she was young), and carrying an an-
tique fan she looked like some lovely French Queen.

My other picture was made by Mrs. Burke Roche. I
can see yet that figure of grace in a gown of white tulle
and silver tulle fringed and fringed in some odd, lovely
way with white violets. Sometimes a ballgown achieved
such poetry that it could only be set to music—and was,
of course. Mrs. William Astor blazed with the celebrated
diamonds—tiara, necklace, bracelets. A trio of unob-

trusive gentlemen hovered ever near her. They looked like vestrymen; they were detectives.

I wish I could remember what Mrs. Harrison, our new President's wife, wore that night. But, perversely, I can see only her son's wife, Mrs. Russell Harrison, very fresh, very *panachée* with blue ostrich tips in her hair—and blue slippers to match. Those were the days when we "matched"—or perished.

Music and champagne went on until five o'clock in the morning. A special legislative concession had taken the ban off selling drinks "between 1 and 5 A.M." The spectacle in the supper-room of several thousand people "helping themselves"—service was beyond all waiters—was hardly edifying. The President and his party (their table was on a platform quite apart from the crush) remained but a short time in the supper-room. Two bands helped maintain the note of joy unconfined. Lanciers from "Yeomen of the Guards," I remember, and Strauss's dreamiest waltz, "Vienna Women," and another waltz, in honor of Mrs. Harrison, called "Carrie" (it always evoked applause), and the "Pearl of Pekin." Strains floated after us as we went out from the ball to meet the morning star. General Sherman was with us. "I like this new music," he said. He confided to me that if they stopped altogether playing "Marching Through Georgia" he would *quite* forgive them.

But in the soul of the real Centennial lists nothing that yet had happened compared in importance with the big march. Parades across the ages, from Noah, look pretty much alike in the sun. And always the crowd's the thing. Here, in April, 1889, New York met for the first time, I believe, a crowd that was too much for it. People covered Manhattan Island like insects. They swarmed into the side streets, when Fifth Avenue was finished, and home-steaded there; trucks, wagons (and their horses) and brownstone stoops looked like Arizona anthills. Men and boys roosted like rooks in the trees of the Square. From my place just opposite the President's reviewing-stand I could see the crowds on top of the Hoffman House, the Fifth Avenue, the Madison Square Bank Building and other "skyscrapers."

"Very dangerous," said Mr. Chauncey Depew, point-ing to a row of men lying on a near-by roof, looking down at the scene "Very dangerous indeed. Must be one hundred and fifty feet!" He removed his top hat and wiped his brow. April dropping briefly into a July mood.

We waited a long time among our lunch hampers and rugs. Bands played the usual deceitfully-encouraging see-the-conquering-hero-comes music that is written for parade-waits. The crowds, impatient, hungry, matched pennies for small beer, mobbed sandwich-sellers, and at every tuneful sop thrown by the bands, surged over everything like a dam breaking. The soldiers threatened to ride over their heads. Let 'em! Folks had come to see this here parade and they were a-goin' to see it. Finally a group of dignified gentlemen appeared on the Presi-dent's stand: Vice-President Morton, Chief-Justice

Fuller, and members of the President's Cabinet, with Mayor Grant of New York. They had come from solemn commemorative services at the Sub-Treasury, or at St. Paul's. At the latter Washington's ancient prayer-book had been used; Archbishop Corrigan had pronounced the benediction. The Cabinet group suggested, oddly, good citizens who had been to church and were now ready for Sunday dinner.

When at last *they* came, the President of the United States and the armed array of the nation, heralded by a roar like the Deluge, sentiment and comedy conspired slyly to slip into the impressive scene a few smiles. As President Harrison's carriage passed the Morton house, Mrs. Harrison and Mrs. Morton stepped to the front of the balcony and waved and blew kisses, and the President stood up and beamed and bowed and waved to them, looking strangely, humanly, rosily emotional. His silk hat was bashed in at the brim. He had been lifting it on and off for hours. But he looked a happy man. At the sentimental domestic touch a propinquitous band swung wittily into "Ben Bolt." The crowd loved it. For that flash of a second Benjamin Harrison could have had three terms.

The militia of each state escorted its governor: blazed the blue and scarlet artillery, the blue and yellow cavalry, the infantry blue and white. Regulars and smart volunteers. Governors in the mass can be quite effective. A lone governor outside his own state isn't so dashing. Most of

the forty-eight governors—I am including the territorial
governors—rode. The Southerners and the Westerners
were beautiful horsemen, of course, and picturesque in
their wide-brimmed, soft felt hats. Governor Riggs of
Delaware looking like, with his long white hair and air
of tempered benignity, the ghost of Henry Ward
Beecher, turned continually in his saddle, grandly sweeping the ground right and left with his hat. His hat got
quite dusty. Governor Beaver of Pennsylvania rode like
a centaur, though he'd lost a leg somewhere in the valley
of the Shenandoah. He took applause like an old actor,
bowing to the balconies with his hand pressed upon his
heart, even, Irving-like, raising his eyes to the roofs—the
"gallery." Gordon of Georgia, conscious that he never
appeared so well as on a horse, made the most of that
picture. He threw kisses to Mrs. Harrison, liked the
effect, repeated this tender homage as he passed Mrs.
Cleveland—then looked around for Mrs. Hayes. A
great First Ladies' man, old Gordon.

Among the riders there was one who would have
shone with greater luster in a carriage. This was Governor Hill of New York. I imagine that this was his début
as horseman. Two orderlies, one on each side, walked
beside his horse. When the Governor approached the
President's stand he prepared to salute by dropping the
reins and raising his high hat. His horse stopped dead.
The orderlies grabbed the reins and prodded the horse to
move on. The Governor remained stiffly aloof from this

maneuver, holding high his hat. There was a suppressed titter from the crowd; very suppressed. Sssh! This was our host, the Governor of New York! The salute finally was accomplished, the orderlies prominently assisting. It was one of the gayest sights.

But an end to confetti. When Governor Oliver Ames of Massachusetts appeared with the Ancient and Honorable Artillery of Massachusetts marching with the Marylanders, then it came over us what we were parading for. People caught the significance of that union. It was the Marylanders, we remembered, who stained Baltimore streets with Massachusetts blood, the first blood shed in the Civil War. General Fitzhugh Lee, beplumed and débonair, with his Virginians, struck the same historic-patriotic chord. So did, in a different way and youth-heightened, the West Point cadets and the Annapolis lads. Mr. Cleveland had not permitted these pets of the nation to march in President Harrison's inaugural parade; the crowd, always a little hysterical when they appear, now devoured them with cheers.

There was other cheering which seemed to my ears not the least musical of all. It grew to a roar as the object of it, Governor Foraker of Ohio, followed by the gorgeous Cleveland City Company known as the Cleveland Greys, and the Ohio troops came into Madison Square. Every horse in that contingent was a Kentucky thoroughbred. My husband rode a very valuable horse owned by George A. Garretson, captain of the First Troop Cavalry of Cleveland. After that demonstration I felt that I could get through the day. I didn't mind it when Mrs. Grover Cleveland, nurturing the old "rebel flags" grievance, turned her back on the Foraker column. The Ohio Society waxed very wroth at this gesture. But dear me, I could not! She was a very young woman. I only felt sorry that she missed seeing all those beautiful horses.

That night a quite Lucullan banquet took place at the Metropolian Opera House. The last scene of the pageant. The menu interests one now as a "museum bit." There have been bigger banquets since then, but this one, eight hundred men sitting down at tables arranged double-horseshoe fashion, was the biggest ever at that time. The menu, eight inches long, was in French; sixteen thousand dollars' worth of wine flowed; twelve different kinds. There seem to have been but three liqueurs. Bishop Potter "asked the blessing" on this Bacchic feast. I was among the ladies invited to sit in the balcony and hear the after-dinner speeches made by President Harrison, Mr. James Russell Lowell, Mr. Joseph Choate, and others. Mirrors were set ever so often in the centre of the tables, bearing masses of red and white flowers. We ladies looked down on the scene. The blossoms were reflected in the mirrors; so were the bearded faces of the men. There were the time-honored thirteen toasts, and one silent toast—to George Washington.

I think it was General Miles who told me that as everybody was going home, satiated and tired, he noticed a man standing on the corner and surrounded by a little group; he was talking eagerly in a quite charming voice, though rather falsetto when raised, and pointing to the sky.

"It was young Roosevelt," said the General; "he was introducing some fellows to the stars." In 1889 you could still discern the Big Dipper in the New York sky.

At the Centennial Ball the night before, Governor Francis of Missouri, a very handsome man and dapper, had asked my husband how he should dress for the parade.

"Ask my wife," said Foraker; "she collects centenials."

It did look as if I had gone in for that sort of thing—instead of old silver. During the Governor's terms the days brought just one hurraying parade after another. In September, 1887, we attended the Philadelphia Constitution, or Industrial, Centennial. In 1888 we had four centennials in our own State—one in Cincinnati, two in Marietta, and one in Columbus. Into the bargain we had under our political roof the National Guard Encampment and that of the Grand Army. In 1889 came the New York celebration just recalled. What with, besides, inaugurals, political conventions, national and state, cornerstone dedications piling upon cornerstone and other ceremonies, and myself looking, if not with biblical idealism, then as best I could, to the ways of my household, truly they were lively years.

Of all the centennials in my "collection" Philadelphia was the best-managed, New York the most brilliant, and the two Mariettas the most interesting and to me the most enjoyable. At Marietta I had the fun of running a hotel, my only experience as a hotel-keeper. As the affair was a success and as there were no financial returns to bother about, I am unable to regard the hotel business as anything but one long pleasant picnic. It's a point of view.

In 1888, Marietta, earliest settlement in Ohio, dramatized its history in two stirring scenes. The first took place on April 7th. It celebrated the end-of-a-century since General Rufus Putnam and forty-eight New Englanders floated down the Ohio on the *Mayflower II* and, greeted by seventy Indians, landed at the mouth of the Muskingum. The second scene was staged July 15th; it reënacted the inauguration of Arthur St. Clair, first Governor of the Northwest Territory and so, first Governor of Ohio.

I had reason to be keen over Marietta's jubilee beyond all others. My own people were of the Marietta pioneers. My maternal great-grandfather, Captain John James, was one of Putnam's men. He came out with his wife and ten children in the Fourth Company, 1789, the year before the Indian wars in the Territory ended. They lived first in the famous "Farmers' Castle," a stockade consisting of thirteen houses built 'round a square. Great-grandfather lived in Number Two with three other families, twenty-nine people in all. His son William, leaving the protection of the stockade for a camp in the rich river land called the "Bottom," was killed one night at dusk when all arms were stacked, by a band of Indians. My mother's mother and father were married at Marietta; my father's mother and father settled in that wilderness in 1815. Father was born there. Marietta was my legend.

The town had been asleep in the dog fennel for a hundred years. Now it woke up to receive with flowers and flags and music and in Sunday clothes the thousands who came to pay its history homage that April day. A dreamy old town with beautiful, austere early houses, patriarchal trees, and along the ridge that forms the background the fine Indian mounds that mark the boundaries of the ancient forts.

Governor Foraker welcomed the assemblage; then Edward Everett Hale led the oratorical lists with the proud reminder that, next to the signing of the Declaration of Independence, the opening of the Northwest was the most important event in American history. And T. Randolph Tucker of Virginia, planter *par excellence*, rose to say that that was indeed so, and to add that it was Virginia, who had a title of conquest to the Northwest, who was the mother of them all. And ex-President Hayes spoke, of course (no ex-President was so omnipresent and so useful), and Orton the geologist, very erudite about the mounds, and Howe the historian, and crowds of others, all eloquent. Senator Hoar of Massachusetts spoke learnedly and to our delight; he seemed another man on this occasion. Oratory flowed on and on. Hunger was its only rival. Just at noon, the hour at which Putnam's party was said to have stepped off the *Mayflower of the Northwest*, a salute of one hundred guns was fired. Marietta trembled—then rang a dinner bell.

After the banquet—and the champion cake-makers, pie-makers, ham-boilers, and chicken-fryers of the whole countryside saw to it that the multitude was fed—oratory was resumed with renewed vigor. Not until shadows lay across the ancient greens did it abate. Then in lovely April twilight we wandered, carriage or afoot, about the ancient sites: the old cemetery—is it not the only cemetery in the country in which there is an Indian mound?—the first church built in Ohio; the land office, one of the oldest houses in the country still standing on its original site (now owned by the Colonial Dames); the log cabin in which the treaty of peace with the Indians was signed; Campus Martius, the ancient fortifications where the settlers fled from the savage redskins.

That April celebration was remarkable for the many very old, old people who had come from different parts of the United States for this event. There was Thomas Porter, eighty-nine, son of the last living survivor of

Putnam's party. And Mrs. Phœbe Bryan, ninety-two, born in Marietta. Like a withered snowdrop was Phœbe Bryan. She had traveled all alone from Beaver, Pennsylvania; hadn't been "home" for sixty years. And there was Mr. McIntosh. How old was Mr. McIntosh I do not remember. He looked like a ravaged Lear. Douglas Putnam, grandson of General Israel Putnam, the one they called "The Wolf," had raked the universe for Marietta pioneers. If they could travel, he saw to it that they came. It was Methuselahland. One can imagine the reverential impression made by these ancient men and women, all born in the eighteenth century, all part and parcel of the events we young centennialists were here to commemorate.

During our twilight tour of the past, Senator Hoar found an arrowhead. He looked at it as at an open book. "The hand of fate was on the Indian races," he said; "they had to give way."

The sun dropped behind an Indian mound. A salute of thirty-eight guns reminded us that the day was done. But it was only the beginning. We were coming back in July, really to celebrate. This time it was the centenary of Governor St. Clair's inaugural. Enthusiasts allowed that this would take one whole week.

Spring of 1888 found us desperately put to it to find a house in Columbus suitable for a governor and an expansive family. Our lease of the Ewing Miller house was limited. Dear me! What a time! "Ohio's Governor," said old Dennison, "hasn't a place to put down his grip." One day Foraker came home beaming.

"I've got your house," he said; "it's in Marietta."

This took some clearing-up. The centennial committee had decided, it seemed, that at the July celebration the thing for the thirty-ninth Governor of Ohio to do in honor of the first Governor, was to take a house, entertain all the distinguished guests, and help Marietta make a royal event of it.

All right. But if that was to be my job I wanted to do it well. General Axline and I raced over to Marietta to have an early look at the field. The General had to organize a tent-community for the regular troops and the National Guard, which were coming. The house we were to occupy was the old Grafton house, standing high, with a fine view of the Muskingum Valley. Two families were then occupying it; there were two very small kitchens, two very small stoves.

"You'll probably have a couple of hundred people for dinner every night," the General said, casually.

Well, didn't I sail in! A gas range was installed, great quantities of china provided; I supplied the linen, the silver, and all the servants except two, natives, who went with the house. I turned the barn into a laundry, with extra space providing barracks for men workers. (One to two hundred napkins a day was a trifling item.) A great many people were to be our house guests; if we couldn't "sleep them" we were to give them meals. If this wasn't to be the "Imperial Hotel" of Marietta, what was it?

Cooks. Men make history, but cooks make the centennial. I imported my Irish treasure from the capital and added several other experts. We were ready for anything —and it came. A second and third table for most meals. I learned about catering. I learned that twenty-five pounds of ground coffee make eight hundred cups, that five hundred chickens went like lightning in seven days—and that orators were imposing cake-eaters. Two Marietta women whose cakes took prizes at the fairs baked for us every day. We froze our own ice-cream, baked our own bread—we even "jelled." To ask pioneers to eat anything but the home-made was an anachronism. All over the grounds was General Axline's tent-city for staff officers, newspaper men, and men of the National Guard. These we fed, too. When, on July 15th, the door was opened, all down the dusty road stood carriages, ready to take people anywhere; lemonade was on tap; a band under a big sycamore was playing "First Heart Throbs," popular new piece—and perspiring. It was hot.

That hotel of mine ran without a hitch. The horn of plenty hung inverted over us. Farmers' wives came from as far as fifty miles away with butter, broilers, eggs, and honey. They all wanted to see the Governor's wife and I was delighted to see them and to chat about chickens and children over a market basket. A Marietta lady furnished us with cream—an auriferous supply; she furnished us also with a little innocent fun. Every day at the same hour she would arrive with the cream cans and tell me, and the usual large audience present, that this cream was so heavy it could be lifted with a knife. Every day she would go in and warn the kitchen.

"Be sure to thin this cream," she would say; "it's so thick you can lift it with a knife."

After a week of this our chief dairy maid, a dry old maid from Warren County, announced that she had "that knife ready. But," darkly, "it ain't for the cream."

Our own trip from Columbus to Marietta was something that, just to recall it, makes me feel young again. Blue sky and blazing sun. The train stopped at every cornfield, almost. There were crowds. Calls for "Foraker! Foraker!" The Governor would appear, then I. Immediately some one would call out, "Where are the children? We want to see them." So, Benson, Florence, Louise, Julia, a blushing, bobbing, smiling, stepladder of a family, would troop out onto the platform. The children had a great success. "Oneacre! Twoacre! Threeacre! Fouracre!" the crowds yelled. It was all great fun. The enthusiasm kept up until we were fairly inside our new home.

A great many people sat down to supper—and what a supper! that first night. Strangers all. We did not know them, and they, apparently, didn't know one another. Representatives appointed by the governors of other Northwest Territorial States—Michigan, Indiana, Illi-

nois, and Wisconsin. Advance guard of the governors
themselves. At first they were all stiff as ramrods. Then
I made a little speech. I said that we had a week together
ahead of us, that the house was theirs; I hoped they would
find it a comfortable home and treat it like a hotel; that
we had tried to think of everything—sorry there wasn't
a barbershop, but it was a nice walk—and that I only
wanted them to enjoy themselves. Not a very original
speech, perhaps, but it broke the ice. At once the table
began to hum like a sawmill.

For five long July days we were bombarded by the
eloquence of our country's great speakers. All the Northwest states sent their crack orators; the others sent their
best ones, too. Whatever the Northwesterners didn't remember to mention, the others did. Our endurance
stamina under forensic fire was heroic in those days. Mrs.
Mary A. Livermore made a Civil War speech. A dramatic person. She told about the great Sanitary Fair in
Chicago when Western farmers stripped their fields and
brought in every green eatable thing to save the Union
boys from scurvy; when women worked the potato
patches—and wept. And Senator Evarts of New York,
polished and delightful man, talked about the simon-
pure Americanism of the Northwest. He quoted George
Rogers Clark:

"In the part of Ohio known as the Western Reserve
there are more people of Connecticut blood than in Connecticut." . . . "The superior mettle of Ohio men was

due to the fusion of the best people of all European races. . . . Foreign immigration did not reach the Northwest Territory until 1830."

John Sherman was in his prime then, and I never have heard a finer address than he made on that occasion; a scholarly, panoramic marshaling of all the events in the Northwest's one hundred years.

"I saw the last Indian tribe leave Ohio in 1840," he said; "a sad remnant of the once powerful Wyandotte nation."

This week of noble words had its picturesque reliefs. On Tuesday night two hundred Mariettans, all descendants of the first settlers, presented a most remarkable pageant. Every race linked with our national history, from the Mound Builders to the people of the present, was represented: Columbus and Isabella; George and Martha; Governor Arthur St. Clair, his secretary and two judges appointed by Washington; Aaron Burr plotting with the rich Irishman, Blennerhassett, at his island "castle" on the Ohio; Lady Blennerhassett, played by a Blennerhassett in a long red riding-habit, with a sweeping feather in her hat, a contemporary costume. What a defile it was! Scenes and costumes were archæologically accurate; types had been sought for every character. One of the quaintest scenes was that of the first Sunday school. It was interrupted by an Indian raid. Rang again the very same bell that in the early days rang to warn the settlers of the Indians' approach. One of the governors, name forgotten, had brought his little son with him.

"Now you see what terrible dangers children went through when they attended Sunday school in those early days," said the Governor, impressively; "and yet, you see, they went." The child had his own view of it. He wouldn't mind going to Sunday school, he said, if he could have a crack at an Indian.

General Grosvenor the following day, referring publicly to the pageant, spoke of the next anniversary pageant, the two-hundredth. "On that day," he said, "the historian will announce that it is Governor and Mrs. Foraker who head the procession." It gave me a queer sensation, being flung ahead a hundred years like that. I wondered who would represent me? . . . And would she like to wear my dress? It was of "ashes of roses"; a delicate flowered silk elaborately draped over a deeper-toned foundation and preening itself with hoops in the bustle and a labyrinth of cording and piping. A modest V-neck, elbow sleeves, a nineteen-inch waist boned with shad-like lavishness. Costume for a hot night in that year of grace! Doubtless it will as little resemble woman's dress in 1988 as in 1888 it resembled that of Pocohontas.

Dinner parties. Every night we entertained in honor of this notable or that: a dinner for Senator Daniels of Virginia, for Governor Wilson of West Virginia, for Senator Evarts of New York, for Senator Sherman of Ohio. For the moment there were but two kinds of peo-

ple in the world—those fortune-favored souls who were
born in the "Northwest"—and the other kind. There
were so many officials from various state capitals in
Marietta that week, one wondered how state business was
being carried on. Our house was the meeting-center; the
most glittering guests stayed with us and every visitor of
note came. One night the government official who had
charge of the valuable historical relics sent by the Smith-
sonian Institution to this centennial brought over for our
interest some rare manuscripts. One referred to the St.
Clair inaugural, July 15, 1788. By the use of forest
branches a "bower" was erected on the site of Marietta,
the seat of government. There all the inhabitants gathered while the Governor took the oath of office. What a
noble scene! Marietta named for the French queen,
Marie Antoinette, possesses a quite rich little historical
museum of its own.

Presentations. A gavel presented to Governor Foraker,
made of various woods from the old fortifications of
Campus Martius, St. Clair's house and Blennerhassett's
castle. Sealed with other mementoes of this occasion and
deposited in a fire-proof vault in the Marietta County
Treasury "awaiting the Judgment Day"—or the next
bi-centennial. A gold "St. Clair and Foraker" badge
presented to me. This was a complete surprise. Judge
Cassidy of Wisconsin was speaking; suddenly I realized
that he was addressing me. I looked wildly about me.
Where was my husband? He must reply for me. But he

wasn't anywhere in sight. So I had to make my own speech. It was, I think, my first. I had mild stage fright. This "Northwest" badge was the start of my collection of badges, which grew in extent, variety, and interest as political years rolled on.

Fireworks. From a fleet of barges in the middle of the Ohio River rockets, Roman candles and historic "pieces" illumined the West Virginia hills and the mossy rises beyond the Muskingum with strange beauty and turned the turgid, yellow Ohio into a golden stream. Thousands of people were massed, ghostily, on the banks. There was a moon.

The departure of one of our guests, Senator Evarts, provoked a situation interesting to recall today. Senator Evarts had brought with him his secretary, a colored man. The Senator made a point of his being treated with respect. Why not? He was intelligent, educated. We were a crowd that day for luncheon; Senator Evarts was leaving immediately afterwards. Where to place his *protégé* was a question. So many souls sensitive to black! The matter ended by the Governor's staff officers inviting him to their table. I happened to look across at them during the meal; the colored secretary was talking and the officers were listening with intense interest. "Much ado about nothing."

We wound up festivities with a reception on the last night. All Marietta, and most of the Northwest Territory, it would seem, came to our party; Major Kellog of the army furnished the government band. It played under the trees on the broad lawn; played, with tact, old waltzes, old Scottish airs and Irish—"The Flowers of the Forest" and "I would I Were the Tender Apple Blossom." It was very soothing. People had begun to tire just a little of patriotic music.

Yes, people were tired. After all, seven summer days are long enough for the celebration of anything. The staff officers were worn out delivering messages to important people who arrived all through the week and must be invited to dine or lunch with us, and with managing formalities for the Governor. They wore their gorgeous uniforms all the time and the weather was more for white linen than for gold lace. Colonel Baldwin of the staff expressed the general Saturday mood:

"I'm tired of this war," he said. "We've got the Marietta people whipped. We might as well go home."

We went. Our departure died away in music and waves of farewell. Good-by, pioneers and your Indian mounds! Good-by, Ohio's Plymouth Rock! A great silence settled upon the party in our car as the train pulled out, the silence of a henroost after sunset. It had been a radiant and glorious week—and now let us not talk any more.

But I, I was not done with commemorating Ohio's first Governor. In 1892 I had a little celebration of my own—my youngest son was born. I called him "Arthur St. Clair."

THE 'NINETIES
AND ON

CHAPTER XII

GANGWAY FOR THE QUEEN

THE opening 'nineties saw the old *régime*, Anglo-Saxon, conservative, making its last stand at the White House. The Harrisons gathered around them a fine best-families group: women who could give all their time to social perfections undistracted by suffrage, divorce, interior decoration or other extraneities. We went in heavily—and breathlessly!—for "Delsarte," but there ended our responsibility towards the Greeks and things. We still exchanged recipes, had not yet begun to discuss diet, except as a delight, changed our dress exhaustingly-often during the day, and were, altogether, as conventional as a sideboard. It was a nice period.

Among the distinguished women of that administration Mrs. Morton's suavely sophisticated personality must have my special tribute. The wife of the Vice-President was extremely handsome, wore her lovely French clothes with a great air, had something of the dictator's temperament, and had lived abroad long enough to have acquired a completely continental point of view about social usages. She Europeanized many Washington customs. For one thing, it was she who killed the fashion for artificial light and evening dress at daytime entertainment.

Atrocious! Upon her edict that no one should appear in evening dress before six o'clock, smart society hastily took to hats and boned collars, powdered for daylight, and began to comment upon how sweet it was to look out and see the blue sky—and weren't the magnolias lovely this year?

The Mortons had three charming girls. They were dressed always with the most smiting simplicity, the eldest (sixteen) in white with gloves (at public affairs), the next two younger in plain dark frocks and no gloves. The eldest married William Corcoran Eustis and lived in the famous old Corcoran house which young Eustis had inherited from his uncle. I attended many delightful entertainments in that house. Most delightful of all were the garden parties given in the lovely old walled garden with its fine box. The Calvin Brices and the Depews also had this notable house at different periods, and were my hosts at entertainments which have their place in the Washington portion of this narrative.

Mrs. Harrison was a lovely woman, well bred, above all too kind of heart ever to neglect the amenities. Her tact and good manners saved many an occasion when her husband's dourness was freezing people stiff with discomfort and offense. (There was a famous feud between Mrs. Harrison and a powerful rival with an imperious hand; it was provoked and kept alive by administration jealousy, it penetrated officialdom and dictated to those

in high places. But only the Book That Will Never Be
Written can go into that.)

The Harrisons had made a quaint beginning of their
life together. She was Caroline Scott, a professor's daughter of Oxford, Ohio. Her marriage to Benjamin Harrison
took place in that country-college town, practically—and
romantically—at dawn. This was in order that the bridal
pair could "catch the five-o'clock bus." It was the only
way there was of getting out of Oxford that day. As they
drove off in that pearly light neither the bridegroom nor
his bride nor their friends who waved good-bys and
threw rice could have had (in spite of John Calvin) any
thought that that lumbering old omnibus was carrying a
future President of the United States.

Mrs. Harrison had two completely absorbing interests.
One was china-painting, the other was her grandchil-
dren. The Harrison-administration china, made in
France from the First Lady's own design, stands out
agreeably among the sorrows of the White House china-
cupboard. And the idolized "Baby McKee" was permitted to take away a great many scenes from the President himself.

Towards the very end the Harrison administration
flared with a brief, exotic sparkle. This was when Hawaii
made us aware of her. To annex or not to annex became
the question. In the cold, snow-stormy winter of 1893 it
was pleasant to think about owning those dream-like
islands, and the President was known to be preparing a

favorable treaty to send to the Senate. We heard a great deal, too, about the islands' picturesque queen who, decidedly, had a mind of her own:

> "Come, Liliuokalani,
> Give Uncle Sam
> Your little yellow hannie ——"

people hummed on their way to dinner parties for the Hawaiian Commissioners. In Washington then I heard Hawaiian music for the first time. It was like idling under the Southern Cross. We were never to be quite the same after that.

Mrs. Harrison's death in 1892 made the second time that the wife of a President had died in the White House or during her husband's Presidency. The first was President Tyler's first wife, born Letitia Christian.

CHAPTER XIII

WASHINGTON

THE god of change was very busy that rare spring of
1897 when President Cleveland moved out of the
White House and President McKinley moved in. Had
Mr. Cleveland looked back, it is unlikely, he would have
seen a Republican Congress with a gleam in its eye that
was thought to bode prosperity, and a far-flung nation
eager that no grass should grow under congressional feet
in bringing prosperity about. Indeed, we had come
through some hard times. "Nothing worse since Buchanan." Not to be compared with the Black Friday
crisis of 1869 nor the panic of 1873, of course; but always,
when we Republicans had been out of power, and hence
worried about the country's welfare, we used to drag in
poor old Buchanan.

The new administration was quite splendid; the gold
plank swung like a bright charm on Uncle Sam's pon-
derous watch chain; there was a fairly successful effort to
veil with sanguine rose our concern about the Spanish
war-cloud, no larger than a man's hand, that hung over
the unlucky State Department. Rest assured, my friends,
all would be for the best under the best possible of parties.

Foraker succeeded Calvin S. Brice as United States

Senator from Ohio. His term began with the inauguration of his old friend, William McKinley, whom he had
nominated first for Governor of Ohio in 1891, then for
President in 1896, and was to renominate for a second
term in 1900. There was plenty of stress in store for us;
the glass registered storm much of the time; yet they
were years of glamour. What woman would not have
thought herself lucky to have gone through them on the
crest—though murderous Fate *was* waiting 'round the
bend!

We settled down in a big yellow house in Sixteenth
Street; built it ourselves because of special needs. There
were no good Senate office buildings in Washington then.
Foraker, like Senator Elkins, met the lack by having his
official quarters under his own roof. Then we had our
lively young people, a trio of girls coming-out; there
would be cakes-and-ale and "sound of dancing on the
floor."

Contact with what I thought at the first, and still
think, the most charming feature of Washington life,
grew out of an anxious circumstance. Foraker's health
needed watching; for this reason I had the habit of going
with him when he made the rounds of official appointments. Ohio was peculiarly intrenched in the McKinley
administration; my husband's duties would take him
from the White House to the State Department, or to
the War or Navy; from a conference with the President
to a meeting of the Foreign Relations Committee or that

of our insular possessions, or another. You may imagine
that a wife would learn a good deal about what was going
on nationally and internationally in those short, interrupted drives. And the intervals, when I waited in the
carriage, were full of delightful social interchange. What
is so rare as a Washington morning in the season? The
sunshine, the soft, sweet air, the brilliant come-and-go.
Smart equipage! Horses! And the whole distinguished,
cosmopolitan world abroad! Everybody knew everybody
else. There was a great smiling and waving of greetings,
a great many informal levees held at brougham doors. I
know little about the life of European queens (there
were more then), but I doubt if any of them ever held
gayer matinée courts than we Washington women of
the 'nineties.

Of the ninety Senators in Congress then, only about
seven or eight had large houses and entertained on an
important scale. (A number of Senators were there without their wives.) The hospitable crowd included the
Depews (they had the old Daniel Webster House with
its fine public rooms), the Elkins, Wetmores, Hales,
Roots, Fairbanks, Burroughs, Keans, and Knoxes. Both
Mrs. Eugene Hale and Mrs. Elkins enjoyed the distinction of being daughter, wife, and mother of a Senator.
You may imagine that they knew their way about! Generally, however, in the government set and outside of it,
the period was notable for many brilliant hostesses. A
rush of reminiscences comes at the thought of them; only

a few can detain me here as the kaleidoscope turns: flashes of personality, fragments of wit, gleams of candle-light on flowers and faces long faded.

White House dinner parties. Everybody was under a certain strain when the McKinleys were hosts; Mrs. McKinley, so physically unequal to the thing she bravely was attempting to do, and the President, masking his tender concern about his wife under a deferential solicitude for his guests that went to our hearts. With his successor a different key was pitched. At the Roosevelts' there was a great bubble and hum in the air, with Mrs. Roosevelt, loveliest and wisest of hostesses, keeping table talk off the rocks in spite of our monologistic, aggressive, brilliant host; helping each of her guests quietly to shine or, rather, making him *feel* that he shone, which, after all, is the art of it. Two small Roosevelt dinners I particularly remember. At one my escort was Mr. Whitelaw Reid, our ambassador to England. I sat on the President's left. "I regard your husband as a very remarkable man, Mrs. Foraker," he said; "I am counting on him to become my administration Senator." It was not thus to be.

The second dinner was given for Mrs. Leonard Wood, wife of General Wood, Roosevelt's great friend. It was just after General Wood's promotion from brigadier-general—won by gallant leadership at the battle of Las Guásimas—to major-general. The Roosevelt-Wood alliance precipitated one of the most trying and hard-fought cases that came up while my husband was in the Senate.

EDITH CAREW ROOSEVELT
Wife of President Roosevelt, 1901

An appointee of President McKinley and a friend of Senator Hanna was serving under General Wood, then military administrator in our government's effort to bring order out of Cuban chaos. Hanna's man, Major Rathbone, was determined to discredit Roosevelt's man. Senator Foraker, chairman of the Military Committee, conducted the investigation. This was one time when my husband's work in the Senate met with approval of the President of the United States. The warm friendship between Leonard Wood and Theodore Roosevelt dated from the Spanish American War, and never faltered. Foraker devoted his time and ability to the Wood case for months. Had his services in that affair been estimated on the basis of an attorney's fee, our financial status would have taken a lively leap.

President Roosevelt stressed ceremony at social functions as none of his predecessors had thought necessary to do. I remember the first time we received an intimation of Mr. Roosevelt's ruling that ladies were to remain standing in the Presence. After dinner we had been conducted, as usual, to the East Room. What had happened to the old East Room? There were no chairs, only a bench or two against the wall. Mrs. Hanna, limping from an accident, and frail Mrs. Jesup sank down on a bench. Mrs. Roosevelt and all the rest of us remained standing, waiting for the President and the other gentlemen to join us. Then shortly we were to leave. Ladies stood whenever the President was on his feet.

An invitation to the Roosevelts was a royal command. We all tried to plan our parties with a vigilant eye on the White House calendar; even so an eleventh-hour invitation from the President might come. Senator Kean was giving a large dinner one night. Kean was a bachelor; his mother and three sisters lived with him. Late in the afternoon the Senator came to Foraker and begged him to take his place as host. Mr. Roosevelt had just invited him to dine at the White House that evening. One of those conferential men's dinners which the President liked to give; impromptu, often. Something would come up that he wanted to talk over; no man asked would dream of refusing. Two ambassadors were to be among Senator Kean's guests, Signor des Planches of the Italian embassy, and the Russian ambassador, Count Cassini. No matter—it was the "President calling."

Foraker took over the dinner. It happened to come on the same night as a thousand-and-one other functions. As we got into the carriage, my husband said to the coachman: "Drive to Senator Kean's. Come back at ten and take us to the White House. Come back at twelve and take us to the British Embassy." Then wearily, half to himself, "Come back at two—and take us to the Insane Asylum." I wanted to know which one. There is always a choice.

Perhaps if those affairs had been dull a man couldn't have stood the season's pace. It is inanity that kills. But how could a dinner party "bog down," as Hanna used to say, when there were international beauties to make the picture, the gold embroidery and foreign ribbons of the diplomats and the gold of our army and navy to splash in the color, and national and international wit to furnish the sparkle? Moreover, Washington's magical short distances made it easy to keep up with its gay gregariousness.

My dinner partners in a season ran a varied gamut. Of the Diplomatic ones Sir Julian Pauncefote, British ambassador, was so intensely, pompously, pre-war Victorian that not until the fish course was I able to overcome my crushing sense of racial inferiority—and decide that he was really nice. Even Lady Pauncefote, though a timid little mouse of a woman, could, in evening dress, convey that same impression of superiority along with the implication that it belonged exclusively to the English. In street clothes Lady Pauncefote was less successful in "putting over" the superiority attribute. She always wore a large Paisley shawl over her day costume, "gift of the old Queen." Sir Julian was a stern stickler for precedent. The only person who ever really got ahead of him on this score was Mrs. Hobart. Mrs. Hobart believed that as the wife of the Vice-President the Pauncefotes should call on her first. No matter what had been the custom, such was to be the custom now. The Pauncefotes insisted that the British Empire called first only on the Divine Being. Neither would give in. Finally, Sir Julian, quite put to it, consulted King Edward. "Better call," said that wise monarch. The Pauncefotes called. At a reception at the British Embassy one night guests were greeted by a very beautiful effect of candle-light, every-where; even the staircase was wreathed with candles. "Ah! one of your charming English customs!" twittered an anglomaniacal lady. "No," said Lady Pauncefote, dryly, "bad wiring."

Sir Michael Herbert, Sir Julian's successor, had an American wife; she was Miss Leila Wilson, sister of Mrs. Cornelius Vanderbilt. A witty, worldly Englishman, Sir Michael; gave us champagne for a change after thirteen years of port. Sir Mortimer Durand, following, was another delightful person with a wide experience in the foreign service. He was a great amateur of rugs. I remember talking rugs with him in our library one night after dinner, and his telling me of the valuable collection of Oriental rugs he had made during his years of residence in the East. In moving from some diplomatic post to another all those rare rugs were lost. Lord Bryce, who came along duly, was simple and nice, admired American women's interest in genealogy; thought it strange: "Only the nobility really care about family records in England," he said. Admired the "D. A. R.," and was enormously entertained by native American stories "told by the Man from There." One story, current in the cloakroom, though this was considerably later, was, Lord Bryce told me, the best in his collection. This was of the

Senator from one of the northernly-southern states who
was candidate for a second term. From the returns coming in it looked as if he were not going to get it. At the
last hour he received a telegram signed by a local district
leader: "Psalms 121:1" was all it said. The Senator called
for a Bible and found the reference to read thus: "I will
lift up mine eyes unto the hills, from whence cometh
my help." A perfectly clear political tip. The Senator's
henchmen hurried to the mountain districts of the state,
insisted upon a recount, got it—and sent the Senator
back to Congress in triumph!

"But it's almost a pity that he won," said Lord Bryce,
"for if he hadn't there's such a marvelous verse from
Jeremiah that he could have telegraphed back to his
friends who quoted from the Psalms: 'Truly in vain is
salvation hoped for from the hills and from the multitude
of mountains.'"

Something tells me that this revised English version
of the tale is the one that has been handed on to diplomatic posterity.

In the foreign embassies our great friends were the
Jusserands. We liked to get the French ambassador to
address the Washington meeting of the Daughters of
the American Revolution. The D. A. R. always seems to
astonish and charm foreigners. M. Cambon, who preceded the Jusserands, was a friend of Mr. Roosevelt's in
pre-presidential days. What a book he could have contributed to Rooseveltiana! He admired the President

enormously, but he had several amusing stories of occasions when his French formality was rather startled by him.

While I am with the legation crowd let me recall a vivid figure: Sir Chentung Liang-Cheng, Chinese minister between the two "Wus." He had been educated at American schools—liked to tell about the game his three-base hit won for Phillips Academy, Andover— and knew English beautifully. He prided himself on being the complete Occidental. But how Chinese he remained at heart! He gave many dinners and always had white servants; thought Americans didn't like Chinese servants. I remember one night when we ladies were in the legation drawing-room, the men had gone off to smoke somewhere, one of the group found she'd left her fan in the dining-room and went back for it. She returned looking rather startled. "Do you know there are about thirty Chinks in that room," she said. "Every white has vanished." As soon as the guests were out of the way the real staff of the establishment swarmed in for the clean-up!

Terrapin, a lavish amount, was a feature of the minister's dinners. "I know it's expensive," he said, "and that I am very extravagant. But I adore it, so I always order a large quantity for a dinner, thus there will be always some left for me next day. Luckily," he smiled, "one must give dinners."

Sir Chentung was a widower, young, with sons and

one daughter. We used to see the boys playing baseball in front of the legation in Nineteenth Street. A mere surface touch. It was after one of his dinners that we realized how very Chinese our English-bred host was. His daughter, sixteen, perhaps, lovely as a bit of Chi'en Lung porcelain, would be brought into the drawing-room to speak to each lady. With a nurse on either side of her, the child fluttered timidly forward on tiny, bound feet. She spoke not one word of English.

Sir Chentung's wife had died years before. He missed her. Some one asked him why he did not marry again. "I long to marry," he said, "but my mother-in-law won't hear of it." He was as Chinese as *that*.

At the Depews', as at the Roosevelts', one was certain to meet the prettiest women. I think quite the most notable were those of the diplomatic set who were American by birth. The Baroness Speck von Sternburg, wife of the German Ambassador, was lovely Lily Langham of Louisville; the beautiful Baroness Moncheur, wife of the Belgian minister, was a daughter of Senator Clayton of Arkansas. Baroness von Sternburg was ethereally blonde, with a skin like milk and a voice of music. She was slightly lame. "Ah, but of course," a wit said, "she is much too beautiful to go about like ordinary women." Mrs. Crackenthorpe, wife of an *attaché* of the British Embassy, and daughter of fiery General Sickles, had great looks, too. Her mother was a famous

Spanish beauty. It was because the son of Francis Scott Key, author of "The Star-spangled Banner," permitted himself a too-frank admiration for Mrs. Sickles' lovely looks that old Dan Sickles shot and killed young Key in front of the Sickles house in Lafayette Square, now the Cosmos Club.

The new Mrs. Depew was ravishing; like a marquise, and with the manners of one. Today, I am told, we should call her a "platinum blonde." I should never have thought of it myself. In the flowery younger ranks certainly Alice Roosevelt was beautiful; so was Marguerite Cassini, niece of the Russian ambassador, in whose drawing-room on Sunday afternoons the more dashing diplomats gathered like bees around honey; and Mathilde Townsend, and Louise Foraker, and —— but there! How I run on! One couldn't move for pretty girls in those gorgeous old Washington days. "Alas, that youth should vanish with the rose!"

Depew, historic diner-out, never ate anything; this left him free as chief entertainer. One night at the Charles Emory Smiths' (he was Postmaster-General in McKinley's Cabinet) the Senator told a story concerned with a night when he dined with King Edward VII. One of the anecdotal gems with which Depew diverted His Majesty that night was the story of the New England spinster taking her first ride on a railroad train. There was a collision; the dear, old thing found herself sitting in splinters. She straightened her "bunnit," looked 'round for her reticule, then asked innocently if the train always stopped like that? "How the King laughed!" said Depew.

The Senator happened to mention the fact that the American humorist, Mark Twain, was stopping at his hotel. Thereupon the King, evidently enjoying himself, asked Depew to come back for dinner the next night, and invited, also, Mark Twain. They came. "And what do you think that man Clemens started off with?" said Depew. "*My* story! My identical story of the old lady in the railroad wreck! Said *he* was there, too! And of course I had said *I* was there! How the King laughed!"

Depew himself laughed to tears as he told this; his host emerged from a conversation at the other end of the table . . . wanted to know what the fun was about. And Depew told the story all over again. While the Senator talked, Mrs. Depew, across the table, was watching him with adoring eyes. A great romance there. Mrs. Depew (second) had spent most of her life in Paris. Her mother was a very fascinating widow, near Senator Depew's age, and when the American Senator's visits became very frequent the daughter, thinking that it was her mother he was courting, kept quietly in the background, true French fashion. But it was to her that he proposed, and as she had been in love with him all along, it was very nice that it was so.

The first dinner we gave in our Sixteenth Street house was for President and Mrs. McKinley. Our guests, be-

sides the McKinleys, were the Vice-President and Mrs.
Hobart and the members of the Cabinet and their wives.
A great many entertainments were to follow. We had a
household staff that enabled us to give impromptu parties, the pleasantest of all, I think. Often I returned about
half past six from making calls, to be told at my door
that there was a dinner party on for from ten to fourteen
guests. One of these dinners, arranged by my husband
after I left the house at three o'clock, was given for
the Philippine Commission in January of 1899. Senator
and Mrs. Hoar were invited to meet them. Senator Hoar
was opposed to our taking over the Philippines, and
Foraker wanted him to have an opportunity to talk over
every phase of the situation with the Commission. It
was an instructive night.

Foraker and Senator Hoar rarely saw eye-to-eye. On
one occasion their differences had a comical climax. The
Senator and Foraker had had a spirited battle in the
Senate over the former's attempt to block some Roosevelt
legislation; had he succeeded, it would have given the
Democrats a chance to get in a measure long maneuvered. Foraker's speech rather annihilated Senator Hoar.
When the two men met afterwards in the cloakroom,
Mr. Hoar's manner was lofty and wounded, not to say
stuffy and sour. Both men at the time happened to be
staying at the Arlington Hotel. That night Foraker was
awakened out of a sound sleep by some one coming into
his room and turning on the light. Senator Hoar! Very

confused by the intrusion. "Why-why-why! Wasn't this *his* room?" Foraker had forgotten to lock the door and the Senator had wandered in, mistaking the room for his own. He had practically broken off diplomatic relations with Foraker a few hours before, but now, since also he had broken in upon his privacy, well, there was only one thing to do and that was to laugh. The two men remained fast friends after that.

Among the important affairs given at our Sixteenth Street house was Foraker's reception in honor of the Secretary of War, William Howard Taft. Mr. Taft had just returned from the Philippines, where, as Governor, he had added to his laurels. Invitations read, "To meet the Secretary of War." Those sent to the ambassadors were engraved without the "To meet" line. This was to circumvent the tradition that an ambassador cannot be asked to meet anyone except the President and the Vice-President of the United States. Several hundred guests came to that reception; they included the entire government who's-whodom of Washington at that period. My husband was happy in being able to give this expression of regard for his distinguished fellow-Ohioan and old friend.

Among the unusual number of notable weddings of the McKinley-Roosevelt administrations were those of the daughters of Lord Pauncefote, Chief-Justice Fuller, Major-General Miles, Secretary of State John Hay, Secretary of the Interior Hitchcock, Secretary of War Alger, of the niece of the Russian ambassador, Count Cassini (a Greek ceremony, memorably beautiful), of Miss Alice Roosevelt, daughter of the President, and of my own daughter Julia. The marriage of Senator Warren's daughter to Captain John J. Pershing belongs also to this period. (What a stir there was in army circles when President Roosevelt promoted young Pershing from captain to brigadier-general over eight hundred and sixty-two senior officers!) Nobody at the Pershing-Warren wedding held the crystal that could have revealed the tragedy lying in wait years ahead for those favored young people: The death of General Pershing's wife and three of his children in the burning of the *Presidio* in 1915.

Julia Foraker's wedding to Francis King Wainwright, of Philadelphia, took place at noon in the ballroom of our house in the presence of President and Mrs. Roosevelt, the Justices, Diplomatic *Corps*, the Cabinet, and a few other officials and certain private friends. A very large number came to the reception which followed, the Senate not convening until two o'clock that day in order to give the Senators an opportunity to attend the Foraker wedding.

The wedding of Miss Roosevelt, the second White House wedding since that of President Grant's daughter Nelly, is internationally remembered. Notably, it afforded the President an opportunity to display his dominating, undeniably picturesque personality at its best. "At a funeral," said Princess Alice, "father always wants to be the corpse, and at a wedding he always wants to be the bride." Wedding presents from foreign shores, pouring in by shiploads, led Mr. Roosevelt to announce that presents from other countries could not, correctly, be accepted. "It was so like him," said Senator Lodge, "to come to that decision after the gifts were on their way." And Mrs. Cowles, the President's sister, expressed her delight that "at least Theodore didn't issue his awful ban before the string of pearls from Cuba had arrived."

The Judiciary furnishes first-class social lights. True, one can't mix 'em with Diplomats without tripping up on precedence, but by themselves they are stars. Chief-Justice Fuller's large old-fashioned house in unfashionable G Street was a distinguished center. The way Mrs. Fuller managed on a Chief Justice's salary was one of the Seven Wonders. I can think of but one woman who rivaled her as a household executive; that was my friend Mrs. Lawrence Maxwell, of Ohio, wife of the Solicitor General under Cleveland. The salary was seven thousand. On twelve thousand Mrs. Maxwell maintained one of the most beautiful and hospitable houses in Washington and a reputation for being almost the best-dressed woman at the capital. Mrs. Fuller was one of the few women who went to market herself; went early, got the choicest cuts, the freshest vegetables, the dewiest flowers. I attended many lavish entertainments, but I remember none more beautifully done than one of Mrs. Fuller's luncheons; nine tables, at the head of each a Justice's wife, with a Senator's wife at her right; masses of forget-me-nots and moss roses; and Mrs. Fuller's famously delicious terrapin made without sherry! The Fullers had seven daughters. "Not until my girls grew up," the Chief Justice used to say, "did I know that there was anything to a chicken but wings. You see, I served the chicken— to the chickens." This with an unjudicial wink.

Another delightful member of the Supreme Court was, happily still is, Mr. Justice Oliver Wendell Holmes. I remember sitting next him at a White House dinner. Something started him off on his early days as a lawyer; how meager the fees were, how hard up he always was. He adored the theater, and often, after a hard day's grind, he felt that he just had to see a play—or die of dullness. He would wander about the town, looking at all the different theatrical bills. No, the price was too high. He'd end up by buying a pint of ice-cream, hurrying home with it, and he and his wife would eat it together, jeer at riches and— "Well, it was as good as a comedy," he said, "the fun we two had." Mrs. Holmes was a woman who brought people to her feet by sheer force of wit and sparkle. Everybody wanted the Justice Holmes' for their parties. They forgot to come one night. Mrs. Stanley Matthews, widow of the Justice, was hostess. The dinner was given for the British ambassador. A telephone inquiry brought the Holmes' about salad time and with the usual electrifying effect. I had a Confederate general on my left that night, a Union general on my right; they talked across me about justification for the *lex talionis* in civil war. Directly opposite, on Mrs. Matthews' right, Lord Bryce talked across the table to me about the justification for American women's existence as expressed by the D. A. R.—"American women are both pretty and patriotic. That is enough." Every successful dinner is like that one—a true brook for babble and everybody at once.

Table talk wasn't all politics, by any means. I remember a dinner party at John Hay's which started off with a discussion of some momentary excitement about somebody's lost jewels. Everybody was led to contribute a jewel story: the story of Mrs. Elkins' ruby ring that turned out a wrong one; stories of the sinister powers of the emeralds of the Russian ambassador's wife; Mrs. Hay's story of the pearl dog collar that broke a woman's heart.

The novelist, Henry James, was present. He and Foraker came together sympathetically over recollections of Christine Nillson on the Swedish Nightingale's first American tour. Her voice *and* her face, said Mr. James, were "transcendences infinitely to be remembered." It was the time when the author of *Daisy Miller* was addressing American university audiences on *The Question of our Speech*. Mr. James had a charming light side. Two young girls, guests of ours, walked home with him from tea somewhere. They were crossing the White

House grounds at dusk, when they were stopped by a policeman—no, they couldn't go through there. It was a short cut; it was getting late; the girls demurred a little. But the policeman was firm. "How can you resist the pleadings of two pretty girls?" said the novelist, gravely. "I can resist any number of pretty girls, sorr," was the reply. "Ah!" sighed Henry James, "would that I were you!"

Occasionally one drew a dinner companion who shone perversely by silence. The two most silent men I ever met at dinner were Mr. H. C. Frick, Carnegie partner and patron of art, and Mr. Marshall Field. Mr. Frick spoke once, recalling (I think it was he), the twenty-nine-course dinners (we were at the White House) of Grant's day—wine served with every third course; and Grant's dislike of French dishes, preferring, himself, "pork and ice-cream with canned peaches to any parly-voo on earth." Of Mr. Field my recollection is that, for his part, "when the silence fell it was not broken." Still, to be able to listen is eloquent, and necessary too.

Language was amusingly cut out by Vice-President Hobart one night at a dinner at the Chinese Legation. Hobart sat next to Madam Wu Ting-Fang. She understood no English, so the Vice-President devoted himself to her in pantomime. No one enjoyed this more than penetrative Minister Wu. He managed to find out everything about everybody; would have found out whether or not he and the other person knew one syllable of a mutual language.

Mrs. John B. Henderson, wife of the Senator from Missouri, led socially as "a character." The Senator was very much of a person himself; one of the seven Republicans who voted against the conviction of Andrew Johnson and secured the President's acquittal, May 16, 1868. And what wily skill he showed as the permanent national chairman of the exciting Republican convention in 1884! Henderson was a breezy believer in Southern hospitality in all its glory, but his wife stood out for vegetarian living, high thinking, and no smoking. Nary canvas-back nor succulent tenderloin for the always twenty-eight guests at her dinners. We ate lentils and yams ingeniously dressed as staying entrées, and from huge turnips that had been cooked for eighteen hours and could be carved like turkeys (which we wished they were!), and feasted our eyes on her beautiful tablecloth of heavily-embroidered white Chinese silk, and protected our furbelowed frocks, against the wicked rich dishes that were not served, by vast napkins of the same silk.

Mrs. Henderson created some consternation as a widow by her prohibition gesture that sent flowing down the gutter the entire contents of her husband's fine wine cellar. It was thought at the time that hospitable old John B. must have been made restless by this sacrifice. People remembered that he was the author of the Thirteenth Amendment which freed 4,500,000 slaves. As an apostle of liberty they had loved him.

In the rich political crowd were certain types which contributed to the gayety of our foreign critics. Calvin Brice stressed display with the greatest frankness, I think. The Brices had the Daniel Webster house before the Depews took it, and gave us a lavish greet-the-coming dinner there. "See those roses?" Mr. Brice said to me as we took our places. Did I see them! There must have been five hundred American beauties on that table. "Cost a dollar apiece," he said. A kindly, simple, very shrewd man who was proud of having made money and saw no reason why he shouldn't brag a bit. "Got the hang of the old barn yet?" he asked me, leaning over the railing of our box at the Horse Show. He wore smart London clothes; a red carnation; he was chewing a straw. Brice expressed his point of view by an expensive house. You could *see* that. A friend found him alone one night in his elaborate New York establishment. "Fine house you've got here, Mr. Brice," he said, taking in the assembled splendor with his eye. "Fine house, yes," said Brice, gloomily, "but where's all the folks? Where's the family I built it for? Paris! . . . Tangiers! . . . up the Nile!" He located all the Brices but one. "Now where's Kate?" he burst out, suddenly savage. "Where the devil is Kate?" Fine houses make fine itineraries.

Outside the government set were many hostesses of scope and effectiveness. In the Roosevelt years Washing-

SENATOR AND MRS. FORAKER
Washington—years 1897-1908

ton became the fashion with the New York crowd; the Perry Belmonts, the Goulds, the Vanderbilts, and the Stuyvesant Fishes were among those who took houses at the Capital. The Fishes took the old Morgan house for one month during an engineers' convention. Brought *chefs* and every sort of equipment from New York and kept princely open house. Mrs. Fish had a genius for giving entertainments; she was despairingly nonchalant about it, no matter how important the affair was, nor how large. This casualness is a social gift.

Among the distinguished, politically-detached hostesses was a personage who would have enchanted Mr. Disraeli. This was Mrs. Richard Townsend, daughter of Scott of Pennsylvania, coal Crœsus. Mrs. Townsend gave one a curious sense of power, like a woman out of the Italian Renaissance. Apparently she chose not to use it save as it was expressed by the brilliant, cosmopolitan world she drew about her. Her dinners for thirty guests had great pomp; such crowds of presentable-looking butlers and under-servants—dear me, it was a bit disconcerting!—and an all-silver dinner service; porcelain only for the salad. Mrs. Levi Z. Leiter, mother of Lady Curzon, wife of the Viceroy of India, and of Daisy, who married the Earl of Suffolk, displayed imposing silver on her table, too; no one had anything to top her old Adam urns; she gave dinners that were up to them. Mrs. Leiter had fewer malapropensities than legend charges her with. But she hated your missing any of her opulent dodges. I remember at one dinner she called our reverent attention to the fact that we were in the presence of "imperial Southdown mutton—a saddle." As who should say, "His Grace!" One mocker rose and saluted.

Mrs. Thomas Walsh, who came into the field somewhat later, gave rosy, fabulous dinners, too. She had met and married Tom Walsh of the Midas touch when he was a miner in a Western town and she a school-teacher there. She was the cleverest woman with her hands I ever knew; she could make anything. Dining at her house, Mr. Justice McReynolds said he bet *he* could send her something she wouldn't be able to make anything of. The bet was taken. Mrs. Walsh won. The Justice sent her a battered old top hat. Mrs. Walsh converted it into the most chic and practical of motor bonnets; subsequently at a war bazaar it sold for twenty-five dollars.

A clear-cut figure, hardly in any definite set, could one say, was Miss Davis, niece of Jefferson Davis, President of the Confederate States. Frosty and bright, on the tall side, and every inch the Southern lady. She and Mrs. Joseph Pulitzer were sisters. She lived in an old house on Connecticut Avenue, then a residence street, among her beautiful old mahogany, her old silver rubbed by generations of colored butlers, her memories. A dispenser of Mississippi hospitality at its succulent heyday. Comes back to me the scene of a luncheon she gave for Mrs. Pulitzer. Eighteen or twenty ladies; a lively love feast of the North and South in chiffons; a long, narrow, glittering, groaning table. Chocolate was served. And what chocolate! Something derived from angels was in it to give it that transcendent taste. A detail of the service were five cups of a rare old pattern. I noticed them not without satisfaction, as I had seven exactly like them. And I—I don't know what possessed me—I gave Miss Davis my seven cups to complete her set.

But do you think that the bright and frosty niece of Jeff Davis would tell me how she made that chocolate? She would *not*.

The 'nineties, which had come in like a lamb, went out in one of the finest blizzards that this country has ever produced. It was the night of the Charity Ball. Of the hundreds and hundreds of guests prepared for, only about seventy-five managed to get there. Mrs. John Hay was one of the few hostesses who appeared. I forget how she made it, but I do recall that the two daughters of Alexander Bell waded through the snow in boots and knickers, carrying their ball dresses in their arms. In all Washington not a wheel turned. Drifts of snow six to eight feet high blotted out the universe. Charity began at home that night.

Some day some one will write an erudite exposition of the psychology of precedence. The subject is one to which every woman who goes through official life at our national capital owes at least one wrinkle. Lest I be carried away by my remembrance of the many situations created by this sacred punctilio of place I shall restrict myself to recalling one precedence tangle in my own experience which to this day hasn't been straightened out. I was giving a dinner of twenty-two. In arranging places I found that twenty-two people could not be seated according to precedence except very awkwardly. However, I juggled the cards, a gentleman would have to escort his lady to her place, then walk all around the table to take his. In despair I consulted David Jayne Hill of the State Department. Plainly he was as routed as I, but, manlike, tried to conceal his complete blankness by a cloud of words so braided with "depending upon" and "in consequence thereof" and "thus accordingly" that he left me more at sea than ever.

This was my fix: it was a long table; Mr. Wu, the Chinese minister, was guest of honor; Sir Wilfrid Laurier, in this country on an important mission, represented a great power to be considered; Mrs. Nelly Grant Sartoris, daughter of ex-President Grant, must be regarded. Well: Mr. Wu goes in with me; Madame Wu with my husband; Sir Wilfrid, who takes in Mrs. Sartoris, must seat her on my husband's left, then come clear back to the other end of the table to take his place at my left. I turned the puzzle over to my husband; he worked at it, applying all his ability and insight as a resourceful lawyer. Even *he* wasn't any good at it! We just had to give it up. Precedence had us beaten.

There were a few diners-out in Washington, vague,

charming souls, whom one was always on guard against. The Speck von Sternburgs had a little way of regretting a dinner and then coming to it! As the hostess already had filled their places, the sight of them was not an undiluted joy. The German ambassador and his wife were immensely popular; presumably their engagement-book was difficult to keep. They sent regrets to one of my dinners. I took no chances on their arriving, anyway. My table seated only twenty-four, every place was filled— and we were having quail. You know quail; there are always just enough. A few days before the dinner date I gave a large luncheon, invited the baroness (she accepted), placed her on my right and during our conversation stressed my infinite regret that she and the ambassador could not come to my dinner *on the tenth*. Even so I didn't breathe easily until we were all at table that night—and no von Sternburgs! Mrs. George Westinghouse was another fatal person. Mrs. Westinghouse was always late. I remember her coming to one of our dinners given for certain of the Diplomatic set, and dropping into her place, blonde, untroubled and smiling. We'd had to go in, of course. Time, tide and Diplomats wait for no man—nor woman.

There is, I consider, but one real fly in the Washington amber. One is penetrated at first by the charm of everything. How fluid and colorful the life is! So much movement! Such delightful people from all over the world! And then, presto! as by a swarm of locusts the land is darkened. The office-seekers have come to town! Every four years this phenomenon turns our exquisite national capital into a merry-go-round with a hoarse-voiced, brand-new crowd clamoring for place. The first two weeks after Foraker took his seat in the Senate he received more than twenty-five hundred letters from men who wanted a political office. This number was augmented, of course, by crowds of others at the official gates.

One rather languid day, after Congress had adjourned, my daughters discovered a large box containing photographs of men who had written their father about jobs, and inclosed pictures to help matters along. The girls found that you could make up very good "hands" with these photographs; you played your pictures like cards; the ugliest face was ace and took the trick. They called the game "Office-seeker." One day a Cincinnati youth happened to call. They played the new game. The Ohio lad thought he held some positively winning face cards, when Florence trumped with the prize ace in the pack. "Oh, I'm going to *tell* on you!" cried the boy. "Do you know who that is? That's—" and he named an official of some local importance in our old home town. I think Foraker often wished that he could sweep the office-seekers back into the box along with their photographs!

An office-seeker is a man who can't do anything but hold office. And he never really quite gives up. I used to

receive a great many begging letters, myself. One I remember was from a woman who wrote me that her
husband had voted for my husband at every election; he
had just died. Now would I send her "a widow's mourning outfit, complete and up-to-date, and send so that *I'll
get same by Wednesday*, madam." The italics are hers.
So you see, even after an office-seeker dies his widow car-
ries on.

CHAPTER XIV

"OH, DEWY WAS THE MORNING"

ONE April morning in Washington, 1898, crowds of people, in carriages and afoot, were to be seen making their way towards the Senate. The Cuban crisis, precipitated by the blowing up of the battleship *Maine* on February 15th, made the "War Senate" of that spring a place where anything exciting might happen. On this occasion Senator Foraker was to speak on his belief that it was the duty of our government to recognize the Republic of Cuba. There were many who disagreed as to that duty; President McKinley himself was wary of intervention; the salt of opposition intensified expectation.

A diverse and colorful mass packed the Senate gallery. Hours before the Senate convened every seat was taken and people were being turned away by hundreds. To recall some of the faces in that assemblage brings back a vanished world of picturesque figures: In the Diplomats' Gallery was the Hawaiian Queen, Liliuokalani, somber and yellow and fateful; she looked like a pythoness that day. And Mr. Wu Ting-Fang, abyssmally inquisitive Chinese ambassador, who stood in the gallery aisle the whole time, surveying the scene with the expression of an

ironically amused Buddha. And all around these two
every shade of bronze-and-beige-complexioned diplomat
from Señor Don José Andrade of Venezuela, to Mr.
Matsui of Japan and the eager-eyed Cubans, Señores de
Queseda and Estrada Palma. Somewhat withdrawn from
these countries one observed the Honorable Sir Julian
Pauncefote, so shining clean and gentlemanly, so delightfully Great British, and M. Jules Cambon, ambassador from France, with anemones in his coat, and Dr. von
Holleben, the Kaiser's envoy, using an opera-glass.

Indeed, Herr Doktor, there were some arresting ladies
in the Senate gallery: In the front row, center (appropriately), was an exotic-looking young woman, waist
very small, eyes and pearls very large, enveloped in white
fur. She stood with her back to the railing and looked
down at the Senators over her left shoulder. One of the
Senators was looking up at her, his mouth slightly open
in amazement and admiration. This was dear old innocent Senator Cullom, and the dazzling apparition that
had entranced his usually preoccupied eye was the actress,
Miss Anna Held. The Reverend T. DeWitt Talmage
was in the gallery, too, I remember, and near him another
actress, Miss Cissy Fitzgerald, demure and vespers-like
(Church of England); and, off by himself, William
Jennings Bryan, the most impressive head in that crowd.

Foraker's speech in the Senate was thought to be of
such importance that we sent for my daughter Julia, at
school at Dobbs' Ferry, to come and hear it. For the first

few minutes after Foraker began speaking the Senate Chamber was as still as dawn; nobody even dropped a pin. Then the heckling began. The opposition was led by Senator Elkins, otherwise Foraker's staunch friend. Questions and challenges came fast and furious. Foraker had quoted from some authority; a Senator demanded the reading of the entire quotation from the book. My husband had no one to help him find it; he had to put on his glasses and turn over page after page, while the vast assemblage waited, until he came upon the desired passage. A moment when family and friends wished that they might be swallowed up—like Cervera's fleet. "I thought I should die," said tragic Julia, "before papa found that page." But Foraker, to use John Hay's expression, was one who "did not propose to get lost."

That war is the "great war" which touches closest our hearts. The last Sunday in May we saw our son Benson off on General James F. Wade's staff for Camp Thomas, Georgia, the old Chickamauga battleground. The station was jammed. The old, old story. Here was a father carrying two swords; he was giving two sons; and here a gray-haired mother actually with a pack on her back, getting onto the train with her soldier boy; hundreds and hundreds of tense, silent people parting with all that they loved best.

How Santiago de Cuba stirred us! I remember being awakened at three o'clock in the morning by cries of "Extra! Extra!" and hurrying down two flights of stairs to get a paper. It was brilliant moonlight, a hot, still July night. As I waited for the newsboy an officer in white linen swung jauntily down the deserted street, whistling the "Star-spangled Banner." Well, if the army could whistle, everything must be all right. And then the cannon began booming. The next day was the Fourth, you remember; here was reason enough to plunge right into the racket. The first American killed in that battle was a sailor named Meek, from Clyde, Ohio. A rich Cuban had said that he would give one hundred dollars to the family of the first sailor killed in the war. Months afterwards a monument was erected to Meek; Senator Foraker made the memorial address before ten thousand people.

When our family scattered that war-summer we left our Washington house open. In August, all of General Wade's staff (Captain Benson Foraker was Assistant Adjutant-General) were ordered to the capital. Benson turned our house into a club for these officers, and most of them lived there. Among these was Colonel Lloyd C. Griscom, distinguished in the foreign service, ambassador to Italy in the Roosevelt administration. I was in Kirksville, Missouri, with my son Arthur, a delicate child of six, when word came that Benson had been ordered with General Wade and Admiral Sampson to Havana. The whole country at that moment was sweltering in a hot wave of particular ferocity. That forty-four-hour trip to New York was something of an endurance test. The

Grand Army were swarming to an encampment at Cincinnati; trains were packed to suffocation. I rode backwards the whole way to New York, my section overflowing with women, children, lunch-baskets, and bananas. However, when my family met me late Sunday afternoon, I had managed to change my dress and felt as fresh as a daisy. That was one of those hottest-on-record nights in New York. No sleep for anyone. All night long ambulances clanged up and down Fifth Avenue, picking up prostrated people. The next day Benson sailed.

Late October found us back in Washington; the day after our return I received a piece of news that knocked me out as nothing before or since ever did. Benson had yellow fever. The War Department was wonderful. Colonel Ward kept me informed by constant cables of my son's condition. I sat by the telephone all day; as soon as I heard from the War Department I called my husband, who was keeping his station by long distance in his Cincinnati office. Foraker was on a speaking tour when the news came; he abandoned everything, forgot everything, wanted to leave for Havana at once. But if the worst was to happen, it would happen quickly; still it might mean something to Benson to know that his father was coming to him. Before anything could be decided I had a cable from Colonel Griscom that made me crazy with happiness, "You need have no further uneasiness about Benson." Colonel Griscom was splendid through all that perilous time. A few years before, as one of Richard Harding Davis's "three Gringos in Central America" —the third was Somers Somerset, son of Lady Henry Somerset—he himself had gone through some severe form of jungle fever in Brazil. We knew nothing about yellow fever then except that it was mysterious, horrible, and usually fatal. That was before research, ennobled by the martyrdom of Dr. Lazaer, had identified for the world's betterment the *anopheles* mosquito.

A considerable number of men assigned to special duty in Cuba had contracted the infection. Of the whole number Benson was the only victim who did not die. Not before late November was he able to take ship for home. When he resumed his post as secretary of his father's committee (Benson was a favorite with everyone from President McKinley down—his sweet temper, his bubbling spirits and amusing exploits!) he was thought to have fully recovered. Later, physicians thought that in that earlier battle was laid the foundation of the trouble which so prematurely robbed him of life. War is yellow fever—to us.

In the aftermath of the Spanish-American War were many heartaches. The Sampson-Schley controversy was one of the first war quarrels to reach the Senate. Intervention already had broken the friendship between Thomas B. Reed and Theodore Roosevelt. The Dewey reaction made its ugly sensation.

Of all the public men I ever met, Admiral Dewey was the simplest, the most genuine, the most completely inno-

cent of political canniness and worldly guile. He was bewildered by the nation's emotional state over him. Do
you remember the Dewey frenzy? . . . the "Dewey
Done It" buttons that polka-dotted our universe? (They
must have fixed that ungrammatical atrocity in millions
of minds) . . . the babies christened "Dewey"? the
Dewey fans? the Dewey flags fluttering in the breeze?
and the Dewey pun that everybody was chanting?:

> "Oh, dewy was the morning,
> Upon the first of May,
> And Dewey was the Admiral,
> Down in Manila Bay.
> And dewy were the Regent's eyes,
> Them orbs of royal blue,
> And dew we feel discouraged?
> I dew not think we dew!"

I remember a garden party; the Admiral seemed to
be enjoying himself so much when out of the air appeared a little girl in flounced muslin who curtsied and
presented the hero with a large bouquet. "My father ith
a Vermonter," she said. The Admiral smiled at the child,
then his eyes took on the tell-tale glazed look, for the
little muslin girl, after another curtsy, was beginning—

> "Oh, dewy wath the morning"

Magnificent in war, this sort of thing was too much
for him, and he had to endure a great deal of it.

He was just as much puzzled by the public's fickleness

as by its favor. If people meant it all so lightly as that, it were better to have let him alone. "I was just a sailor doing my duty," he said to me. When he made over to his wife the Washington house presented him by the nation, the hue and cry that followed left him dazed. He understood criticism of his action no more than he understood why he was taken up with immense enthusiasm as a presidential candidate and then coldly dropped. At a time when the Dewey reaction had set in I remember Mrs. Dewey showing me a room in their house at K and Sixteenth Street which was filled from floor to ceiling with magnificent gifts from the Admiral's admirers. One struck me as somewhat ironical. This was a large jar, quite five feet high, made of ten-cent pieces contributed by children all over the United States. "In God we trust." Yes, of course—but look out for the fickle public!

If our treatment of the hero of Manila lacked charm, so did the measures President Roosevelt employed to retire General Miles. The General had a long and honorable record before the Spanish-American War; he added to it thereby his masterly handling of troops and supplies. Until Mr. Roosevelt became President, General Miles was regarded as the hero of heroes among military men. But the General happened to express himself unfavorably about one of Mr. Roosevelt's army appointments; for that the President reprimanded him, before a roomful of people at the White House, as sharply as if General Miles had been a private on inspection. All

Washington was excited over this episode. Mrs. Miles was a Sherman, niece of Senator John and General Tecumseh Sherman. When I went to see her I found a crushed, pathetic figure. In Bishop's *Roosevelt* a version of the famous humiliation is given in which Miles is pictured as the fiery aggressor and Roosevelt the temporizing, soothing lamb. Quite the reverse was the case according to people who were present. Among these was Miss Isabelle McKenna, daughter of Mr. Justice McKenna. In her book of Washington reminiscences, privately printed, she gives an account of the encounter quite different from the one in Mr. Bishop's book. Mr. Roosevelt could not, would not, allow himself to be put in the wrong. But Washington hasn't yet forgotten. Its older contingent still like to recall the General as he was at the military wedding of his only daughter, Cecil, when he walked up the church aisle, the bride on his arm, a brilliant, distinguished figure.

One of the pleasant memories of that period concerns Mrs. Gridley, widow of that Captain Gridley to whom Admiral Dewey, at the battle of Manila Bay, addressed the famous command, "You may fire when ready, Gridley." Mrs. Gridley was a little woman of quiet charm, devoted to the memory of her husband; they had been separated three-quarters of the time during their married life. Once I said to her, "If I can ever help you, Mrs. Gridley, please let me." One day—this was March, 1899—as I reached my house at luncheon-time I saw a slim figure in black standing at the door. Mrs. Gridley. She had come to tell me that her pension bill was to come before the House that afternoon. It looked hopeless. One hundred and ninety pensions ahead of hers! The chairman of Pensions had said that he would fight it; thought she was not entitled to more than thirty dollars a month. Quite hopeless.

This was at one-thirty. Foraker was out of town. I had to act alone. I got my husband's committee-room on the telephone; the secretary on the wire: "Go to the House of Representatives," I said; "find General Grosvenor, General Shattuck, or Judge Bromwell. Tell them that Mrs. Foraker is intensely interested in Mrs. Gridley's pension of fifty dollars passing this afternoon." At exactly three o'clock Judge Bromwell telephoned me: "Mrs. Gridley's pension has just passed the House. Fifty dollars a month."

Dear me, I wish I had asked for a hundred! But I was very pleased that it was Judge Bromwell of Ohio who had put through the pension bill for the widow of You-may-fire-when-ready Gridley of Pennsylvania.

CHAPTER XV

THE MAN WHO'D HAD EVERYTHING

WHAT Roscoe Conkling called the "United
States of Ohio" played a bold hand in the first
McKinley administration. An ambitious woman's harassing activities were in it, too; but that which brought
about the strangest, most poignant chapter of all in the
history of that hour was the sacrifice of John Sherman.

For ever so long the Shermans and General Miles had
formed an invincible alliance. They were the heads of
what was known for thirty years as the "Ohio influence." The General had married a sparkling Sherman
niece; his and Senator Sherman's years of power together
read like a play. It might be given the echoing title of
The Two Noble Kinsmen. It was known that Sherman
and Miles could get anything from the government that
they wished.

Suddenly the combination failed to click. Certain
prominent members of the clan arrived from Ohio and
indicated certain prominent honors it would please them
to receive. But no honors came; none. True, the Ohioans
had been indiscreet enough to talk; a padlock on the
mouth is wise, they say, in seeking preferment at the
court of princes. But the real reason was something quite

irrevocable; it was the shift of control to a new leader "which knew not Joseph."

One must go back to the long years of Hanna's adoring friendship for William McKinley. It was natural that Hanna, god in the machine that put Mr. McKinley into power, should be in a position to ask for anything on earth that he wanted—and to get it.

As it happened, the one and the only thing that Hanna desired was the nobly-silvered head of John Sherman on a charger. Not because he was Sherman—"grand man"; Hanna admitted this with everyone else—but because he sat in the United States Senate. All the years that Hanna was raising millions for the Republican cause, slaving for it, as was thought, with utter disinterestedness, he had secretly cherished the Senatorial dream. My husband had been Senator-elect for more than a year. Unless Sherman got out, Hanna could not go in.

One biting winter day in Cleveland, Mr. Hanna, sitting under a picture of McKinley in his office, astonished and shocked my husband by telling him that Sherman was to be "elevated" to the position of Secretary of State. Yes, President McKinley had agreed to this. He, Hanna, was to succeed Sherman in the Senate. Only one or two little things awaited adjustment in order that this happy consummation be achieved. One was to induce Senator Sherman to resign, and to take the First Minister's chair in the Cabinet-room. The other was to persuade Governor Bushnell of Ohio to appoint Hanna for the vacancy thus created.

The checks encountered in rounding this political Hellespont were many and not without their comedy touch. In the first place, Senator Sherman did not wish to be Secretary of State. He would rather be right than be Senator, but after that he shared the universal feeling that to be Senator was to have the best. He was seventy-four years old; he had served the country for forty-three years; a great many of these years had been spent in the Senate Chamber. He thought he knew where he belonged and that he had the privilege of choosing where he would be. When the President told him how vitally his counsel was needed in the Cabinet, John Sherman smiled a little cynically. The Shermans were soldiers, executives, and financiers, not diplomats. None knew that better than Mr. McKinley.

At first Senator Sherman said he wouldn't resign; then he said he would, but only on one condition—that he be allowed to name his successor. This rather dashed the intriguers. Finally, for party harmony Mr. Sherman did resign and left the field free.

Now enters the Governor of Ohio. It is he who must appoint Mr. Hanna to the vacancy. But alas and alas! Hanna had opposed Governor Bushnell's nomination, in his honest, gloveless fashion, and the Governor wasn't too keen on turning the other cheek. Other men, friends this time and ardent Bushnell supporters, wanted to be

Senator quite as much as Mr. Hanna did. Had Mr. Hanna thought of that? Moreover, the Governor's power to say who is to fill out an uncompleted term is one of his choicest perquisites. Mr. Bushnell hinted that he proposed to exercise it deliberately. And he did.

With a characteristic *volte face* Hanna turned to my husband. The two men, political leaders of northern and southern Ohio, had known each other intimately for years, the barometer of friendship running up and down, according to how the wind blew. Hanna was fond of pronouncing my husband "dead" when "Forakerism" blocked his plans; now "for these courtesies" he beseeched him to throw himself into the breach and use all his suddenly galvanized influence to speed the glacier-like Bushnell.

It was a difficult and disagreeable position for Foraker. He was a life-long friend of John Sherman; he had nominated him for the Presidency in 1884, and in 1888 had sacrificed his own presidential nomination through loyalty to Sherman. Bushnell also was my husband's friend. He had nominated Bushnell for Governor in the dashing Zanesville Convention, 1895, the scene of the last big contest between the warring Republican camps. The victory of the Foraker men over the Hanna men at Zanesville was satirized by somebody, who knew his Bret Harte, in widely quoted verses called "The Smooth Joseph B.": . . .

Yet the cards they were stocked
In a way that I grieve,
And my feelings were shocked
At the state of his sleeve ——
Which was chuck full of Asas, et cetera,
And the same with intent to deceive.

Luck was with the parodist. Asa Bushnell was the Foraker candidate for Governor, and Asa Jones for Lieutenant-Governor.

And now Asa Bushnell took his own time about
bestowing on his opponent the gem of gubernatorial
bric-à-brac. In an interval of several weeks in which my
husband was under a fusillade of urging letters from
Mr. Hanna, and Hanna, so his biographer states, was in
an "agony of suspense," in all this time Bushnell was, one
imagines, remarkably enjoying himself. Finally, under
my husband's persuasion, the Governor yielded. Marcus
A. Hanna was appointed to succeed John A. Sherman in
the United States Senate. That's the way it was.

Poor Sherman! He knew his highly specialized work
in the Senate like the palm of his hand. But he was
beyond "Pier 70"; his memory was faithless at times; his
strength was limited. My husband's disapproval of the
appointment was not based on opposition to Hanna as a
Senator, but on the circumstance that the State Department at this particular time, with Cuban, Nicaraguan,
and Hawaiian complications looming, demanded a chief
at the height of his powers. The thing was unfair to

Sherman and unfair to the State Department. Sherman's wife implored her husband not to accept the Cabinet office; the humiliation he was to meet there undoubtedly hastened her death. As months went by the President more and more conferred with William R. Day, his life-long Canton friend, whom he had appointed Assistant Secretary of State. He saw less and less of John Sherman. Upon the declaration of war with Spain Mr. Sherman tendered the President his resignation, and the President accepted it.

Senator Sherman came often to our house; he and my husband were friends to the end. The old statesman never again mentioned the President's name, nor that of Senator Hanna, nor the administration, nor any of its policies. For him it was as if they did not exist. This complete blotting out of all that had been his long life was rather terrible in the flash it gave of bitterness of soul.

Mr. Sherman died a few weeks before the turn of the century. At his funeral, in Mansfield, Ohio, we met a stonily-sorrowing family. Flowers had come from the White House; the Shermans refused to receive them. Flowers cannot come from the dead.

Statesmen are rarely deposed on the score of age; or it is that in politics there is less age sensitiveness. In 1904 did not Henry Gassaway Davis, with all his eighty-one years, "run" for the Democratic Vice-Presidency? The Senate at the time Sherman was dislodged was particu-

larly distinguished for its wise old men. There were,
notably, Senators Cullom, Hoar, Teller, Morrill, Allison
—a council of patriarchs. So long as Sherman remained
in the Senate, and they needed his ripe judgment there,
he would be protected; if there were hesitancies of memory his colleagues, who loved and admired him, would
be alert to meet them. He was surrounded by the sympathy and deferential thought which is the attitude of
the Senators towards the older members. In the Cabinet-
room, alas! the sun shines cruelly on every wrinkle!

Among Sherman's private papers was found, after his
death, a letter written in November, 1898, to some un-
identifiable "Dear Sir" and never posted. The letter was
given my husband by General Miles, whose wife was a
Sherman, to use as he wished. As Sherman's ruthless and
brutal sacrifice was a blot on the McKinley administration—the administration knew this; it tried desperately
to keep the matter secret—the letter is interesting as making clear an old mystery and showing that Sherman himself had no illusion that he was not bending his head
to the block:

"No doubt I ought to have remained in the Senate
during my term, which would not have expired until the
4th of March next. At that time I regarded McKinley as
a sincere and ardent friend whom I had assisted and
whose election I had promoted. When he urged me to
accept the position of Secretary of State, I accepted with
some reluctance and largely to promote the wishes of

Mark Hanna. The result was that I lost both the position of Senator and Secretary, and I hear that both McKinley and Hanna are *pitying* me for failing memory and physical strength. I do not care for their pity and do not ask them any favors, but wish only to feel independent of them, and conscious that while they deprived me of the high office of Senator by the temporary appointment as Secretary of State, they have not lessened me in the good will of the great Republican Party of the United States."

Thus was hastened the "elevation" of this gallant old public servant to his far home.

If John Sherman with all his qualities had had Tecumseh's charm, he would have been, I think, one of those defiantly-great men with whom liberties are not taken. But it would seem in his case that the volatile fairy charged with presenting this magic at christenings must have said, "No, John, you have enough. Just look at your gifts—all sterling. I shall save charm for your brother Tecumseh."

But Washington has time for everything save tears over a dead lion. Another drama which touched that of John Sherman once now occupied the Administration.

CHAPTER XVI

"THE ABROADER THE BETTER"

THE first hint Senator Sherman had of the Hanna coup came from Mrs. Bellamy Storer.

Mr. McKinley had hardly been elected to the Presidency when Mrs. Storer felt justified in taking a fast train to Canton and making a request of him. In her bright, birdlike eyes was a look of conscious priority which impressed, not to say worried, the crowd. There were always plenty of people about; they overflowed the McKinley porch with its trumpet vines, its hickory rockers showing hard wear. . . .

This lady swept right in. What did *she* want?

The Storer claim takes us back to 1893, when William McKinley, very popular and as happy, probably, as he was ever to be, was about to begin his second term as Governor of Ohio. Disaster chooses ripe moments to strike public men; it struck William McKinley now.

One spring-haunted February day, the Governor, very débonair, a Lawson pink in his coat and in his pocket some notes for a graceful speech, started for New York to address the Ohio Society at their Washington's Birthday banquet. On the train a telegram was handed him. As he read it, a fellow-traveler remembers, the peculiar granite

stare of his eyes became fixed in gray horror. The telegram informed Mr. McKinley that notes negotiated by
a friend, one Walker, gone bankrupt in tin cans, were
signed by William McKinley . . . that these notes were
falling due . . . that they amounted to something over
one hundred thousand dollars. The Governor telegraphed the Ohio Society that he couldn't come, and
turned back.

It is one of Jove's sardonic laughs, the thing William
McKinley had done to get himself into this pit. This
was the way of it: During his years in Congress he had,
at the beginning of successive reëlections, borrowed
money from Walker—two thousand dollars—to pay his
campaign expenses. He agreed to pay back this sum during the term, one thousand dollars each year. This he
did. The obligation was fully discharged when his friend
embarked on a business enterprise and asked McKinley
for a small loan, a thousand or so. Yes, of course, said
McKinley. The man could not meet his note; however,
he appeared from time to time with blank notes which
he asked McKinley to sign; he assured him that these
signatures were merely to be extensions of the original
note and of the dates of interest.

William McKinley, in his faithful attendance at Methodist country churches, must have heard more than one
preacher develop the text, "He that goeth surety for a
friend shall smart for it." He had an astute mind capable

of mastering the intricacies of tariff. Yet he signed blank notes. His friend filled them out for varying sums of money and raised money on them in one bank after another in northern Ohio.

The blow would have ruined an ordinary man. But McKinley had a star. Every dollar was paid. McKinley's devoted admirers (he was always rich there; the man's genius was for friendship, for judgment of men, for their management)—Hanna, Herrick, Kohlsaat, many others—and Mr. and Mrs. Bellamy Storer.

After all, a check for ten thousand dollars is not such a bagatelle. With McKinley President, the time had come for Mrs. Storer to realize a long-burning ambition. When she mentioned to McKinley the choice of distinguished posts which she desired for her husband, he was all sympathy. He was entirely sensible of the rights of such loyal friends and eager to recognize them; but such an appointment as Mrs. Storer sought would be made by the State Department. Then in confidence he added, "Senator Sherman is to be my Secretary of State."

Was he, indeed! Mrs. Storer fairly flew to Washington. She told Sherman. What? Secretary of State! The Senator frowned. Incredible and undesirable. He wouldn't even talk about it. He bade Mrs. Storer a cold good morning.

Now began that storming of the administration by two ambitious Americans that was to involve as many exalted officials as the making of a treaty and to become such a tortured issue in the Roosevelt reign as to spoil, while it lasted, the social atmosphere of the White House.

President McKinley called my husband to discuss with him a suitable reward for Bellamy Storer. He must do something, he said, wearily. Would it be agreeable to Senator Foraker if Storer were made Assistant Secretary of State?

Unfortunately, no, it would not be agreeable. Senator Foraker's position on the Foreign Relations Committee took him constantly to the State Department. There were reasons why it would give him no pleasure to see Bellamy Storer there.

The reasons ran back to a certain morning a few years before when a man bearing a letter of introduction from Senator Lindsay of Kentucky was shown into Foraker's law office in Cincinnati. The caller was an old Blue Grass farmer with a long white beard and a mild manner. But there was nothing mild in the nature of the business which on Senator Lindsay's advice had brought him to Ohio. This business was a suit based on most sensational charges which he proposed to bring against a prominent Cincinnati family that included among its connections Bellamy Storer.

Foraker instantly declined to touch the case. In that type of law business he was not interested. Realizing, however, that the man would easily find a lawyer who would have no scruple about exploiting his case, Foraker, acting on a friendly impulse, detained him until he could get hold of Thomas McDougall, lawyer for the family involved. He told McDougall what was afoot, advised him to take the man in hand at once and try to come to a private settlement. McDougall thanked him; agreed; tried to compromise. It proved not so easy. McDougall then appealed to my husband, since he was the one, and the only one, who knew the facts, to help him by representing Senator Lindsay's client. He asked this as a personal favor on the plea that a highly respected family would be spared painful publicity, etc., etc. The case would "never be allowed to come to trial," said McDougall. Under this impression Foraker yielded.

McDougall broke his promise. To Foraker's disgust the case did come into the courts. Foraker found himself trapped into an aggressive position towards an old Cincinnati family, a position which he loathed and would never have been in but for McDougall's misrepresentation. McDougall was a shrewd Scot; it may have added more to his prestige with his clients and to his own profit to have the case come to trial, and to win it, than otherwise. I cannot think that mere professional jealousy made him so "double-cross" a rising colleague. Whatever was back of it, the family, naturally, resented any representative of the man who was making trouble for them and never understood I am sure, the circumstance that brought Foraker into the affair at all. Bellamy Storer, clansman, was henceforth politically hostile.

The affair was fixed in my mind by one of those tragicomic incidents that enliven trying days: My husband was told one morning as he was leaving for New York that the case would be argued two days later. This brought him back from New York just in time to go to court. I went to his office about four o'clock that afternoon and found him munching a red apple. There hadn't been time all day for even a sandwich. He had an engagement to speak in Cleveland that night; had expected to meet this on his way back from New York. He told me he had ordered a special train to take him to Cleveland and was leaving in a few minutes. That *was* a ride! It was a perilous day of sleet and ice; but the train got there on time, a seven-hour run in five hours. Newspapers all over the country published pictures of the train and of a tired but contented man receiving an ovation from a crowd who had heard of the Foraker dash.

It was so good an advertisement for the Big Four that M. E. Ingalls, president, declined to accept my husband's check. But that wouldn't do. "Some day," said Foraker, "I may have a case against you, and I shall want to charge a good fee." I smile as I think of that hungry, harassing, horrible day; that red apple; that five-hundred-dollar train.

Aside from the unlucky lawsuit, Bellamy Storer

fancied that my husband was responsible for his being dropped as Congressman. The reverse was the case. When nomination time came Mr. Storer was so sure he would be reëlected that he remained happily at the seashore, somewhere cool, anyway. About this time, George B. Cox, Cincinnati ward-leader, told my husband that Storer was off the ticket. He had suffered from the zeal of a Catholic priest who, just before the last election, had instructed his congregation to vote the straight Democratic ticket except for Congressman; for Congressman they were to vote for Bellamy Storer. Foraker went straight to McDougall, same old family watch-dog, told him of this plot, and advised him to telegraph Bellamy to come home and mend his fences. McDougall jeered, "They wouldn't dare to drop Storer." They did dare. And Charles P. Taft, brother of William Howard, went to Congress in his place—and served one term.

We women were friendly. Mrs. Storer sent me red roses when Arthur, my youngest son, was born—twenty years after my eldest—and I admired her always for her daring in initiative and for other talents that, undeniably, shone best in limelit places.

"No, Mr. President," said Senator Foraker, "I shouldn't care for Bellamy in the State Department. But," he added, "if you care to send the appointment to the Senate, I'll take care of it there."

The President got very red. "I couldn't do that," he

said. "People would say you and I weren't friends." He tapped the desk with his pencil and gazed into space. Then it came to him, "How would something abroad do for the Storers?"

"Good!" said Foraker. "The abroader the better."

CHAPTER XVII

A LADY AND A RED HAT

STORER thinks," Senator Lodge had written Mr.
Roosevelt in 1895—"Storer thinks that we shall lose
Ohio and the Senatorship on account of Foraker."*

Indeed, that would have been too bad. For it was
Senator Foraker, as I have told, who was to act as im-
petus to the Storers on their diplomatic travels, and who
was to be still holding Ohio when the fanfare of their
departure had died away in the silence of their return.

The affair is so fast-threaded through my memories
of the 'nineties that I cannot disentangle it from this narrative. It involved popes, presidents, cardinals, and statesmen, ran through two administrations, provoked vast
rages and many laughs, was a seven days' wonder in London, Paris, Rome, and Berlin, talked to tatters in Washington, and ended most unhappily.

In 1899, when President McKinley transferred the
Storers from Brussels to our legation at Madrid, a personage joined their alliance. This was John Ireland, archbishop of St. Paul. I remember meeting the archbishop—
"a lovely April day," my journal says—coming from the
Capitol: a tall, powerful figure in a shabby black cloak

* Roosevelt-Lodge correspondence, vol. i, p. 178.

that flapped about his heels. There was a touch of the
Indian sachem about his bearing. And what a face the
man had! What a look intellectual fire and spiritual
grace can give to blue eyes! He walked abstractedly; the
sycamores threw salaaming shadows across his path.

Ireland was a national figure then. We saw him often
in Washington. Nobody had forgotten his fearless pio-
neering in Minnesota when he took the toughs "by the
collar and by the hand" and dragged them out of the
saloons and into the Church. When he exercised his
power in favor of the Republican Party we were all immensely pleased. He supported the McKinley ticket in
1896. Three years earlier his influence in Cleveland had
helped Hanna to a victory with the immense foreign
vote. A kick of the beam at a crisis. Guests at the famous
Platt banquet in March, 1902, told with pride that they'd
"had the archbishop with them." Moreover, as a modern-
ist and the most American Roman Catholic of them all,
he was a coming cardinal, if ever cardinal was coming.
And this very generally was recognized as excellent public policy.

Alas! Could he have been but saved from his friends!

After the war with Spain the Philippines troubled
Congress very much. In the long-drawn-out settlement of
the "friars' lands" (the Franciscans, Dominicans, and
Augustinians owned some four hundred thousand acres
on the islands) the archbishop was of great help to the
government. Thousands of letters poured in from Catho-

lics all over the United States, seeking to run up the price
we were to pay for this property. In the end we paid the
friars $7,239,000; this sum satisfied the Catholic island-
ers and pleased Rome. But the policy of both President
McKinley and President Roosevelt was sharply attacked
by the Democrats; my husband, with characteristic thoroughness, flung himself into the subject of the Philippines and led the debates defending the administration.

Washington dinner tables are lively forums for the discussion of public affairs; in the first year or so following
our war with Spain we heard a great deal about the
Philippines between the clams and the coffee. About
Aguinaldo, only thirty-one when Funston captured him
that March day in the mountains; a romantic figure in
spite of the annoyance he caused us. And about some new
citizens we were threatened with—the Igorots.

The benightedness of the Igorots greatly excited Mrs.
McKinley's sympathies. I went to call on her one day
during the Philippine agitation and found her full of
plans for saving the Igorots, particularly the children. I
had my little son Arthur with me that day; she always
liked me to bring him, and I remember her offering him
a rose and Arthur, a little shy, hesitating to take it, and
Mrs. McKinley being hurt by this and showing it, tears
coming into her eyes, and my embarrassment. Her love
for children and the tragedy of her own loss made her so
sensitive that she suffered if a child, through diffidence,
was for a moment unresponsive. People today have for-

gotten about little Katie and baby Ida, those children of the McKinleys' who never lived to grow up; ghosts in long-ago moonlight, yet playing a strangely real part in the national career of the man who became our twenty-fifth President.

Mrs. Admiral Dewey at this period more than shared the limelight with the President's wife. Childless too; adored children; spoiled them; was quite without sentimental philanthropy. On one occasion, Mrs. Francis B. Loomis, wife of the First Assistant Secretary of State, had her baby brought down to the drawing-room to meet Mrs. Dewey. The child became fascinated by a glittering jet pendant that was distinctly the ornamental *clou* of the costume worn by the Admiral's lady. He clutched at this furbelow . . . didn't want to let go . . . screamed. Mrs. Dewey was enchanted; instantly she detached the ornament. . . . There! . . . and young Loomis, all sunshine again, bore it off with him in triumph.

To return deviously to the Philippines: I find in my notes reference to a dinner party at the Senator Burrows' (Michigan) which was diverted by the Japanese minister, Mr. Takahira. The first *ambassador* from Japan was his successor, Viscount Aoki, who had a German wife. Mr. Takahira was very dignified, and with unconscious drollery told us more about those Igorots: their fancy for making all the unmarried women live together . . . the amorous prerogatives granted their chiefs . . . their head-hunting. Head-hunting! Somebody remarked that politically, if not Igorotically, Washington knew all about that.

On my morning drives with my husband I heard Philippine news, too, and strangely mixed with it a great deal about Archbishop Ireland's intervention in the interests of his friends and converts, the Bellamy Storers.

Madrid, it seemed, was not the pleasantest place of residence for an American minister, just after the Spanish-American War. Distracted as President McKinley was in 1901, he was pressed to do something, and at once, to brighten life for the Storers in Spain. If Madrid were an embassy, now. An embassy has more prestige, and prestige is amusing. Secretary Hay was, I know, instructed to suggest this change to the Spanish Minister, Brunetti, the Duke of Arcos. Spain must, of course, send us an ambassador first. Unamiable, she did not so honor us until twelve years later.

But Madrid didn't matter. A mere stepping-stone. The Storers' determined orientation was towards an important embassy, Paris, preferably; if not Paris immediately, then as soon as may be; in the interval, London or Berlin would serve.

"The sin by which the angels fell" was no new thing to the State Department; the ambitious place-seeking of our minister to Spain was memorable only for the fiercer, grander aim enmeshed in it. That aim was the cardinalate for John Ireland. Mrs. Bellamy Storer swept into history on the arm of the archbishop. Beside her desire to see him wear the red hat, her desire to see her husband ambassador to France fades to a trifle. Defeat was waiting for both of these craftily-woven plans; but the circumstances attending it were more dramatic than ever victory could have been.

One can understand poor, badgered McKinley promising anything to the Storers: Paris . . . the moon! But Fate grimly stayed his loyal intentions. Upon President Roosevelt devolved the difficulties of finding a way out of the labyrinth into which he was led by Mrs. Storer's importunate demands—she was the Roosevelts' friend, too—and by the archbishop's suave, steady, and most telling pressure on the administration. Only we in the inner circle knew how deeply Roosevelt was involved. He wrote to Mr. Root, icy to the whole matter, apropos of a letter from Mrs. Storer "suggesting the embassies of London or Paris. . . . There is a certain element of the comic in their attempt to get me to remove Mr. Choate or Mr. Porter."

Mr. Roosevelt deserved sympathy in this onset and at one time he got it from everybody. "I feel sorry for the President," my husband said to me one day. I smiled. "*You*, sorry for the President! Are you joking?" This was before the Brownsville chasm yawned (I am coming to that) but the statehood tilt—admission of Arizona and New Mexico—and the Hepburn railroad-rate bill clash had flashed "Danger" at the hairpin bend those two were rounding. "I'm not joking," said Foraker; "he's having the most awful time with Mrs. Storer. He told me today that she was making perfectly amazing demands. She seems to think he ought to wreck the administration to please her. And what do you think he said to me? 'Mind you, Senator,' he said, 'I don't think any more of Maria than you do.'"

At this very time, as later was shown, Mr. Roosevelt's letters to "Dear Maria" were full of soothing injunctions to patience, of friendliness and promises. But one could not blame the President. The affair got to be too much for him. King Solomon himself, in similar stress, would have fled to Ophir for an indefinite stay.

Washington society is sophisticated; it doesn't take its gossip too solemnly. The Storers' storming of the administration citadel came as near to rocking it as anything could. The very White House cat was christened "Maria." It was thought the cream of *esprit* to ask about her. Wits depended upon a new Theodore-and-Maria story for their dining-out success; if the story took a topical turn, so much the better. Sometimes it vaulted the barrier of taste. There was a certain Cabinet member's little leap at a dinner at the German Embassy. My daughter Louise was present on this occasion, sitting next to an *attaché* of the British Embassy. Dr. von Holleben, the Kaiser's bachelor ambassador, was a capital host, though he is best remembered for his attempt and failure to charge Sir Julian Pauncefote, British ambassador, with intrigue against this country in the Spanish War crisis. The dinner was given about the time of the Jamaica earthquake, and the subject of the hour was the boorish behavior of one Sir Alexander Swettenham, British Governor of the island, toward United States Rear-Admiral Davis, who had gone to Jamaican relief.

Things were going gaily when our Cabinet officer called down the table to a Senator's wife, "The President said something very funny at the Cabinet meeting to-day." Instantly everybody was alert. The story-teller savored this, looked 'round the table, beamed; he felt that he had a good one. "He said that if it wasn't for Bellamy he'd give Maria to Swettenham!" Well, the Cabinet may have roared over this. Von Holleben's guests were frozen by it. Those who didn't try to look at their very anti-British German host out of the corner of one eye, watched the very anti-German British *attaché* out of the corner of another. Then everybody at once began talking about something else, that excessive animation which betrays a slip. Dinner hostesses had a stop-look-and-listen gleam in their eyes in those days.

Diplomatically, Vienna was the nearest to Heaven that the Bellamy Storers ever got. Still, Mrs. Storer was the wife of an important ambassador, the Austria-Hungary capital an excellent place for directing intrigues, and dreams now promised to turn into exciting reality.

Plainly the administration was fascinated by Archbishop Ireland. All except Mr. Root; he was Catholic-

fascination proof. In the summer of 1903 the Secretary
of War was in Rome, joining Bishop O'Gorman on a
Philippine mission to the Vatican. The affair demanded
just the wisdom and delicate handling which Mr. Taft
brought to it. On Leo XIII the Secretary made a most
favorable impression. Later (there was a new Holy
Father then, Pius X) Mr. Taft was so agreeably struck
by the prelate who negotiated the matter of the lands
that he intimated he might help to have him made a
cardinal. But I think nothing came of this. We are not
cardinal-makers, I fear, we Republicans. The events of
the Roosevelt reign should warn us to keep hands off.

With Mrs. Storer things were going marvelously at
Vienna. She was at the zenith of her power, moving
great personages, domestic and European, like so many
marionettes. Then, presto! something happened that
was to bring the roof of the ambassador's handsome
Viennese *palast* about his head.

Archbishop Farley of New York called one day upon
President Roosevelt. He had heard, he said, that Archbishop Ireland had the President's backing for the cardinalate. Also, that Mr. Storer, ambassador to Austria-
Hungary, had, at the President's request, visited the Pope
and asked him, as a personal favor to the President of the
United States, to make Archbishop Ireland a cardinal.
Archbishop Farley merely wished to know where he
stood in this noble scheme. Was he not also under the
presidential ægis?

The President felt himself on very thin ice. Instantly
he let it be known that he would be pleased to see Archbishop Farley a cardinal as well. This made Rome faintly
smile. The Americans didn't want much, did they? Only
two cardinals at one consistory! Well, no American was
honored by the red hat in 1905.

Roosevelt raged for a minute, then he acted. His letters to "Dear Maria" and the archbishop's letters to Mrs.
Storer, as their subsequent publication was to show, were
full of the President's desire to have Archbishop Ireland
made a cardinal. The President now denied, and his denial was widely broadcast, that he had ever "officially"
written or said anything to any person that would au-
thorize him or her to speak for him at the Vatican on
the archbishop's behalf. He had sincerely favored the
archbishop ever since the days when he was Governor
of New York, but everything he had written or said on
the subject was strictly as friend to friend. The Storers
were violators of confidence and unwarranted meddlers
in matters of state. And he wrote the ambassador and
Mrs. Storer at Vienna a letter. It must have been a letter
in all ways remarkable, for it was never answered.

"I cannot have an ambassador who does not answer
my letters," snapped Theodore Roosevelt. And then, in
spite of a long, close friendship, in spite of the Storers'
lavish devotion to the Roosevelts, and the early days
when anything the Storers had was at the Roosevelts'
disposal—their Washington house, offered rent free, if

not accepted; their horses, their dinner table, their cellar, their chef; in spite of the fact that Bellamy had played Bassanio so handsomely—

> My purse, my person, my extremest means
> Are all unlocked to your occasions.

and that it was Bellamy whom Roosevelt had begged to propose him to Mr. McKinley as Assistant Secretary of the Navy in his first Cabinet—though Roosevelt always said that he had never asked for any office save that of President—then, in spite of all this and more, the President did a curiously brutal and undignified thing. He recalled Ambassador Storer in a peremptory cablegram. That was the end.

Now the social atmosphere of Washington was indeed stormy. My husband and I were not so often at the White House in 1907 as we had been before then. The "Brownsville" engagement at the Gridiron Club occurred in January of that year. But I heard enough from my friends of the dinner parties there to feel that we had known the White House in its pleasantest days.

About the Storers the President was undoubtedly very unhappy. They had been close friends for so long, he said; Mrs. Storer was so devoted to Mrs. Roosevelt, and just think of the lovely things she had always done! There was that time when they hesitated about going to President Cleveland's reception on account of the expense; Mrs. Storer not only sent Mrs. Roosevelt a daz-

zling new Paris dress—in which Edith looked a dream
—but she sent her own carriage with two men on the
box; and so on and on and on. Ah, no one would ever
know how hard it was for him to do what he did in
having Bellamy, dearest, staunchest, and most generous
of friends, dismissed from the foreign service. But duty
was duty.

Well, whether it was or not, the tide of sympathy
now raced to the Storers. They had intrigued daringly,
perhaps, but they had been cruelly and ruinously re-
buked. Worst of all, between the Roosevelt partisans and
the Storerites there was a great gulf fixed that blocked
social intercourse. I remember meeting Mrs. Don Cameron one day at luncheon. She said, plaintively, that she
had come back to Washington for a few happy months
among her old friends, the Roosevelt-Storer crowd, and
what met her? An edict that no person who had anything
whatever to do with the Bellamy Storers would be permitted to cross the White House threshhold. "The
Roosevelts are my dearest friends," said Mrs. Cameron,
"and the Storers are my dearest friends, and now . . ."

That Archbishop Ireland never wore the red hat, and
that Mrs. Maria Longworth Storer never graced with her
undeniable distinction the American Embassy in the
French capital, was an unravelment, fantastic and sad.
So much passion had been spent on these ambitions, so
many grand wires pulled, there were such heart-
burnings.

CHAPTER XVIII

A KNIGHT OF THE 'NINETIES

I CANNOT leave the McKinley years without re-
cording my remembrance of the two tragic personalities who occupied the White House from 1897 to
1901. Films of memory begin with a happy scene: the
east portico of the Capitol, where the President first took
the oath, with the budding trees beyond; William Mc-
Kinley's priest-like face with its curious look of strain;
his wife, Dresden-like, touching, always her lonely gray
eyes fixed on her husband. And Chief-Justice Fuller,
graver only in his robes than Mark Hanna, whose so-
lemnity on that day amounted to awe; and the Hobarts,
the Vice-President so kind it was a sort of genius, and
Mrs. Hobart, elegant, tactful, alert, keeping close to Mrs.
McKinley's side, and General Miles, gold-bright in the
Executive wake—the whole brave assemblage in the sun.

Sunshine and flowers liked William McKinley. Blos-
somingly the White House welcomed him; the snow-
drops were wonderful that year, and the magnolias. The
house still had its Adamsonian simplicity—a fine, human, home of a house where a man, who was also a
gentleman, might hope for happiness. Mrs. McKinley
told me that as they drove up to it after the Inauguration

ceremony, "she was so tired . . . it looked nice to her
. . . almost another Canton." A couple of old colored
servants from Grant's time stood at the door, like bronze
fates.

We had known Major McKinley through long, Ohio
days. His genius for winning the regard of men displayed
itself early; his close friendship with Hayes and Blaine
must have been very useful to him. And even at that time
the public was weaving a halo for him out of his devotion
to his invalid wife. I remember my first meeting with
McKinley one day in the 'eighties when he came to our
home in Cincinnati. He wore a flower in his coat. My
little girls trooped in from school. How charming the
"Major" was to them! Charmed, himself, too, I think.
His face softened; a flash of longing. Whatever the qualities, the circumstances, that led him to the highest pin-
nacle of fame, the thing that endeared McKinley to the
nation was his slavish protectiveness towards the woman
to whom the best had been given—and taken away.
The unbroken guard he kept, his patience and gentle-
ness in circumstances of the most trying nature, affected
Washington, affected the whole country as nothing coming from the White House ever had done. It was an
idyll of pure chivalry that in an era disputatious and
material flamed like a rose.

"Ida was the most beautiful girl you ever saw," the
President said to Mrs. Storer, and he added, "She is
beautiful to me now." Indeed, she must have been lovely

that long ago day when, in a flounced frock of sprigged challie, she looked through the cashier's cage of her father's bank at Canton and saw the spruce young officer who had come in to negotiate his last army pay. By the time she reached the White House, however, illness and sorrow, and the fact that for years her husband had been a shield between her and reality, had made of her a pathetically spoiled and difficult woman.

We were often at the White House from the beginning of McKinley days there. A worldlier note had crept in since my first acquaintance with it in Hayes' time. Instead of the Hayes hymn-singing, highly-paid artists were intrusted to furnish the music. I remember Nordica singing "Home, Sweet Home" one night; it was at Mr. McKinley's rather diffident request, with a narrow glance at his wife for fear the song might make her sad. Apprehension checked the spontaneity for which we were so ready when, with the Roosevelts, it very brilliantly came.

Mrs. McKinley knew what she liked and she got it royally. White House interiors had been freshly redecorated, of course, for the new President. A good deal of sunshiny yellow had been used in Mrs. McKinley's own apartments. Now for yellow Mrs. McKinley had Olivia's antipathy, " 'tis a color she abhors." When she saw her yellow rooms she stopped dead, refused to step foot in them until they had been done over in blue. Blue, hastily, they became.

The homage lavished by her husband Mrs. McKinley repaid with an adoration that quite upset values, just as the indulgence she had received made her look upon herself as different from all other women. Indeed, one had to watch one's *p's* and *q's* in conversation! I remember the confusion of a young English girl, guest of the Hobarts, at a White House dinner party. In reply to some bantering question she had admitted that, even after seeing America, she still loved England best; for her it was the place above all others in which to live.

Mrs. McKinley looked at her severely: "Do you mean to say that you would prefer England to a country ruled over by *my husband*?" She waited for an answer. There was no answer but an English blush. It may have been at the same dinner, or at another, that my husband, sitting next to Mrs. McKinley and doing his best with the difficulties of small talk with his hostess, remarked: "Your husband is lucky. He doesn't have to go home to vote. Now I have to drop everything and go out to Ohio (spring election) to vote."

Mrs. McKinley: "Well, I'm glad to hear that. I think it's about time you men did something. My husband has carried the Republican Party for twenty years. Now I'd like to see somebody else do something."

When anyone referred to the President's resemblance to Daniel Webster or to Napoleon, Mrs. McKinley waved the compliment aside as one not so much honoring McKinley as the other man. Her husband was the Hero of all Time—why "drag in" anybody else? Whatever the President felt about such rebuttals, his face betrayed nothing.

One day I was calling on Mrs. McKinley and, as usual when I went to see her, I had Arthur with me. The child behaved very well that day. (I have told about how very bad he was on another occasion when timidly he refused a rose she offered him.) Mrs. McKinley seemed very happy; she always seemed so with children. In the midst of our visit a delegation of women from Kansas appeared at the door. The audience had been arranged for, of course, but whether it was because Mrs. McKinley was enjoying herself talking to a child, or found herself out of the mood for receiving delegations from Kansas or elsewhere—whatever it was, her reception of those Kansas ladies was of a nature that they were not likely to forget. The leader of the delegation, a smiling, confident woman, advanced, her mouth framed for a charming speech:

"We are so glad to see you again, Mrs. McKinley. We remember what a pleasure it was to meet you when you were in Kansas City."

Mrs. McKinley: "I was never there."

The confident spokeswoman colored, hesitated, but held her ground. "Oh, don't you remember? It was the time the city gave a big banquet to President McKinley and you ——"

Mrs. McKinley: "I tell you we were never there. If my husband went I went with him. But he never went."

The delegation leader faltered, the delegation ladies stared at one another, there was a general sunflower droop. It was quite painful. It was rare that Mrs. McKinley was left without some one to act as a buffer between her and people, innocently-eager and loyal, whom she felt suddenly disinclined to encourage.

One day I took a group of young friends to the White House, just to show it to them. I did not ask to see Mrs. McKinley; as a rule such visits are arranged for in advance. Out of courtesy, however, I gave my card to an usher. He at once brought down word that Mrs. McKinley wished to see me. We went up to the south room with the round windows on the second floor, overlooking the gardens, which the McKinleys used as their private sitting-room. Mrs. Abner McKinley, wife of the President's brother, was there, stiff as ice, perfectly wordless.

Mrs. McKinley was exquisitely dressed in blue, always in silvery blue, her short hair, naturally curly, worn Greek-youth fashion, her hands (she had lovely hands) busy knitting her famous and everlasting slippers. She knitted expertly; if she liked you she would knit you a pair of slippers, the color of your personality; it was she who decided what that color was. I presented my young people, then made some remark about the beautiful fall weather.

"Beautiful?" said the First Lady. "I don't see anything beautiful about it. We've had nothing but rain, rain, rain." Nervously I thought of something else. The McKinleys had some young guests at the time, their niece, Mabel McKinley, and her friends. The President and Mrs. McKinley must find it pleasant, I ventured, having all these gay young people in the house. "Not at all," Mrs. McKinley took me up, her needles clicking: "Young people are always on the go, always out, always coming in late. What pleasure is there in that?" Mrs. "Ab" sat there, hearing these blasts, but making no effort to check them. It just wasn't Mrs. McKinley's day. At her occasional happiest, however, she could be quite different. She had a certain wit, she had been well educated, and one could not forget that once in a far-time when "professional women" were rarities, she had been one and with a clever grasp of finance.

Her husband was a saint. We know that now. Why, the man never even had a bed to himself! During the Spanish-American War he was, many a night, in his office until two o'clock in the morning. When, after those long hours, exhausted, unhappy, too, for he hated our intervention, he sought his own apartments, rest still was denied him. Mrs. McKinley slept badly. When he found her wide-eyed, nervous, it soothed her to have him, in a half sitting-up position, put his arm around her, comfort her, chat a little. Then perhaps she could drop off.

But he mustn't take his arm away. Dear me, no! She could only sleep if it were there.

The tragic thing about that household was that while Mrs. McKinley was always in her husband's thought, tenderly enveloped by his sympathy and interest, there was no woman to whom McKinley could really *talk*. What Samuel Johnson called "the enduring elegance of female friendship" was not for our friend. He could *talk* only to men. It explains a good deal. No matter how troubled he was by administration affairs, he never entered his wife's presence without a reassuring smile. "It's all right, Ida; everything's all right." Ah, the masks he wore!

Her exigence could hardly be kept wholly veiled. Once, during a crisis in the Canal Treaty conversations, I think, a dentist went to the White House to do some work for Mrs. McKinley. The President sat with her while the work progressed. Finally he arose; he would have to go; a person of importance was waiting to see him. There was an outburst. Go, of course, if he cared more for some mysterious "person" than for her! The President sat down again; stayed on some time; then, "John Hay is waiting to see me," he said at last. "I cannot keep him any longer." He walked out in complete silence.

We were in the Adirondacks when, September 6, 1901, we heard that President McKinley had been shot at the

Pan-American Exposition, Buffalo. The assassin—"a man with his hand tied up." Those close to the President in the receiving line said that "the man held out his left hand which the President took with a glance of sympathy at the other." Reports changing from favorable to grave put an end to our summer—to everybody's summer. On the twelfth we were in Buffalo. Bulletins were issued all the following day from the house of John G. Milburn, McKinley's host: the President was sinking.

Soft, winey, intoxicating September weather. In my room, shortly after midnight, the stillness of the town, quiet as a meadow under the stars, was broken: newsboys were racing up and down the streets, crying, "McKinley dead! McKinley dead!" I thought of another tumult which the name of this man had raised. In June, 1896, when, at the Republican convention, St. Louis, Foraker proposed "William McKinley" for President of the United States, there burst a perfect tornado of applause. The shouting kept up for thirty minutes (not since the celebrated cheering at Chicago in 1880 by the supporters of Grant and Blaine had there been anything like it). That was only five years ago, and now they were crying, "McKinley dead!" Odd bits of the man's talk came back to me. A quaint story of his childhood. He lived in a little place, Niles, Ohio, and used to drive the cows to and from pasture, outside the village. He was always barefoot; his feet used to get so cold, he would press them into the earth where the cows had lain. Nothing, he said, ever gave him such a thrill of pure *luxury* as the remembrance of the feel of that warm, meadow earth. Now he was our President, dead.

All the next day, Saturday, I sat on the porch of the Hotel Lenox—an old-fashioned hotel porch with ranks of rocking chairs. A great many people whom we knew were there, rocking and waiting. We knew that the Exposition would be closed. I had left cards at the hushed house, where the McKinleys had stopped. Now there was nothing to do but take the train and go home. We could not leave until six o'clock. Among the friends who joined me that long afternoon were General Sickles and Senator Fairbanks. The General, gruff, fiery, towering, had lost a leg at Gettysburg in the hot fighting around the Peach Orchard. As we sat there, Mabel McKinley, the lame niece of the President, went in and out of the hotel, in and out a great many times on her crutches. The sight set General Sickles off on his favorite theme—the art of making crutches. Most people's crutches were all wrong —too short, too high, too heavy. Mabel McKinley's were very wrong. The General had given valuable suggestions to surgeons; he had designed his own crutches; he seemed prouder of his skill as crutch expert than of his conspicuous bravery at Chancellorsville, or of his success as a duelist and a romantic.

Senator Fairbanks sat there and said not one word.

Just sat there stiffly, a Hoosier schoolmaster figure in a very high collar. How people at momentous moments, when hearts are heavy, seek refuge in trivialities! While General Sickles was telling me things about crutches that otherwise I never would have known, my mind wandered in another channel. Mr. Roosevelt was hurrying back to Buffalo from Mount Marcy in Vermont, where he had rejoined his family after coming to Buffalo immediately upon receiving word of the shooting. The Vice-President was reassured, we were all reassured, that Mr. McKinley would recover. When Cortleyou's message came, telling of the President's change for the worse, Roosevelt was at a little lake higher up in the mountain, called—how odd!—"The Tear in the Clouds." There was no truth whatever in the widespread report that when the President was sinking Roosevelt was hunting somewhere in the big woods and could not be found. Roosevelt had no heart for sport those fatal September days. While General Sickles rambled on I kept thinking of the Vice-President's dash down the mountain from a leafy camp to this grim scene. A sudden, absurd worry possessed me: would Roosevelt have a silk hat, a proper silk hat, one that would fit him? I worried about that silk hat. It was monstrous.

There was something sinister about the closely packed lines of people at the railway station, lines and lines of people waiting for trains to take them away from that place of woe. A pall hung over life. The universe lowered its voice.

I doubt if the death of any public man ever caused more genuine sorrow in the hearts of his followers. McKinley had an almost mesmeric quality that made those who came under its spell add to the fine traits he possessed others more or less godlike. At the moment when Fate touched him with martyrdom these worshipers sometimes parted with their sense of humor to an extent that would have made their loved-and-lost hero himself smile. There was Captain Clark Toner, an old army comrade whom the President had appointed to the Indian Office, or maybe the Land Office. . . .

"He was the *purest* man that ever lived," said Toner. "Often, often I've heard him say, 'Boys, if there's any dirty work to be done, don't tell me of it. *Do it*—but don't tell me!'"

Tears streamed down the veteran's furrowed cheeks.

The world's sympathy went out to Mrs. McKinley. It thought her crushed. Yet how marvelous she was! How erect in grief! Suddenly deprived of the prop of life, she seemed to draw strength and self-control from very remembrance. No one would have said that she could have lived with so much courage through the lonely years that followed. She who had been shielded from every sort of responsibility and weariness now recognized reality, even took an interest in certain of her business affairs. I think it was the same steel tenacity in that frail little woman that made her insist upon assuming her place as head of the White House, made her hold it, made her go with the President again and again on his official trips. McKinley stuck to his front-porch presidential campaign because he would not leave his wife. When he had to leave her at the last she behaved like a Roman.

Hanna, on the other hand, was defenseless against loss. For a long time every stab dealt by the caricaturists' pencil at the man he had so loved glowed dully in his face like a scar.

CHAPTER XIX

THE BATTLE FOR THE BLACK BATTALION

ON JULY 12, 1906, a great wrong done to an innocent French soldier was righted. Dreyfus was rein-
stated in the French army, from which he had been discharged twelve years before.

One month from that date, on August 13th, exactly,
something happened in a Texas town that resulted in
the discharge of one hundred and sixty-seven innocent
soldiers from the American army. The injustice of this
mass dismissal excited the country for years. It was never
repaired.

Everybody alive and awake a quarter of a century ago
remembers the Brownsville scandal—President Roosevelt's discharge without honor of a battalion of the
twenty-fifth United States Infantry, colored, following
the shooting up of Brownsville, Texas.

There was nothing in the air that hazy August to hint
that an army brawl involving negro troops was to lead
the President and Senator Foraker into an impasse of
hostility. Up to that time the relations of Mr. Roosevelt
and my husband had been of the strive-mightily-but-eat-
and-drink-as-friends order. They had not seen even half-
an-eye to eye on joint statehood; the very year of the

Brownsville breach they were hardly speaking the same language when the subject was railroad-rate legislation. But in politics, as in law, friendship survives strife, and the cordiality of the two men's relations was unaffected by their conflicts of opinion on public questions. My husband admired the President for his intellectual gusto and his courage, and granted him, for his admirable dexterity in tight corners, a claim to genius. What Mr. Roosevelt thought of Foraker he expressed in a personal letter which, in its own place, I shall quote. It was written long after the President's virulent hostility had spent itself, written when nothing further mattered at all. So perhaps it was sincere.

Roosevelt and Foraker first met at the Republican National Convention of 1884. Roosevelt was twenty-six, scowling and raspily positive; he had, markedly, fire and a point of view, and Foraker, always attracted by this combination, and himself attractive to younger men, liked the New York Assemblyman. He wrote John Sherman, from whom Blaine had taken away the presidential nomination, that young Roosevelt had worked like a nailer to throw the Edmunds vote to Sherman. . . . Wouldn't Mr. Sherman write and thank him? They spoke of John Sherman as "the old man" then; he was sixty-one.

That 1884 convention was a memorable threshold for coming-on-leaders. Hanna and Foraker, meeting for the first time, and Major William McKinley and Henry

Cabot Lodge, who, it was admiringly remarked, used "mighty fine grammar," and Original Mugwump George William Curtis, anti-Blaine and party-bolter then and there; and, besides Theodore Roosevelt, other Harvard swells such as Hamilton Fish, Jr., and dandified little William Walter Phelps. These Eastern striplings wore their hair banged, pronounced "either" with an *i*, and said "rawther," and this provoked derision from the plain-people delegates. The annoying thing was that the banged boys spoke extremely well, knew what they wanted, showed a very beagle's flair for political tactics, were determined to be heard in the din, and were heard, loud and often; they got as hoarse as anybody else.

I have a vivid memory—this was my first national convention, if you know what that means—of Theodore Roosevelt and "Willy Wally" Phelps standing on chairs, yelling arguments and shaking their fists. At least, Roosevelt was shaking his fist.

An incident of this convention—apposite here since Brownsville was coming—was the proposal to appoint a colored delegate from Mississippi as chairman. This move, pure political strategy, of course, was to get a test vote to find out how strong Blaine really was. The National Committee had named Senator Clayton of Arkansas as chairman. Clayton was very Blaine indeed, and the plot to displace him launched a lively fight between his henchman and the test-voters. Foraker was in this latter crowd, and Roosevelt, smelling powder, hurried over to his camp and helped put the vote through. Mr. Lynch, colored, became chairman.

So, oddly, a black Congressman figured in the events that first brought Roosevelt and Foraker together, and it was a black battalion that disrupted their friendship in the end. This last time the black did not win.

At the first news that Brownsville had been "shot up" in the dead of a moonless summer night by mysterious raiders, everybody believed that the soldiers had done the shooting. Here was a Southern community with a military post; here, against popular clamor, three companies of a colored regiment had been stationed. This was two weeks before the raid.

Brownsville is on the southern tip of Texas, just across the Rio Grande from Matamoras, Mexico. Gold-seekers fitted out at Brownsville on their way to California in 1849. "Old Rough and Ready" Zachary Taylor fought all over the place. Until captured by Federal troops in 1863, it was a center for Confederate blockade-runners. General Taylor established the fort there. It's a picturesque old thing. Brownsville is proud of it. There, you see, are the scars of repeated bombardments from Mexico in Santa Anna's time. It's almost a hundred years old, our fort.

Brownsville got Texas-excited when told that a black battalion was coming; it protested to the Secretary of War, Mr. Taft. They didn't want colored soldiers in their town . . . white soldiers had always been sent before; no blacks for Brownsville, please. Strangely, all this was ignored. A number of people, Senator Culberson of Texas, for one, flaired danger and said so. The War Department did nothing. And then Brownsville had its revenge.

The black battalion had come down from Fort Niobrara, Nebraska. There and at every other post where the men had been stationed they had left a record as very decent, well-disciplined soldiers. One of them, Sergeant Mingo Sanders, had so noteworthy an army score that before Brownsville subsided he had figured in hundreds of cartoons. The one best remembered was by W. A. Rogers in *Harper's Weekly*—"Dishonorably Discharged"—a full-page drawing of this powerful, coal-black negro, covered with medals, standing like a dazed child, his discharge papers in his hand. Sanders had served almost thirty years—in the Indian wars, in the Philippines, in Cuba.

But, good or bad, Brownsville hated the battalion even before its black shadow cut across the state border; almost at once there were inevitable minor clashes. So, when raiders went through the town that night (from eight to twenty they thought, but who shall say? it was pitch-dark), firing recklessly, killing one man, injuring two, and petrifying the rest with fright, when that happened everybody cried, "The soldiers!" A local grand jury promptly sat upon the outrage.

There was nation-wide disgust at this disgrace to the

army; there were muttered I-told-you-sos from the southern Jeremiahs. The President ordered an investigation.

The President's subsequent action was to excite the
country as nothing had excited it since Civil War rancors.
The report resulting from the investigation was based on
the unsworn testimony of Brownsville citizens, on a
statement that shells and clips were found on the ground
like those used by the soldiers, on the "eye-witness" report of Major Blocksom, the only inspector who was sent
to Brownsville (Major Blocksom was the son of a "Val-
landigham Copperhead Democrat"; the strain instills no
love for the colored race). In conclusion came the findings of General Garlington, Inspector-General of the
army, whom the President had sent to Reno (the battalion had been shifted to this station) with instructions
to force the men to "tell on" one another, under penalty,
if they did not confess, of being mustered out without
honor.

The soldiers swore to a man that they had had nothing
to do with the "shooting up." They denied all knowledge
of it; stuck to this denial in the face of persuasion, promises, and threats; "The men," said General Garlington,
"seemed banded together to suppress the truth." He
could not get a single one of the entire one hundred and
sixty-seven to say anything but that he was entirely innocent of the crime. Thereupon the General recommended
to the President that "as an example to the whole army
the whole battalion be discharged without honor."

"Punishment as example" has an unfamiliar and barbaric sound to American ears. Yet, making an example of these wretched men, the President did discharge the black battalion without honor. Discharged it solely on the Blocksom-Garlington report; discharged it regardless of the correct procedure laid down by Congress for exactly such crises as these. And thought that he'd heard the last of Brownsville.

I have always understood that Mr. Roosevelt acted wholly on his own in the matter of the Brownsville discharge; that he did not consult his Secretary of War. During the progress of the affair, petition after petition, protest after protest from societies and movements interested in the welfare of the negro race, presented itself at Washington in an effort to have the decision revoked. An incident at the beginning showed the emotionalism of the colored people themselves over the dismissal. One morning a gaunt, excited negress, mother of a boy in the battalion, went tearing into the War Department, got to see Mr. Taft, wept, and begged him to persuade the President not to discharge the men. "Dey didn't do it! . . . Dey didn't do it!" she sobbed over and over. (I have the story at first hand.) And I know that Mr. Taft was so moved by the woman's storming and tears that he at once tried to get hold of the President, to advise him to hold up the thing. But Mr. Roosevelt was off on a trip somewhere; couldn't be reached. The order stood.

"By George!" the President had said. "The men's guilt is as clear as day!"

Ah, it was not so clear. Suddenly it clouded. That Senator Foraker was to be the troubler of the crystal was a circumstance utterly without political or personal bias. In the first weeks of the Brownsville excitement my husband took the general view that the black troops had done the "shooting up." He knew that the South was prejudiced against colored soldiers; that Brownsville had resented the battalion. When it was forced on it, doubtless the citizens nagged the men; doubtless, in reprisal, the negroes shot up the naggers. Even a colored worm will turn. Foraker hadn't read the testimony—but the President must have known what he was about.

In the gravity of the charge, however, in the harsh punishment inflicted, there was something murky, something extravagant and wrong. This conviction haunted my husband into reading the testimony. He was amazed. It seemed to him flimsy, insufficient, unreliable. Was it possible that on such evidence the President had discharged the battalion? Mr. Roosevelt had been misled, that was all; in his hasty, executive action there was danger of a cruel injustice. Stronger proof than this must be found to justify such a sentence. It was not enough that the men refused to confess. The guilty must be ferreted out and punished; the innocent must be acquitted. Anglo-Saxon law is as simple as that. Well, Mr. Roosevelt was the last man to permit injustice to stand. The

man who would help him to correct injustice was one of
Roosevelt's Own. It was with this belief that Foraker
threw himself into the Brownsville affair. He went into
it with the zeal of a Canaanean and with all the reserves
of knowledge and insight which an experienced lawyer
brings to the study of a baffling case.

I remember, for one reason because it upset my social
calendar, how absorbedly my husband gave himself to
Brownsville that November before the Congress convened: writing, wiring, sending men out to Texas to take
sworn testimony, to secure exact details; spending hours
and hours in a thickening jungle of newspapers, clip-
pings, letters, and calf-bound books. I remember, as he
read on and on, his unconscious ejaculations of dissent:
"No, that isn't true. . . . That doesn't follow at all.
. . . No, no, there is nothing in that."

The thing was too much for Foraker's sense of justice,
too much for his legal sense. Here, on the one hand, was
a mass of gimcrack evidence. One of the four so-called
"eye-witnesses" was blind in one eye and limited of vision
in the other, yet he was a very cat at identifying black
soldiers in the black of night at a distance ranging un-
certainly from thirty to one hundred and fifty feet; and
there, on the other hand, was a crowd of colored men in
the uniform of the United States army protesting that
they knew nothing about the shooting; sticking to that
oath though they were to be ruined by the government
they had honestly served.

These men, wards of the government—as Secretary
Taft said of white soldiers who once shot up the town of
Athens, Ohio—were entitled to the protection of the
government in all their legal rights. They had not had
that protection. They had been dealt with in the dark.
They had been treated like Salem witches; the only
alley of escape offered them was confession. They said
they had nothing to confess. And Foraker, the deeper
he went into the affair, came terribly to believe that they
were telling the truth.

When Congress met in December my husband had
completed his investigations and prepared his case. He
intended to submit this to the Senate after he had had an
opportunity to consult the Senators as to the proper moment. When Congress convenes, the first Monday in
December, it is customary for it to adjourn immediately
the formalities of the opening are over. No business is
begun on that day. On this occasion, however, this precedent, so far as could be recalled, was broken for the
first time. The Vice-President was on the point of proposing adjournment when Senator Boise Penrose sprang
upon the Senate a message from the President of the
United States. This message was a request that the
Brownsville matter be left wholly in the President's
hands. The Senate would be so good as not to concern
itself with Brownsville.

The Senators stared. They knew of Foraker's work,
of course, and of his plan. The President must have

known, too, for here by a *coup* he had spiked all Brownsville guns. Yet, not all. Senator Penrose had hardly finished when Senator Foraker leaped to his feet. By sheer
chance—or was it fate?—my husband had in his coat
pocket all the notes on his case which he had expected to
present a few days later. Later? It was now or never.
Then and there Foraker let the Senate have "Brownsville" in a new and startling light. Senator Penrose was
not remarkable for mobility of countenance, but at the
Foraker stroke it was reported that he looked cranberry-
ish and indignant.

The President had thought to smother Foraker before
he had a chance to move. What he did was to give him
a very prince of openings. The Senator's resolution, following immediately, directed the Secretary of War to
send to the Senate all his information on the subject of
Brownsville. It went through electrically. My husband
had the Senate generously with him on that occasion.
The Executive screw, Senator Lodge, chief engineer, that
was to reduce the number, had not yet begun to turn.

It is beyond doubt that Mr. Roosevelt, with his lightning flair, knew of Foraker's Brownsville research at the
outset. Senator Lodge, in a very pro-administration
speech in the Senate, had gone back to "bloody Winnemucca," stated that colored troops had been guilty of that
Nebraskan outrage, and that, consequently, with a just-
like-the-blacks logic, the twenty-fifth battalion was born
but to shoot-up Brownsville.

The newspapers were hardly out with the Lodge speech when a Nebraskan woman called at our house. Colored troops were not guilty at Winnemucca, she said; the War Department had investigated the affair and cleared them; all the testimony was on record. Foraker at once asked to have the Winnemucca details sent him. The War Department, with customary politeness, promised the information at once. It didn't come. After repeated requests, trailing over two weeks, Foraker telephoned the Department that if he did not receive the papers within a half-hour he would fetch them himself. They came in fifteen minutes. Such a putting off of a government official was unheard of; only superior orders could account for it. The records proved that the black troops at Winnemucca had been completely absolved. Senator Lodge simply was mistaken; a man of perfect honor, incapable of an assertion that he did not believe to be true.

Brownsville was smoldering most ominously when the President launched his celebrated broadside at Foraker on the night of the Gridiron dinner. The heather flamed at that match. I admit that it was pretty dry. All Washington began at first whispering about the Gridiron sensation; then the town rang with it. Gridiron happenings are supposed to be inviolate, but as no other President had ever challenged a man to debate before a large audience, and as this audience was composed of distinguished financiers, statesmen, writers, and artists, the news was

too good to keep. And then telegrams began coming in
to my husband from all over the country. He couldn't
move for Brownsville. My reception day that week was
a suffocating crush.

Until this public breach, the social *status quo* had managed to hold up its head. But now President Roosevelt,
whom my husband, in investigating the charge against
the battalion, had thought only to serve, turned against
Foraker the full force of his very dangerous enmity.

There were many easy reprisals open to the President:
Foraker's recommendations for appointments were not
honored; the malice in this was its aim to discredit my
husband with the people of Ohio. The case of the "judge-
ships" is in glaring point. Invitations to the White House
dinners ceased. Unimportant but for the fact that the
President's official dinners always have significance. Mr.
Roosevelt gave a great many informal dinners for men,
ten to fifteen guests. Presumably questions occupying the
government were discussed. In the first Roosevelt years
my husband was repeatedly asked; after Brownsville,
never.

That year, too, was the first time my husband and myself were omitted from the Diplomatic dinner at the
White House. This was so raw a neglect of surface
amenities, I cannot but think that it had to do with an
incident of the preceding dinner for the Diplomats. That
invitation "commanded" us on a day when my husband was to plead before the Supreme Court of Ohio,

an engagement of months. He could hardly put off the Supreme Court. That ended it. I was not entirely inconsolable; Foraker's fee for that argument in court was ten thousand dollars. Sometimes a crown is not worth a mass. Invitations to White House receptions, all the trifling big things, came as usual. Naturally, these we never thought of accepting. Plainly a war was on.

But it was not until official venom penetrated our family life that we learned what we were so deeply in for. "Brownsville" was to run for almost three years. For a long part of that time we were to live in an atmosphere of spying and furtiveness that was like something out of revolutionary Russia.

CHAPTER XX

UNDER COVER OF NIGHT

AS A clan we were, naturally, enlisted in the Texas issue heart and soul. Foraker's grim thoroughness, the way he probed points, set them up like ninepins or knocked them down, his dive to the very bottom of Brownsville, magnetized us all. I remember my son Benson putting on his soldier's uniform one night, at his father's request, and taking his stand at different distances from the house; the determinable point was how near a person must be to be recognized in the dark. Everybody in the Senator's camp began making these tests. It's rather a good game. The impossibility of identifying anyone at night was proved:

Stand on the sidewalk, across the road, at any short distance in any town (ours was Washington) after dark; unless it is bright moonlight, or unless a person comes under the rays of artificial light, one cannot tell whether a man is white or black, or anything about how he is dressed. What price then, the Brownsville "eyewitnesses" who, though excited by being fired at, could describe details of the soldiers' uniform, take in a mole on a sergeant's cheek, even be able to swear to the color— blue, sir!—of the gun barrels?

Efforts to clear up the mystery carried my husband far into the field of military technique. My youngest boy, Arthur, twelve years old then, was aide here. The child happened to be with his father in the committee-room when the board of military affairs was conducting a microscopic examination of exploded shells picked up in the streets of Brownsville. Even with strong magnifying glasses the Senators on that committee had a wry time of it, trying to catch the minute indentations. So they called on Arthur to do it for them; an easy thing for strong young eyes. It is a vignette on the margin of the Brownsville canvas—a rather frail little boy in a sailor suit, the center of that group of gray-beards.

In this connection I may recall a dramatic point in the testimony, widely known as the "story of the four guns." Every gun, of course, leaves a mark on the shell fired from it which is as individual as the human fingerprint. Shells picked up in the streets after the raid showed under a microscope indentations made by four special guns known to have been issued to Company B. But, on the undisputed testimony of white officers these guns were not used that night. Three of them, when submitted for the inspection which was immediately made, were perfectly clean and bright and were proved not to have been fired. The fourth gun, belonging to a sergeant on furlough from Fort Niobrara, was in an army chest with the lid screwed on under a pile of baggage in a locked-up storeroom. How was it, then, that shells from these unused guns were found in the streets after the shooting-up? Light on this point is thrown by the following paragraph from Foraker's summing up of Brownsville testimony before the Senate:

"Before this microscopic investigation was made or any such question was foreseen, it was established by uncontradicted testimony that Company B took with it to Brownsville as a part of its baggage a box containing from 1,600 to 2,000 exploded shells, with a proportionate number of clips, and that after arrival at Brownsville this box, opened, stood on the back porch of B barracks, where anyone passing might have access to it and remove shells and clips from it. The microscopic report says that the shells picked up in the streets of Brownsville and put in evidence were, beyond a reasonable doubt, fired out of these four guns belonging to B company. If so, then it also follows that they were fired, not in Brownsville, but at Fort Niobrara, and that they were found in the streets, not because they fell there when fired, but because they had been placed there by persons unknown, who had secured them from this box of shells standing on the back porch and easily accessible to anyone disposed to remove them therefrom. In other words, the microscopic inspection shows conclusively, not that the soldiers were guilty of the firing, but that the soldiers were free from such guilt."

The circumstance brought a great many people over to the battalion's side and strengthened the theory that the Brownsville raid was the work of Mexicans dressed in the stolen uniforms of United States soldiers. As it all comes back to me, I wonder if some one who may read this book and who knows the real truth about Brownsville may not be moved to come out and tell it?

Great interest was taken in the Texas issue by officers in the service. Some had been commanders of these same colored troops; many were our personal friends. Officers who had retired felt free to express their support of my husband's side of the case; those still in the service naturally were discreet. Oddly, though, things were to be given a turn that allowed even these officers to show their colors:

Not suddenly, but subtly, a queer change came over the social atmosphere of our house. What was it? People began to change their calling hours from daytime to evening. Men who were for my husband, and helping him collect information, called only after dark. Under night's cover even the active army officers showed their sympathy. Sometimes men who, in the usual course of affairs, would have come themselves, didn't come; they sent their wives to see me. I would receive them and give to my husband the information they brought from their husbands. This undercover approach puzzled us. Then we began to get it—*we were being watched*.

It took very little investigation to learn that Secret Service men employed by the government were keeping their eyes on our house. The name of everybody who

called was put on record; if the visit was thought to have
any connection with Brownsville, it was reported to the
President. Official interferences went even further.
Senator Foraker's mail was tampered with. Letters
showed that they had been opened and resealed. There
must have been general suspicion of this, for at the same
time letters intended for my husband very often came
inclosed in envelopes addressed to me. The Senator himself was warned to look out for postal spies. One day in
the summer of 1907 he was in his office in the Traction
Building, Cincinnati, when a friend in the northern part
of the state called him on long distance. "Be careful what
you say in your letters," he said. "I have learned that they
are being opened in the Post Office at Washington."*
This man knew the postmaster at the capital. He con-
fronted him with the outrage; asked him why he permitted it. The man looked unhappy.

"I am helpless," he said. "I have orders that this must
be done. I am ashamed to do it . . . but I have to obey."

Spies struck at our social life. Very much in evidence
at afternoon receptions, at all functions that could be
crashed, was a "gentleman detective," an American
journalist, afterwards in the World War in German pay.
During the Brownsville period it seemed to me that I
saw this man at every turn. Everybody knew what he
was doing—eavesdropping, reporting, coming back to

* Senator Tillman, in his difficulties with Roosevelt, had a similar experience:
Dunn's "From Harrison to Harding", v. 2, p. 92.

overhear more; "a picker-up of unconsidered trifles" of talk and hurrying with them to official headquarters. One had to be alert. Mrs. Fairbanks, wife of the Vice-President, was an old school friend of mine. I saw her often. Whenever she and I wished to talk at a reception, Mrs. Fairbanks would retreat to a far corner, stand with her back to the wall so that she could keep an eye on everybody, then signal me to come close to her and we would speak in whispers.

Poor Mrs. Fairbanks! She must have been quite worn out by Brownsville. She was, of course, very often at the White House, and constantly meeting the President at Cabinet dinners, where her place was on his right. The President couldn't keep off the subject of Foraker and his wicked interest in the black battalion. He would pound the table at a point. The glasses shivered.

Everybody caught it. General Miles, coming to our house one day from luncheon with Mr. James R. Garfield—a Roosevelt train-bearer—reported the wave of indignation which engulfed Mr. Garfield's generous board because "Foraker was giving us so much trouble." Well, there are many Senators and members who give a President no trouble whatever. They vote amiably for measures as it seems expedient and easy to vote. Simpler, certainly, than my husband's principle of not voting on any bill without knowing all about it. This swallows up one's leisure (Foraker always was slavishly absorbed), but one emerges with a lively and informed, if complicating, point of view.

As time went on everybody on the inside of things adopted the "hush" note. One talked guardedly, looking over one's shoulder. Washington became a haunted house. We lived for months under this strain. Men with a furtive slant to their eyes were on hand when the postman came in the morning; relays were still hanging around when my daughters went to balls at night. Upon my soul, I don't know how we ever lived through those days!

Curious circumstances came to light during my husband's efforts to get justice for the battalion. One day the Senator received a letter from a woman who wrote that she had lived in Brownsville; her husband had been Governor of Texas. She knew Brownsville people well, knew all about the colored soldiers, did not believe that they had anything to do with the "shooting up," and offered new theories as to who did do it. My husband asked me to see this lady. One of the strange things she told me was this: Judge Fletcher, a Texan and a personal friend, had presided over the court in which thirteen of the soldiers had been tried. The trial brought out nothing to show that the men were guilty and the judge discharged them as innocent. Two months later Judge Fletcher was found in his bed, shot through the head. All reference to the murder was rigorously excluded from the government's investigation. Yet curiosity flamed as to who shot the judge. Not the colored soldiers whom he had befriended. Who then?

It was no use. Brownsville became a monstrous labyrinth, baffling, icily hopeless the more my husband persisted in his efforts to get to the light. As an instance, there was the matter of the bullets found imbedded in wood that were fired on the night of the raid. Certain army officers, deeply interested, secured these bullets and sent them to Foraker. The Senator had them analyzed and found that they contained a certain amount of antimony. Consulting the regulations which govern the making of bullets for the United States, he found that no antimony was permitted. He at once called up the munitions firm who had the contract to make our army bullets, and asked them, Did they ever use antimony in making U. S. army bullets? No, they said, they never used antimony; against the law, etc. Foraker asked them to put that statement in writing and send it to him. They said they would. They never did.

Later when all kinds of evidence were being presented in the investigation directed by the President, Mr. Roosevelt sent to the Senate a statement, signed by the same munition-makers who had told my husband that they never had used antimony, in which it was admitted that in February, 1906, they had made a certain number of bullets containing antimony for the army. This started fresh speculation as to Brownsville guilt and general wonderment: why did the munitions-makers give a definite "No" to Senator Foraker and a submissive "Yes" to the President?

My husband was never able to pin an interested official down on a single vital point that arose. What could one do against a block like that? All that Senator Foraker was working for was to get a fair trial for the soldiers before the correct officials. He was out for the truth, only the truth; he did not care whether blacks or whites did the shooting. It simply was not in him, as an experienced lawyer, to sit back and see one hundred and sixty-seven men punished who had not been proved guilty; it was not in him as a man to submit to this decision for no stronger reason than that the President of the United States had made it and refused to retract it.

But Mr. Roosevelt held the strings of power. The country had his decision and, like one "bearing letters of marque from God," as Wendell Phillips said wonderingly of John Brown, he stuck to it, marshaling the government to support him, come weal, come woe. Thus impelled, Brownsville in its course described a trajectory of mischief that would have frightened off a man less fearless than Foraker. But my husband stayed in the fight; the Senators fell away from Brownsville like autumn leaves before a high wind—the wind blew from the White House—but Foraker stayed in the fight. Apostates were regretful in the cloakroom. There was a Western Senator, Turncoat will stand for his name then as it stands today: he assured my husband that he would support him; two weeks later he was sorry, but he couldn't keep his promise. The President was making it too unpleasant. Foraker got quite used to these furtive regrets. There was lone Senator Bailey. Southern pressure enters here. After complimenting my husband on a Brownsville speech in the Senate, he turned to me. "I think your husband is absolutely in the right," he said, a soft, cottonfield voice; "I admire him. I'd like to stand by him. But, Mrs. Foraker, I am a Democrat from Texas." In effect, the Senate had married a wife and could not come.

I suppose all this braiding of I-would-ifs and I'm-sorry-buts, in such quixotic circumstances, was inevitable and understandable, the Fifteenth Psalm's portrait of a good citizen to the contrary.

Outside of the government crowd Foraker had immense numbers of cohorts. Old foes took off their hats. In an article entitled "Cleveland's Opinion of Men," *McClure's Magazine*, April, 1907, ex-President Cleveland is quoted thus:

"I have not known anything in years which has pleased me more than the Ohio Senator's [Foraker] attitude upon current public questions. Whatever may be the whole truth about the Brownsville case, it has been a display of genuine courage for a Republican Senator to take the position assumed by Mr. Foraker. It is due to him that there has been a real discussion of the President's action in all its bearings."

Mr. Cleveland and Foraker, when the former was President and my husband Governor of Ohio, had a spirited tilt on the subject of returning captured Confederate flags to the Southern States. (And for that, though it's another story, Mrs. Cleveland, at the Philadelphia Centennial in 1887, thought she wouldn't return my bow!) But the battalion barbarity was too much for everybody not muffled by self-interest. The unprejudiced public and the strongest newspapers in the North stood by my husband. Yet in the end, officially, Foraker came to press his fight for justice almost alone, to lead the forlornest of hopes. There was something gallant in this that touched the imagination. A man who would act thus, would risk pulling his house about his head, could be moved only by the sincerest conviction that a great wrong was being done.

Mr. Roosevelt alone knew otherwise. Yet in spite of obedient whips he must have felt himself rather badly driven in those days. He wrote a great many letters to editors of religious papers, to learned chancellors, and to others, justifying his stand and attacking everybody who dared raise his voice for the battalion. He was "amazed and indignant at the attitude of the negroes" . . . at the attitude of "short-sighted white sentimentalists" . . . at that of "Northern politicians who wish to keep the negro vote" . . . at that of "self-seeking demagogues in our Northern states."* When Brownsville was over, the only

* Bishop's *Roosevelt*, vol. ii, p. 28.

vituperatives left breathing in the President's large collection were "idiot," "swine," and "liar." The staunch old dears!

Writing to Mr. George F. Spinney, of New York, as early as January 22, 1907,* the President said that he had warned the Senate, who were "insisting that they could not desert Foraker, . . . that I should state most unhesitatingly, and whenever it became necessary in public, that the opposition to me on Brownsville was simply a cloak to cover antagonism to my actions about trusts, swollen fortunes, and the like." This fanciful linking of Crœsus and the colored man pleased the President. He was to use it again at Philippi.

In the interval Mr. Roosevelt kept up an insistent drumming that Foraker was not after justice for the soldiers, but votes for himself. The holier-than-thouism in this is almost awing. On March 13, 1903, Mr. Roosevelt, in a letter to a member of the National Republican Committee, a man with Southern sympathies, said: "The most damaging thing to me anyone can do is to give the impression that in what I have been trying to do for the negro I have been actuated by political motives.†

Ah no! Theodore Roosevelt must not be "damaged" by such an imputation; but let another man, a man whose sincerity, as the nation knew, was only equaled by his courage in backing his convictions—let another man

* Bishop's *Roosevelt,* vol. i, p. 247.
† *Ibid.*

seek to help the negro, and Mr. Roosevelt rushes foaming to "damage" him, right and left, with loud cries of "political motives." All this was long ago, but no one living then, no one left today to remember, could honestly think that Foraker, fighting for the rights of that wretched battalion, gave one thought to votes, black or white.

Yes, I think Mr. Roosevelt began to be sadly badgered by the "Brownsville nightmare"; his phrase. We were growing a little wan under it ourselves, what with spies in Sixteenth Street and the strange, impenetrable stone wall that loomed between my husband and his every effort to bring to light the dark truth. It was at this point that Mr. Roosevelt betrayed what may have been uneasiness over the outcome, in spite of his noble support, or merely sheer exasperation:

He sent Senator Penrose to see my husband. It was in the evening, of course. Mr. Penrose had his own reason for adopting after dark calling hours at the Foraker house. He brought Foraker a message from the President. It was this: if Senator Foraker would drop the Brownsville fight Mr. Roosevelt was prepared to offer him any distinguished post which he might desire. An ambassadorship, perhaps. If so, which embassy would the Senator prefer? This was quite comic, this idea of transporting, or rather, deporting, the troubling Foraker to foreign shores. But it didn't make Foraker smile. He only stared at the Senator from Pennsylvania. A treacled

bribe? . . . from President Roosevelt? Many thanks . . .
he wasn't taking any. Brownsville would be fought to a
finish.

And that, Mr. President, was that.

Brownsville turned on the fact that the soldiers had
been discharged without a fair trial. Foraker would not
give up until such a trial was granted. He finally succeeded in forcing the President to appoint a Court of
Inquiry—six officers. Two and a half years had passed.
In that time the soldiers, scattered all over the country,
had been hounded and harassed by officers and secretly
employed agents of the government. Anything to get a
confession! The men's discharge by the President must
be vindicated!

When the names of Mr. Roosevelt's court were made
public, Senator Foraker met General Corbin. "You've
got your commission," said the General, "but it's packed.
The verdict will be one that will save the President's face.
You'll see."

That is precisely what happened. Everything possible
was done by Foraker to get before the commission *his*
facts, long and laboriously gathered at great personal expense. *He could not get them in.* The trial proved that
"Nobody is guilty." I quote the New York *World*,
"therefore the verdict, *à la Roosevelt*, is that 'Everybody
is guilty.'" Once more those one hundred and sixty-
seven soldiers were thrown out to their dusty wandering,

discredited and sore but obstinately sticking to their denial that they had anything whatever to do with the
"shooting-up" of Brownsville.

During the Brownsville years my husband never went
to the Senate without having with him all his notes on
the case. He never knew what might be sprung. Once,
in a message from the President, a detective sent by Mr.
Roosevelt to gather evidence against the battalion was
referred to by name. Instantly, something like a hiss
came from the newspaper men's gallery. The detective's
reputation was such that no one could believe a word he
said.

Fortunately, before the President's message was read,
Foraker, warned by a telegram, was able to read a statement of his own which was on the calendar for a later
date. Mr. Roosevelt's detective reported (his report was
included in the Presidential message) a "confession" im-
plicating the battalion in the Brownsville raid. Foraker's
statement disposed of this confession as pure pinchbeck.
It had been extorted under terrorizing threats from one
of the wretched, dogged, and bewildered pariahs that the
black troops had become. This was part of the sensational
Macon, Georgia, testimony which was so stultified that
even the White House crowd threw it out.

A deplorable mockery, Brownsville. It ended, like the
true farce it was, in a most cynical climax. For Mr.
Roosevelt, it is well known, won in the finals. Won, in
spite of the fact that not one single thread of testimony

was ever produced to show that the black battalion shot up that sleeping town on the banks of the Rio Grande.

". . . if the Government," said Foraker, "had spent the one-tenth part to discover the men who shot up Brownsville that it did spend to convict its innocent soldiers of a crime they never committed, the truth would have been easily and long ago established."

One thing was established, however. It grew out of Brownsville and became immediately clear. This was Mr. Roosevelt's determination that Senator Foraker, too potent, too plaguey, too unweldable, should be banished from political life.

The decree was dearly to the taste of our own Julius Cæsar, and within his power.

CHAPTER XXI

JUGGERNAUT

AMONG the milestones guiding me over the long
trail that threads my story, I now come to one so
much less happy than any other I could wish not to recall
it. Yet not to do so would be as a traveler who, having
made a journey with a friend he greatly loved, tells everything that happened, but passes over in silence that moment on the road when his companion received a death
blow. What I have to say in chapters immediately following I say in justice to my husband, for whom, before
justice could speak, the end came. I write without bitterness. If I cannot quite write without feeling, I must be
forgiven. It is hard to put things from the heart in irons.

The 18th of September, 1908, remains for me a day of
rare beauty darkened suddenly by a poisonous fog.

That morning, as usual, I opened the newspapers to
mark items of interest to my husband before the papers
were sent to him. No need to pencil the feature of that
date; a choice morsel it was, indeed, running blackly
across the front page. It was furnished by William Randolph Hearst, then campaigning the country in the interest of a party of his own called the Independence

League. The night before, at a political meeting in Columbus, Ohio, Mr. Hearst had read a number of letters written to my husband by John D. Archbold, vice-president of the Standard Oil Company. The letters had been stolen from their files and sold in the market place. They were construed as showing that Foraker, while serving in the United States Senate, had been secretly employed on legal business for the Standard Oil.

Circumstances sensationally heightened the charge. The Standard Oil Company, among other great industries, had been the notorious object of prosecution and punishment by the Federal government. The whole country was swept by a mad rage at wealth. The most damaging thing that could be done to a public man was to link his name with the trusts.

Foraker met the accusation like a whirlwind. The afternoon papers of the same day carried his clear and complete setting forth of his association with Standard Oil from the beginning. The correspondence, of which Mr. Hearst had chosen to read but one side, was given in full. The letters made public told of various services which my husband had rendered the Standard Oil Company and been most conservatively paid for. They dated from 1898. Point by point Foraker proved that his work for the Standard Oil was over and done with long before any Federal legislation against the company was proposed or foreseen. That it had to do with the company's legitimate reorganization under the laws of Ohio.

That his conduct, in undertaking it, was perfectly correct and abundantly precedented. That far from being secret, it was with full general knowledge that he had had these, then, most desirable clients at the time he was reëlected to the Senate.

Myself, I remember how open this fact was. I was very proud of my husband, indeed. Had he not succeeded the great Mr. Choate, leaving to be our ambassador to England, as advisory counsel to one of the powerful industries of the world? The only thing secret about it was my personal thrill that my husband had formed a brilliant connection which every lawyer coveted. I am too humanly a woman not to admit that.

Mr. Hearst, I understand, had had the Archbold letters in his archives for three years. Psychologically he chose the moment for their release: we were on the eve of a presidential reëlection and that of my husband's reëlection to the Senate. A ripening hour for roorbacks.

At St. Louis, on the evening following the first reading, more stolen letters were produced. One of them, the only one of importance, started a shocked hum that must have made Foraker's enemies rock with rapture. The Big News was brief—Mr. Archbold simply referred my husband to an "inclosed certificate of deposit for fifty thousand dollars . . . in accordance with our understanding. . . . Your letter states the conditions correctly." He adds, "I trust that the transaction will be successfully consummated."

A white page with a few words distorted into black insinuation.

For the first, last, only time in my life I saw my husband at a loss. He couldn't remember ever having had such a letter. Couldn't remember ever having received such a sum from Mr. Archbold. (A lawyer's memory for a fifty-thousand-dollar retainer is usually excellent.) Remembered nothing whatever about such a transaction!

We were an excited breakfast-table group that morning. "You can't remember it," said Benson, (to Benson his father was the man who could do no wrong). "Can't remember it, so it never happened. All you've got to do is to deny it." He thought that settled it; he took some more sliced peaches. But his father said: no, he felt that there must have been such a letter; he would find it, or a clue to it, in his files.

In the end my husband called up our house in Washington (his official offices were in the house) and had a search made which resulted in a transaction being recalled that had gone entirely from his mind:

Back in 1902 there had been a movement on foot to buy the Ohio *State Journal*. Mr. J. Linn Rodgers, of Columbus, held an option on it; he applied to Foraker, a friend, to help him raise the money to buy it. The Republican Party needed a paper in southern Ohio to combat the Hanna opposition to Mr. Roosevelt's nomination for the presidency. My husband saw the value of securing the *Journal*; he applied to a number of people for loans (the price was high), including, at Mr. Rodgers' suggestion, Mr. Archbold of the Standard Oil.

At first Mr. Archbold agreed to a loan of thirty-five thousand dollars. Then one or two who were in the venture dropped out; the rest were asked to increase their amounts. Mr. Archbold raised his to fifty thousand dollars. The expressions quoted in the note which went with this check, and which were advanced as proof that Foraker's hands were deep in Standard Oil money, referred to the terms of the loan: five annual payments; five per cent interest; stock proportional to loan as collateral . . . the usual conditions of a usual business loan made, not to Foraker individually, but as the representative of a group of men united in a perfectly legitimate and sound enterprise.

They lost the paper, after all. Somebody, having dined happily, gave away the fact that the "Foraker crowd" were after it. At once, and for a much larger sum, it was bought by the "Hanna crowd." And Foraker, thanks to long-distance and a lynx-eyed clerk, was able to publish in the afternoon papers of September 19th, the true facts, word for word, as given in his reply, February 14, 1902, to Mr. Archbold's letter to him.

"I herewith send you," Foraker wrote (after telling of the project's failure) ". . . N. Y. draft for $50,000 . . . as repayment of the money advanced by you on the above-mentioned account."*

* All letters of this correspondence are in the Library of Congress at Washington.

A complete rebuttal of the whole accusation.

After the newspaper project's collapse Foraker had nothing further to do with the Standard Oil Company except to help frame the Elkins law, under which statute Judge Landis imposed on the company a fine of over twenty-nine million dollars. Nothing proved more conclusively Foraker's complete detachment from Standard Oil interests than his connection with the Federal prosecution of the Standard Oil Company. I may add that another letter, implicatively read, linking the fifty thousand with a mystifying "Jones bill," could not be connected with my husband's name at all. Foraker, himself, was unable to recall the bill, and the letter, if Mr. Archbold ever wrote it, was lost in the unstemable stream of letters which Senators and members of the House receive asking their help to kill or to promote this bill or that—the Smith, Jones, or Robinson bill. (When my husband dismantled his Washington offices, five or six hundred thousand of such letters were destroyed.)

Two days after the loan-letter's appearance was the big Republican mass-meeting opening the campaign for Mr. Taft as President. Foraker had been asked to preside as chairman. We were driving into town, my husband and I.

"I shall not go to Music Hall on Tuesday night," he said. "These letters will have a very mischievous effect. I can help Taft best by staying away."

I reassured him: he would be certain to be able to un-
tangle the thing . . . to clear up the mystery by his files.

"Yes, of course," he said, "but it will take time. And
I shall do nothing that may react on Taft."

The friendship between Mr. Taft and my husband
began as far back as 1878. Taft, just graduated from
Yale, appeared in Foraker's courtroom as a local reporter
for the *Cincinnati Commercial*. There was instant sympathy between the twenty-one-year-old collegian and the
thirty-two-year-old magistrate. Foraker liked Taft's
smile, liked his agreeable manner, liked his type of mind.
It was characteristic of my husband to begin considering
then what he might be able to do to show helpfully his
regard for this delightful new friend, just starting in life.

The chance came when my husband was Governor.
Judge Judson Harmon of the Superior Court of Cincinnati had resigned. The office is elective in Ohio.
Foraker ignored the circumstance of Taft's youth and
appointed him to succeed Judge Harmon, a man very
much his senior. This was in 1887.

In a letter of thanks to the Governor, Taft wrote,
January 31st of that year: "Considering the opportunity
so honorable a position offers to a man of my age and
circumstances, my debt to you is very great." In another
letter, April 5th, about the same appointment, he empha-
sizes "how highly I appreciate your kindness and how

much I value the great opportunity you have afforded me."

By another year the association of the two men had become singularly close. Taft wrote to my husband, June 7, 1888 (in a letter asking his aid towards the appointment of a college friend, William Dixon, as prosecuting attorney of Hamilton County): "I only wish that you could join my wife and me in our trip to Europe this summer." Replying, Foraker urged him "not to get drowned. That would spoil the program I have for you, and if you knew how much store I place by it, you would understand what a serious disappointment it would be."

There was something a little touching about Foraker's quite boyish enthusiasm for young Will Taft; his ambition for him. Foraker's early life had been a stern struggle; in Mr. Taft's background he saw all the brilliance and charm of association that for him had glamour, and that he had missed. The political course of the two men ran differently, too. Except the minor post of supervisor of elections, my husband was elected to every office he held. Mr. Taft was appointed to all his offices, barring his second term as judge of the Supreme Court of Cincinnati and his greatest honor.

September 17, 1889, Mr. Taft writes Foraker to ask "whether you can conscientiously add another to the many obligations I am under to you by writing a letter to the President recommending me for the vacancy on the Supreme Bench." Whether the appointment comes off or not, Taft goes on to say, "I shall continue to be grateful as ever for the opportunity which you have given, both in the appointment and in a renomination to my present position."

In this particular appeal it is interesting that Taft in his earliest thirties and after two years as judge of the Cincinnati Superior Court should present himself for the highest of judiciary distinctions, the bench of the Supreme Court of the United States, an appointment for life. Admirable instance of one heart, one way. Mr. Taft took his own measure for judicial ermine at an age when the average alumnus is bewilderedly trying on careers.

In furtherance of the Supreme Court program Foraker did write to the President. The idea was dismissed, but Foraker's letter admittedly influenced Mr. Harrison to appoint Judge Taft of Cincinnati Solicitor-General of the United States. My husband inclosed his letter to President Harrison with a line to Taft. The latter replied, September 25, 1889:

"I am very grateful to you for the handsome and much too complimentary words of your letter in my behalf to the President. If anything could make a success of what in the nature of things is a very remote chance, I am sure your support given in such an emphatic way will do it."

A letter from Foraker to Taft about this appointment, January 31, 1890: "The special feature of good fortune that I see in it [the Solicitor-Generalship] lies beyond that office in the other position to which I can clearly see that it leads . . . the bench of the Supreme Court. When you reach that ultimate honor I shall be satisfied, and not before." When the honor, so long coveted, so long visioned, came at last, the friend and prophet had gone.

In 1900 President McKinley consulted my husband about the qualifications of William H. Taft for the post of Governor-General of the Philippines. How warmly Foraker spoke of Taft, and what this meant to him, is shown in a letter from Mr. Taft to Foraker on February 11th of that year:

"I am very much obliged to you for the kind words of your letter and the approval of the appointment which you expressed to the President when he consulted you as to its wisdom before he made it. I shall always have a feeling that the course of my life has been largely due to you who gave me the opportunity and first honor from which all that I have had since has easily flowed."

Foraker never relaxed his eager, loyal support. An instance of this will be recalled by every member who was in the Senate on May 3, 1903, when Senator Culberson accused Mr. Taft of evasion and misleading statements in his testimony before the Philippine Committee.

The Senator from Texas had hardly concluded his arraignment when Foraker was on his feet, informing the Senate with blazing vigor that Governor Taft could not be charged with "withholding any truth. . . . If there is a man in all the world absolutely faithful to the truth in any statement that he may make . . . that man is William Howard Taft. I have known him all my life. I know whereof I speak." The Senate meekly subsided. "Foraker fairly pounced on 'em," a newspaper man reported; "Taft has always been his pet rising star."

Mr. Taft remembered this defense three years later when he testified before the Canal Committee. He appealed to Foraker to read his testimony and to again protect him in the Senate if any more shafts were hurled. Foraker familiarized himself with the whole case. Indeed, he was ready for them if they attacked Taft. In him (Taft knew this; it was compact with the sympathy between them) the younger man had at all times an ardent champion.

Foraker, incidentally, never made but one request of Mr. Taft. This was the promotion to brigadier-general of Colonel Kingsbury, husband of the daughter of General Slocum, Foraker's adored old commander. Colonel Kingsbury was not made brigadier-general.

On June 19, 1908, Taft wrote to my husband thanking him for congratulations on his nomination to the Presidency:

"I have never ceased to remember that I owe to you my first substantial start in public life and that it came without solicitation."

Three months later, the disaster that threatened Foraker brought Mr. Taft an opportunity for a rather sounder proof of friendship than the graceful phrases of a well-bred man.

Two or three hours after the explosion of Mr. Hearst's oily time fuse I went to my husband's office. I found the whole force jubilant. "We've got the letter" . . . everybody spoke at once. "I knew you'd find it," I said. Benson was there, laughing and talking with a crowd of newspaper men. "What I couldn't understand," I heard him say, "was father having fifty thousand dollars and not letting the rest of us in on it. It wasn't like father to hold out on the family."

In another room was my husband with Senator Crane and Senator Dick. "We've been trying to find you all morning, Mrs. Foraker," said Senator Crane. "We want you to know just what we are doing." He then asked me to read a letter which my husband had written to Mr. Taft, then in Cincinnati. In it Foraker announced his decision not to attend the Music Hall meeting.

"I take this decision," he wrote, "not because I deem the answers I have made (to the Archbold letters) insufficient, nor because of any lack of loyalty to your cause, but only because I do not wish to do anything that might injure the cause or embarrass you personally."

Senator Crane looked at me. "I don't think that Mr. Taft will consent to such a thing," he said; "we're taking the letter to him." He picked up his hat. "I don't think for a moment that he will consent. Do you?"

I looked at Senator Crane. "If the positions of the two men were reversed," I said, "if my husband were the presidential candidate and Mr. Taft the Senator, I know what would happen. My husband would refuse to believe the charge brought against an intimate old friend. He would recognize it as an election trick and denounce it. He would insist that the Senator appear on the platform with him—or he would not appear. But now——"

I began making points in the carpet with my parasol. Somehow, I could not go on.

Mr. Taft was busy on the telephone when the two Senators arrived. He was talking to Mr. Roosevelt. When he read the letter, he appeared "disturbed and embarrassed." He then asked to be excused from saying more than that he hoped Senator Foraker would be willing to confer with the committee and to abide by their decision.

My husband immediately withdrew from any part in the campaign.

Mr. Taft had but one comment to make upon the Foraker crisis:

"I will not strike a man when he is down," he said.

Reporters' pencils moved swiftly; presses all over the country began to sing, "I-will-not-strike—will-not-strike—will-not-strike-a-man when-he-is down-down." . . .

Taft never added to these words. He stood by in silence, watching the wave engulf his old friend.

CHAPTER XXII

THE PROPHET MICAH AND THE GOOD LIEUTENANT

I AM perfectly aware that Mr. Taft was in a most difficult position. He was the Republican candidate for the Presidency, and a presidential candidate is not a free soul. He cannot give independent expression to fine, natural impulses. He cannot save drowning friends—unless the party needs them. He is in bondage to his backers.

I have always liked to think that in his heart Mr. Taft did not fail Foraker, that he said to himself, as Foraker had said of him when he was publicly attacked and before he had been able to meet the charge against him: "If there is a man in the world absolutely faithful to the truth of any statement that he may make, that man is Joseph Benson Foraker. I have known him all my life. I know whereof I speak."

But out of the heart the mouth did not speak. Mr. Taft at that moment was "such a good lieutenant" (Mr. Wister so quotes Mr. Roosevelt)—that he made no gesture till he received his general's orders. They were quick in coming:

"I have seen the correspondence between Archbold

and Foraker published in the morning papers," wrote
Mr. Roosevelt to Mr. Taft on September 19th, the very
day that Foraker's vindication was published in the afternoon papers. . . . "Personally," the President continues
—"personally, if I were running for President, I should,
in view of these disclosures, decline to appear on the platform with Foraker. . . . I would like to see you in the
strongest and most emphatic way do what I should do in
your place."*

And Taft did.

An effort has been made to shift on to many shoulders
the responsibility for Foraker's defeat. Mr. Hearst had
been two hours late, at least very late, at the Columbus
meeting. His great audience waited for him. Did it scent
trouble? The public loves trouble. It waited patiently.
Long after my husband's death I was told by his former
secretary, Mr. Charles L. Kurtz, that Mr. Hearst's
tardiness was due to the fact that he was at the telephone, talking with the Chicago headquarters of the
Republican National Committee. In view of what
followed, there was something to support the belief that ambushed Republican Foraker-antagonists knew
about the letters and in whose hands they were, and that
Mr. Hearst let the Columbus crowd wait while he conferred with the committee as to springing the sensation
then and there.

* Bishop's *Roosevelt*, v. ii, p. 96.

Myself, I am inclined to think that Mr. Hearst's acute sense of the startling would have needed no quickening to tell him that the moment was dropping-ripe for his own purpose, whatever his purpose was; and hardly would he have risked any preliminary nibbling at such a tidbit as he had to offer. More to the point is the fact that even before Mr. Hearst's concoction began to brew, a demand for Foraker's head upon a charger was in the air.

The Intransigent in that affair was Theodore Roosevelt.

After "Brownsville" the breach between the President and my husband had hopelessly widened; there was no seeing across it to any bayou of peace. As Mr. Roosevelt was then at the height of his popularity and power, he could not only say who should be the next President; he could move very formidably if he decided to crush an opponent. One of his subordinate leaders, Nicholas Longworth, had filled the late summer air with breezy predictions that "Foraker would be a dead one by the middle of September." But, dear me! Foraker so often had been sat upon by political coroners, always with a merry, mortuary note in the findings—

> "The White Turkey is dead!
> The White Turkey is dead!!"
> How the news through the barnyard went flying!

Reports invariably were "greatly exaggerated." Foraker was a very Antæus on the rebound.

Now, however, a new element fortified attack. Mr. Taft's silent acquiescence to the attitude created against Foraker and inimically maintained, in the face of irrefutable facts, turned the tide quite hopelessly.

The promptness with which Mr. Roosevelt, having "read the morning papers," told his lieutenant-candidate what he was to do, showed that, in this instance, bad news was such good news on no account must one wait for a possible denial.

Mr. Roosevelt had complained that there "wasn't enough ginger in the Taft campaign" to suit him. Well, here was his ginger.

Apropos of his quick orders to his presidential candidate Mr. Roosevelt wrote almost in the same breath September 22, to Lawrence Abbott of *The Outlook*: "In this Foraker affair I made up my mind that I would hit from the shoulder inasmuch as Taft did not." The prize-fighting figure is prettily developed: "If a man wishes to win, it is absolutely necessary that he shall knock out his opponent when he has him groggy."*

I think any man, even a man so quite certain about everything as Mr. Roosevelt was, would have been momentarily groggy from the blow of a lie broadcast from sea to sea. With the truth to revive him, Foraker recovered with amazing swiftness. He stood free of the charge; clearly, cleanly-cut free. But all this was as if it were not. "Foraker exonerated" was the last thing the

* Bishop's *Roosevelt*, v. ii, p. 99.

administration ring desired, the last thing in which the great political Dempsey was interested. "Foraker eliminated" was written on the wall.

The retiring President's instructions to Mr. Taft came before Mr. Roosevelt had inscribed in the pocket Testaments given to the first American troops in June, 1917, a verse from Micah, beginning, "What more doth the Lord require of thee than to do justice." Mr. Roosevelt could not have discovered Micah when he struck with injustice at my husband, with that curiously cruel injustice that does not wait until a man has had even the flash of a split-second to defend himself, that accepts with instant eagerness the word of a defamer.

He was not to redeem this wrong for eight years. On June 28, 1916, Mr. Roosevelt, following my husband's just-published *Notes of a Busy Life*, wrote Foraker the following letter:

Oyster Bay,
Long Island, N. Y.

June 28th, 1916.

My dear Senator:

I have just finished your two volumes, which I have read with great interest. Of course, there are certain portions as to which you and I will continue to differ, but if I ever get the chance to speak publicly, I shall elaborate what I said in speaking of you in the libel suit.

Not only do I admire your entire courage and straightfor-

wardness (in the railway-rate legislation I respected you a
thousand times more than I did many of the men who voted
for the bill), but I also grew steadily more and more to realize
your absolute Americanism, and your capacity for generosity
and disinterestedness. Besides, you knew the need that the
freeman shall be able to fight, under penalty of ceasing to be a
freeman.

Too many of our representatives in the Senate and the Lower
House could not be persauded to take any interest in any matter in which they or their districts were not personally concerned. But, as far as you were concerned when the question
came up of dealing with the Philippines or Porto Rico or
Panama, or the navy, or anything involving America's international good name, or the doing of our duty to help people
who had no champion; I knew that if I could convince you
that my view was right I could count upon your ardent cham-
pionship of the cause. I had much the same feeling about O. H.
Platt of Connecticut and Cockerill of Missouri; but in neither
case did they look upon international affairs as you and I did.

There is no use in raking up the past now, but there were
some things told me against you, or in reference to you, which
(when I consider what I know now of my informants) would
have carried no weight with me at the time had I been as well
informed as at present.

Now for something entirely different. If you are ever in this
neighborhood, I wish you would let me know, and come down
for lunch or dinner. I have some questions I wish to ask you
about the battle of Chickamauga; this being in connection with
the work of a cousin of mine now dead, a man named Gracey.

Faithfully yours,
(Signed) Theodore Roosevelt.

That reference to the need of the freeman is significant. "The need that the freeman shall be able to fight under penalty of ceasing to be a freeman" was Foraker's whole code; it was at the root of everyone of his differences with Roosevelt.

The two men never saw each other again.

Considering the extreme bitterness of "Brownsville," which perhaps made it impossible for Roosevelt to act in the Foraker crisis other than as he did, considering everything that worked against unity between the two men, I find Mr. Roosevelt's retractive expression generous. Moreover, there was human-beingness in his implacably pressing the advantage against Foraker, wasting no time on sorries. It was so honestly of the man.

Mr. Taft's attitude is less reconcilable. He was, it is true, hampered by his position; he was hampered, perhaps, even more by the dictatorship. In June, 1907, Mr. Roosevelt wrote to Senator Lodge:

"Taft, thank Heaven, is up to the point of making an aggressive fight against Foraker, and anything you think he ought to say on the subject of Brownsville you can confidentially send him."[*]

Perhaps, then, this last stand was inevitable. Inevitable, perhaps, that Mr. Taft should have allowed the treacherous tide to race against Foraker without lifting his voice in one staying word for the friend who through twenty

---

* Roosevelt-Lodge correspondence, vol. ii, p. 272.

long years devotedly had served him. Pruning official inevitabilities, still the fact stares at one that my husband's complete exoneration left nothing to the circumstances which defeated him but Taft's action.

I am eighty-four years old. I have been in politics always. I have seen many instances of political passion deflecting the loyalties of men. Yet I can recall nothing more cynical than the averted face of William Howard Taft, "not a politician," when Foraker was battling for his life. Most pictures in my gallery of memory have softened like old prints, they've hung so long. Only remains undimmed this single portrait. I wish it were not so. I wish the picture would fade. But it will not fade. For me it was too cruelly etched to change.

Foraker's refutal of Standard Oil complicity brought swift recognition of the fact that the charge against him was a campaign lie and it was nothing more. A rush of sympathy came from fellow members of the Senate and from hundreds of officials who had worked with my husband, who knew him. Not one but understood that he, like every man in public life, was ever at the mercy of the cabalist. Senator Lodge wrote to Mr. Roosevelt his regret that disaster should threaten Foraker, "distinguished American public man and a member of the Senate possessed of brilliant talents and great personal

charm."* Mr. Lodge was Jonathan to Mr. Roosevelt's
David; he and my husband had differed spiritedly; but
Lodge was very much of a human being; when an opponent whom he knew very well and liked very much
met a reverse, he could not but deplore it.

Senator Beveridge (of the opposition, often, but admir-
ing Foraker) took pains to spread his opinion, expressed
personally to me, that the attack on Foraker was a "most
cynical piece of political chicanery" and more "brutal
than I would have believed possible of contemporaries."

In hundreds of personal letters, in letters to newspapers
and in editorials all over this country and abroad, Foraker's dogged uprightness was summoned to his defense.
The public had watched him for half a century. It ought
to know. There was universal derision of the theory that
a lawyer could not practice because he was in the United
States Senate. The public could not and did not expect
him to rely on his salary of seventy-five hundred dollars.
(He was faced at once with a rental of six thousand dollars for a suitable house. We wondered then what we
would do with the other fifteen hundred.) On the contrary, the country was being very ably served by men in
the Senate and in the House who kept their law offices
open and in the vacations took whatever good business
was offered them.

But all this—what did it matter? The loyalty of the
public and of my husband's associates was as naught.

* Roosevelt-Lodge correspondence, vol. ii, p. 317.

The Standard Oil lie had got too good a start. There it went, a very snowball sent spinning, down, even to posterity's outposts, on a track that had been most craftily prepared. The forces against Foraker were ferocious. A god could not have won.

As a family we suffered poignantly that my husband went from life with the wrong done him officially unrighted. To this was added our natural resentment that writers negligently continued to repeat and repeat a falsehood that so sensationally had served its purpose.

With the thought of having the truth respected, of forcing respect by legal action, if necessary, my daughter, Julia Wainwright, consulted Mr. Owen J. Roberts, eminent Philadelphia lawyer.

"This slandering of my father has got to stop," said Julia.

At her request Mr. Roberts gave himself to a most meticulous examination of the whole matter: of Foraker's published record of his entire association with the Standard Oil Company; of the question of writers who went on restating the refuted, baseless charge as fact. The lawyer saw complexities of time and change in a legal process. But in a wise, kind, and sympathetic letter to my daughter, May 9, 1923, he regretted the blocking of steps "which would give you the redress to which you are entitled as a matter of morals," and expressed his own opinion of the whole matter in the following words:

"That your father was right and his detractors wrong I have no question."

Mr. Roberts is now Mr. Justice Roberts of the United States Supreme Court.

In a biography of Mr. Taft, prepared during the last years of his life, the old story of Foraker-and-Standard Oil is revived and permitted starkly to stand without a word about the established truth which had riddled that story through and through. Perhaps from great eminence, and at the end, one does not stoop to salute a mistake. Yet, if Mr. Taft's biographer thus set throbbing again an old wound, Mr. Robert's words make me happier . . .

It was so odd a turn of the wheel, the confirmation of my husband's innocence by one destined for alliance with the high tribunal of which the man who denied Foraker was chief.

CHAPTER XXIII

"WEAVER'S CHOICE"

FATE weaves some very pretty designs when she takes up the political thread. The interested smart ones are no match for her. There is the pattern of the three H's—Herrick, Harding, and Harris, a sort of double bowknot like the old Southern "kiver" design known as "Weaver's Choice." Because of the ultimate Taft link the chapter belongs here, though it makes me come back to say good-by.

In 1893 Myron T. Herrick was among the friends who came so gallantly to the financial rescue of Governor William McKinley. There was no opportunity to reward Mr. Herrick for his generosity until 1902. Then, under the expert management of Senator Hanna, he was made Governor of Ohio. Shortly after Mr. Herrick's inauguration Senator Hanna died. There was an immediate movement to make Governor Herrick the successor of Hanna in the Senate. But, paradoxically, they could not put the thing over without Hanna! It was Charles A. Dick who became Senator. Not a strong appointment. But with Hanna gone, northern Ohio was leaderless.

Governor Herrick was renominated. Now, darkly, the *motif* crosses the warp. To Mr. Harding, the Lieutenant-

Governorship seemed just an echoing gubernatorial tomb. He declined to run again. So, General Harris, an old Civil War hero, was nominated Lieutenant-Governor in Harding's place.

That campaign was ineffectual from the start; limping terribly when Secretary of War Taft came along and gave it the finishing blow. This he did in a very fine speech at Akron, Ohio, in which he said that, should he go to Cincinnati, his home town, to vote, let it be understood that he would not vote for any man connected with the George B. Cox wing of the Ohio Republican organization. As Herrick was a Cox entry, the Taft bomb defeated him. John Pattison, Democratic nominee, was elected Governor. The rest of the State ticket remained solidly Republican. In April following the inaugural Governor Pattison died, and General Harris, the Republican Lieutenant-Governor, that very old man whom no one ever supposed would be asked to do anything but contribute the popular soldier touch—General Harris became Governor.

Years later Mr. Taft, now President, was the guest of Mr. Herrick at his Cleveland home. In an informal after-dinner talk the President said to his host: "Herrick, how would you like to be our Ambassador to France? You needn't stay longer than a year if you don't like it." This offer was thought to be an honorable amend for that fatal Akron speech which lost Governor Herrick a second term. Mr. Herrick was not too eager at first about accepting the President's offer, but the women of his family were keen. "We've compromised," he told Foraker with a twinkle in his eye; "I'm to go." He remained at Paris until Woodrow Wilson became President.

Eight years afterwards, Warren G. Harding, the man who had been Lieutenant-Governor in Herrick's first term, the man who would not run as Herrick's Lieutenant in the second campaign because he was planning to be Governor himself and whose refusal made him miss being so when the Democratic Governor died—Warren G. Harding was President of the United States. He repeated Mr. Taft's offer of the French ambassadorship to ex-Ambassador Herrick, his old chief. This time there was no question in Mr. Herrick's mind about "liking it." He had proved himself the ideal man for that important post. And he loved it. His peculiar talents would have been lost in the Senate, where at one time they were all trying to push him. He went back to France, everybody remembers, for many happy years; until death recalled him in 1929.

The Spinner wasn't done yet. When Harding became President, one of his first important appointments was that which made ex-President Taft Chief Justice of the Supreme Court. The appointment was about the most distinguished thing that President Harding ever did, a delightful use of power by any President. For Mr. Taft it was the realization of a life-long dream. Had Harding ever seen carried out his ambition to be Governor of

Ohio, set in motion when he pulled out of the campaign with Herrick and meeting the check of definite defeat when he ran for Governor in 1910, if his own plans had ruled, it is unlikely that he would have achieved the Presidency and with it the piquant experience of appointing, from his supreme eminence, two of his sometime superiors to the position for which destiny had intended them all along.

The "divinity that shapes our ends" is the only artist in public life.

There was intricacy, too, in President Taft's attitude towards the appointment of a chief justice when the matter came before him in 1910. Chief-Justice Fuller died at eighty-three after twenty-two years in the Supreme Court. Only Chief-Justices Marshall and Taney had administered the oath of office to more Presidents.

It was upon Mr. Justice Harlan that it was thought the judicial mantle would descend. Mr. Justice Harlan was exactly the same age as Chief-Justice Fuller (he died one year later), had been on the bench of the Supreme Court even longer, and his past record justified him in expecting recognition at the hands of a Republican President.

President Taft did not appoint Mr. Justice Harlan. He appointed Mr. Justice White. Mr. Justice White was considerably the junior of Mr. Justice Harlan; he was a Southern Democrat, an ex-Confederate, a Catholic, and an Associate Justice of the Supreme Court. In this last

respect the appointment was a complete breaking of
precedent. The appointment was a disappointment to
thousands of Republicans and a bitter disappointment to
Mr. Justice Harlan. It was he who swore in the new
Chief Justice. It was said that he performed this ceremony with a curiously touching dignity. His voice faltered just a little at the end. One may imagine his
emotion. For the very old, as for the very young, disappointment reserves its sharpest edge.

Personally, we were very fond of Mr. Justice White.
He was a great lawyer, an able jurist, and a wholly delightful man. When he learned that he was to be appointed he conscientiously dispatched a message to the
President by one of the district judges protesting that he
thought the appointment unwise. "For three reasons: I
am a Democrat, a Confederate soldier, and a Roman
Catholic." Aside from Mr. Justice White being pre-
eminently fitted to be Chief Justice, President Taft was
thought to have had a deeply personal reason for the appointment. He was looking ahead. The day might come,
was coming, indeed, that brought a Democratic President. Were that Democratic Executive to be faced with
the appointment of a chief justice, and was Mr. Taft,
Republican and Protestant, available, precedent on these
points of party and pew was already established. The
appointment would be given him.

Yet in the end it must be always the Great Democrat

who makes a new chief justice. The death of Chief-Justice White, whom Taft had appointed, was to give the ex-President his coveted opportunity. An ideal consummation. One of those rare, quite perfect things that could not possibly be brought about by human maneuver.

CHAPTER. XXIV

GOOD-BYE TO THE GAME

THE year 1912 is politically memorable for the wrecking of the Republican Party and for the fact that in that catastrophe Theodore Roosevelt let down President Taft as completely as President Taft ever let down anybody. It was tit for Taft with a vengeance. The year is memorable also, of course, for the disturbing appearance of a new Moses. The portentous figure of Woodrow Wilson strode confidently upon a stage that hadn't echoed with a Democratic footfall for so long it had forgotten how ominous it could be. But my story is linked only with that of the great wreck.

Back in 1907 President Roosevelt was predicting fearful things on the score of that most dreaded of all party disasters—division. Whatever happens, the walls of political Troy must be kept intact.

"I have had a perfectly comic time with the Senate," Mr. Roosevelt wrote Mr. G. F. Spinney January 22, 1907. (By that time everything between the President and Foraker was solidly frozen over.) "They've been hopping about insisting that they could not desert Foraker, because it would 'split the party'; and I finally told the most active of the compromisers that if they split off

Foraker they would split off a splinter; but if they split off me they would split the party nearly in two."*

The party was split. The prophecy breaks down only on the point as to who was responsible for the terrible cleavage. The hopping Senators were absolved: certainly the splinter was innocent; the collective calamities which Mr. Roosevelt foresaw if the Senate persisted in its fatally sentimental attachment to Foraker, its old leader, all had been shrewdly averted. Unexpectedly, as everybody remembers, and as fantastic as it was sudden, the strong man in that disaster was Theodore Roosevelt himself.

1908. The President had done what he proposed to do upon his retirement. He had named his successor and, had seen him installed (with the soundest of fraternal help) lares, penates and Rooseveltism complete, in the White House.

This was for Mr. Roosevelt a remarkable personal triumph. The Senate, in the main, almost everybody, indeed, save Mr. Lodge of Massachusetts, had opposed the nomination of Mr. Taft. The opposition was in no degree personal to the popular Secretary of War. The Republicans simply resented the President's fiat that either forced their support of his choice or drove them into a dubiousness of party loyalty. The Democrats disliked quite as much as the Republicans the idea of the retiring President dictating as to who was to succeed him. This

* Bishop's *Roosevelt* v. ii p. 30.

was not a government by dynasty! Most of the Senate, the leading members, anyway, began to consider their own claims as Presidential candidate. The Senate bloomed with booms. Foraker was proposed. Knox was proposed; many others. The clever old Senators would pat their man on the back. "You just stick to it," they would say; "we'll run this thing yet." A pure measure of defense. The Senate determined to beat the nonpareil Roosevelt or perish.

But the Roosevelt drive and the Taft luck were unbeatable—

> Rickety ram, rickety ram,
> Theodore, William,
> And Uncle Sam.

Everybody hummed and looked happy.

In 1912 how the tune had changed! Mr. Taft had shown himself no longer a "good lieutenant," but a man who proposed to call his presidential soul not Theodore Roosevelt's, but his own. He had questioned the text which the retiring President, had done, so to say, in beautiful, bold cross-stitch and left hanging, sweetly framed, in the Cabinet room: the famous Rooseveltian text, "For what can a man do that cometh after the king? Even that which hath been already done." Mr. Roosevelt would brook no such going back on gospel. He stalked off with his Progressives. Mr. Taft carried two States (Vermont and Utah, wasn't it?); the Republicans, thought to be so securely in the saddle, handed the government over to the Democrats for eight years ——

And Foraker, standing afar off, heard his old party break up and go to pieces with a loud crash and thanked Heaven and his star that this time the heat of conflict was not for him, nor the blame.

Defeat is not a pleasant thing. But the 1912 catastrophe turned upon fortune's spite of four years earlier the radiance of a blessing.

In the 1912 crisis they flocked back to my husband; begged him to come over into Progressive Macedonia and help them; begged him to help the "Bull Moose." But Foraker stood by the party. He would have stood by the party though he were, like Macaulay's shivering New Zealander, the last man left. He had voted for Mr. Taft in 1908; he voted for him again in 1912. He was a Taft man to the end; lonely, of course, but incorrigibly loyal.

There is something in the Book of Job which I think may have occurred to my husband in that last rally, "Though he slay me yet will I trust in him." Job said it, speaking for Job, alone. Women did not have the vote in 1912, so that I, personally, was unable to express in the sacred privacy of the ballot booth my suffrage for, or against, the Republican candidate.

Shattering old 1912 was a star year for the return of the soldier. The foes of my husband who, such a short time before, had joined hands and danced a political jig around "Foraker eliminated," now in even livelier

time came back to their friends in private life. Congress
at that period was a place suggesting to these shocked
Republicans melancholy, mischief, and sickening mis-
calculation.

Foraker's magnanimity toward the two men who had
twisted so askew the springs of his national usefulness is
remembered. For myself it remains one of those rare
generosities that keep the rose in one's sky. My husband
was wholly without bitterness against Mr. Roosevelt or
Mr. Taft. If he did not forget—*does* one forget?—he very
finely forgave. Nor did he hold any malice against the
Ohio clique who swung over to the enemy, working
slyly in the dark with the enthusiasm of moles.

I must speak of something repeated so often by writers
that it has become a legend, and this, I think, is the moment. Again and again it has been said that Foraker,
because of his political reverse, died of a broken heart.
No, not that. My husband's end was hastened by an
event that touched him to depths no worldly disappointment had the power to reach. This was the death of
Benson, our eldest son, in April, 1915. Benson and his
father were singularly close; since the boy's childhood
their comradeship had been one of perfect sympathy and
delight. Foraker's health was for years an anxious preoccupation; but always he was buoyed by his happy belief that "Benson would be here," to see his father off, to
take his place at the wheel. That Benson could not stay

was heartache too great for Foraker to bear. The political
past was as nothing.

After the Roosevelt-Foraker coming-together my husband wrote in a volume of his *Notes* which he sent to
his former adversary:

"Notwithstanding our differences of opinion on some
subjects, there never has been a moment since the beginning of our acquaintance when I was not an ardent ad-
mirer of your great intellectual power, fervent patriotism,
and fearless courage."

There are certain persons, says Feuchtwanger, certain
undertakings which have no luck for one. Worldly success depends wholly upon one's quick sense of this and
one's instant pulling off. . . .

Theodore Roosevelt was not lucky for Foraker; he
was disaster. It is curious that every serious breach between the two men had its beginning in a sincere, spon-
taneous desire on the part of the Senator to help his
President: Brownsville . . . the affair of the Ohio *State
Journal* . . . it was to be a Rooseveltian loud speaker
. . . railroad rate. Always it began sympathetically and
always, the President pushing the advantage of superior
power, it ended in strife.

Less of a man than my husband would have dropped
the fight and turned his talents, his position, and his
closeness to the seats of the mighty into a channel that
ran straighter and smoother in the direction of personal
interest. But, different in every other way, Mr. Roosevelt

and Foraker were oddly alike in natural fearlessness, independence of thought and utter inability to yield. If this similarity made their battles inevitable, it made them, also, the odds being as they were perfectly hopeless.

Were it all to be lived over again, I am afraid that everything would happen just as it did.

And I? Oh, I've enjoyed my long journey. There were storms, but when the sun shone the days were beautiful indeed. Now it is calm, yet the scene is not empty; memories gleam companionably. Life is like that. After high winds and buffetings, happily one finds oneself, at the last, safe upon a smooth white beach covered with lovely shells.

THE END

INDEX